Crossing the Creek

UNIVERSITY PRESS OF FLORIDA

Florida A&M University, Tallahassee
Florida Atlantic University, Boca Raton
Florida Gulf Coast University, Ft. Myers
Florida International University, Miami
Florida State University, Tallahassee
New College of Florida, Sarasota
University of Central Florida, Orlando
University of Florida, Gainesville
University of North Florida, Jacksonville
University of South Florida, Tampa
University of West Florida, Pensacola

**Anna Lillios**

# Crossing

University Press of Florida

Gainesville Tallahassee Tampa Boca Raton Pensacola Orlando Miami Jacksonville Ft. Myers Sarasota

# the Creek

## The Literary Friendship of Zora Neale Hurston and Marjorie Kinnan Rawlings

Copyright 2010 by Anna Lillios
Printed in the United States of America. This book is printed on Glatfelter
Natures Book, a paper certified under the standards of the Forestry Stewardship
Council (FSC). It is a recycled stock that contains 30 percent post-consumer waste
and is acid-free.

15  14  13  12  11  10    6  5  4  3  2  1

Library of Congress Cataloging-in-Publication Data
Lillios, Anna, 1948–
Crossing the creek : the literary friendship of Zora Neale Hurston and Marjorie
Kinnan Rawlings / Anna Lillios.
p. cm.
Includes bibliographical references and index.
ISBN 978-0-8130-3500-0 (alk. paper)
1. Hurston, Zora Neale—Friends and associates. 2. Rawlings, Marjorie Kinnan,
1896–1953—Friends and associates. 3. Authors, American—20th century—
Biography. I. Title.
PS3515.U789Z764 2010
813.'529–dc22 [B]      2010007784

The University Press of Florida is the scholarly publishing agency for the State
University System of Florida, comprising Florida A&M University, Florida Atlantic
University, Florida Gulf Coast University, Florida International University, Florida
State University, New College of Florida, University of Central Florida, University
of Florida, University of North Florida, University of South Florida, and University
of West Florida.

University Press of Florida
15 Northwest 15th Street
Gainesville, FL 32611-2079
http://www.upf.com

For George, Christopher, and Andrew

And without my writing, I am nothing.

—*Marjorie Kinnan Rawlings*


I have had to go through a long, long, dark tunnel to come out to the light again. But I had the feeling all the time that you believed in me.

—*Zora Neale Hurston*

# Contents

# Acknowledgments

**M**ANY PEOPLE HAVE SUPPORTED and encouraged my work on this project. I owe a tremendous debt of gratitude to librarians, students, friends, fellow scholars, and family for their generosity through the years I was writing this book.

First and foremost, I want to thank my family. My husband, George Everett, has been with me every step of the way, always providing optimism, good cheer, and all sorts of tangible and intangible support. My sons, Christopher and Andrew, are the lights of my life. Their love of nature has opened up facets of Florida hidden from my view. Together we have boated through the Everglades, collected sand dollars in Naples, hunted horseshoe crabs on Pine Island, swum at New Smyrna Beach, gone hawking in central Florida, and watched shuttle launches at Cape Kennedy. I never would have understood Hurston's and Rawlings's settings without these experiences.

I was first introduced to the work of Zora Neale Hurston by my friend Steve Glassman, a professor at Embry-Riddle Aeronautical University, who invited me to present a paper at his "Zora" conference in 1989. I had never heard of Hurston and did not have time to read all of her works, but I came up with an idea that opened up Hurston's world in ways I never could have imagined. I interviewed most of the people in Eatonville who had known her. I will always be grateful to Mrs. Mattie Jones, Mrs. Annie Davis, Mrs. Hoyt Davis, Mrs. Jimmie Lee Harrell, Mrs. Harriet Moseley, and Mrs. Clara Williams for inviting me into their homes and shining the inside light on their remarkable community. I thoroughly enjoyed getting to know these women and am grateful for the ways in which they made Hurston come alive for me.

After these personal interviews awakened my keen interest in Hurston's work, I benefited greatly from illuminating conversations with many valued colleagues. I am especially grateful to Maurice "Socky" O'Sullivan, a professor at Rollins College, for his mentorship, friendship, and wry sense of humor over the past twenty-plus years. He has always been my leading expert on Florida writers. I also want to thank Barbara Speisman, a professor at Florida A&M University, for generously sharing ideas and theories on Hurston's life and works and for giving me a fascinating tour of Notasulga, Alabama, and the Old South. I've also learned so much from the brilliant scholarship of Cheryl Wall, John Lowe, Robert Hemenway, and Carla Kaplan, and I have enormously enjoyed my conversations with them about Hurston.

I owe Barbara Speisman a second debt of gratitude for introducing me to the Marjorie Kinnan Rawlings Society. I have been executive director of this group since 2005. I cannot express in words how special this group has been to me. Over the years, we've traveled together to Banner Elk, North Carolina (where Rawlings wrote *The Yearling*), Cross Creek, Cedar Key, and the scrub area around Salt Springs, Florida. I'm especially grateful to the society's thirty-six trustees, with whom I meet four times a year. They are dedicated to keeping the memory of Rawlings's life, works, and legacy alive. Among the trustees, historian David Nolan of St. Augustine has taken a particular interest in this book. As a friend of Norton Baskin, a historian of St. Augustine, David has provided guidance, direction, and insight. I've also valued the contributions of other trustees who were acquainted with Rawlings, including Philip May Jr. of Jacksonville, whose father defended Rawlings in her famous "invasion of privacy" trial; Idella Parker, who was Rawlings's servant at Cross Creek and wrote *Idella: Marjorie Rawlings' "Perfect Maid"*; and

Ernest Bass, a pastor at St. Simon's Island, Georgia, who knew Rawlings when he was a child at Cross Creek. All of these friends have enriched my knowledge of Rawlings's life and works. I have been fortunate to serve the society with a remarkable list of presidents, including Marsha Phelts, a librarian at the Florida Genealogy Department of the Jacksonville Public Library; William H. Jeter, an attorney from Drayton Island, Florida; Robert Davis from Indialantic, Florida, and Brent Kinser, a professor at Western Carolina University. Brent Kinser, my coeditor of *The Marjorie Kinnan Rawlings Journal of Florida Literature*, has been a source of joy and laughter as we have labored over journal issues and society conferences. I appreciate his belief in the work on Rawlings that we are doing together. Last but certainly not least, I am deeply grateful for my association with Rodger Tarr, University Distinguished Professor, Emeritus, Illinois State University, who is the dean of Rawlings scholarship. I could not have written this book without his groundbreaking insights into Rawlings's work and his meticulous editing of Rawlings's letters to Max Perkins and Norton Baskin.

Part of the pleasure of working on this book has been the opportunity to explore the treasures of a few of my favorite libraries. I am especially grateful to Florence Turcotte, research services archivist in the Special and Area Studies Collections of the University of Florida George A. Smathers Libraries, who has unfailingly assisted me in locating the gems in the Hurston and Rawlings collections. Her predecessor, Frank Orser, provided much assistance in locating materials for my book and sharing his ideas about my project. I would also like to acknowledge the help of librarians Wenxian Zhang and Gertrude Laframboise of the Rollins College Archives and Special Collections. Finally, while visiting my son Andrew, who is a student at Yale University, I have spent many pleasurable hours perusing the African American archives at the Beinecke Library and am grateful for the friendly assistance of the staff there.

Another aspect of my work that has been especially meaningful to me has been the chance to experience warm friendships with the following Florida icons. I have treasured my visits with artist J. T. Glisson, who as a boy was Rawlings's next-door neighbor at Cross Creek. I have loved sitting for hours listening to Jake's stories about Miz' Rawlings and his magical childhood at the Creek (his book of reminiscences is also titled

*The Creek*). I have also admired the work of civil rights activist Stetson Kennedy, the only living person who knew both Hurston and Rawlings. He bravely rode undercover with the Ku Klux Klan, revealing their nefarious activities in his book *The Klan Unmasked*. I also thank him for the use of the Hurston photographs, which he donated to the University of Florida.

I am also grateful for the support I have received from José Fernández, dean of the College of Humanities of the University of Central Florida. I have enjoyed my association with him for the past twenty-five years. I also want to thank two of my colleagues in the University of Central Florida Department of English, J. D. Applen and Mark Kamrath, for their help in creating the Zora Neale Hurston Electronic Archive. Provost and Executive Vice-President Terry Hickey has also lent his support of the technical aspects of the archive.

Finally, I wish to acknowledge Editor-in-Chief John Byram of the University Press of Florida. I am thankful that he found my work worthy of publication and am grateful for all of his positive advice.

Grateful acknowledgment is made to the Department of Special Collections, George A. Smathers Libraries, University of Florida, for permission to quote from Marjorie Kinnan Rawlings's works, manuscripts, letters, and photographs. I also thank Stetson Kennedy for permission to use photographs of Zora Neale Hurston in the collection he donated to the University of Florida Libraries.

Grateful acknowledgment is made to the family members of the Estate of Zora Neale Hurston for permission to quote from Zora Neale Hurston's letters and from *Seraph on the Suwanee*.

Twenty brief quotations totaling 327 words from *Jonah's Gourd Vine* by Zora Neale Hurston. Copyright 1934 by Zora Neale Hurston; renewed © 1962 by John C. Hurston and Joel Hurston. Reprinted by permission of HarperCollins Publishers.

Two brief quotations totaling 100 words from *Mules and Men* by Zora Neale Hurston. Copyright 1935 by Zora Neale Hurston; renewed © 1963 John C. Hurston and Joel Hurston. Reprinted by permission of HarperCollins Publishers.

Twenty-six brief quotations totaling 412 words from *Their Eyes Were*

*Watching God* by Zora Neale Hurston. Copyright 1937 by Harper & Row, Publishers, Inc.; renewed © 1965 by Joel Hurston and John C. Hurston. Reprinted by permission of HarperCollins Publishers.

Numerous brief quotations from the text and Appendix (1959 words in all) from *Dust Tracks on a Road* by Zora Neale Hurston. Copyright 1942 by Zora Neale Hurston; renewed © 1970 by John C. Hurston. Reprinted by permission of HarperCollins Publishers.

An earlier version of pages 66–71 appeared as "'The Monstropolous Beast': The Hurricane in Zora Neale Hurston's *Their Eyes Were Watching God*," *The Southern Quarterly* 136 (1998): 89–93. An earlier version of pages 92–98 appeared as "The Death of Flag: Mother-Son Bonding in Marjorie Kinnan Rawlings's *The Yearling*," *The Marjorie Kinnan Rawlings Journal of Florida Literature* 14 (2005–2006): 13–25.

# Introduction

O N 6 JULY 1942, A TEN-YEAR-OLD BOY accompanied his mother to a literary tea at the Castle Warden, a posh segregated hotel in St. Augustine, Florida. The boy, Donald Wilson, had been born to privilege and was used to mingling among St. Augustine's elite white society. But, on this hot July day, the guest of honor was not a white author—although a nationally recognized author was present—but a black woman, Zora Neale Hurston. Her host was the Pulitzer Prize–winning writer Marjorie Kinnan Rawlings, author of the best-selling novel *The Yearling* (1938). Wilson recalls the moment he saw Hurston. In his eyes, she was "a very beautiful person" and "absolutely brilliant." She and Rawlings appeared to be "great friends" and "spoke at great ease with each other" (Wilson interview). Rawlings's husband, Norton Baskin, also present, recounts how earlier that day he had directed his "colored bell boy" to escort Hurston to his and Rawlings's private apartment at the hotel when she arrived at 5 P.M. When she did not appear at the appointed time, Baskin called his wife to tell her that her guest had failed to show up. Rawlings replied: "Are you crazy? She's up here and if you know what's good for you, you better come on up; I've never had so much fun" (Boyd 351).

Hurston, perhaps comprehending the racial tension her appearance at the segregated hotel may have caused, had sneaked up the back stairs in a maid's uniform.

*Crossing the Creek: The Literary Friendship of Zora Neale Hurston and Marjorie Kinnan Rawlings* tells the story of the complicated inter-racial friendship between the daughter of an Alabama slave, Zora Neale Hurston, and a transplanted upper-middle-class Yankee, Marjorie Kinnan Rawlings, during the 1940s, when both women were at the height of their literary creativity and fame. In 1942, both had just published memoirs—Hurston's *Dust Tracks on a Road* and Rawlings's *Cross Creek*—to great critical and popular acclaim. These memoirs followed on the enormous success of their arguably greatest novels, published within one year of each other—Rawlings's *The Yearling* and Hurston's *Their Eyes Were Watching God* (1937). Shortly after their meeting in 1942, Hurston would win the John Anisfield Award in Race Relations for writing "an admirable autobiography revealing the flexibility, the sensitiveness, and the emotional color of the Negro race in America" (*Saturday Review* 20 February 1943). Her face would appear on the cover of the 20 February 1943 issues of *Saturday Review* and the *Saturday Evening Post*. Rawlings, too, from 1930, had basked in the glory of being one of Charles Scribner's Sons' prize authors, together with Ernest Hemingway, F. Scott Fitzgerald, and Thomas Wolfe. She could count on her novels being picked up by the Book-of-the-Month Club and condensed in *Reader's Digest*.

Nevertheless, after this period of national recognition, both authors struggled emotionally and artistically with their subsequent creative work. Although Hurston in 1947 published *Seraph on the Suwanee*, a novel with an all-white cast of characters (dedicated to Rawlings), she never completed the works closest to her heart: a biography of Herod the Great and another novel about Eatonville, her childhood home now surrounded by Orlando, Florida. It took Rawlings more than ten years to publish her next novel, *The Sojourner*, in 1953, a few months before her death. Both authors were in a process of moving away from material centered on the communities that had originally inspired their greatest work to a discovery of a new way to define themselves as writers and as human beings.

The similar way in which they describe their communities, in fact, is important in making a connection between these two very different writers. In a letter written shortly after they had met, Hurston defines their affinities: "Whether it pleases you or not, you are my sister. You look at plants and animals and people in the way I do. You are conscious of the three layers of life, instead of the obvious thing before your nose. You see and feel the immense past, what is now, and feel inside you something of what is to come. Therefore you are not pacing the cell of the current hour. You are free because you have made your peace with the universe and its laws. You are deep and fine" (*Hurston: A Life in Letters* 486).

Hurston praises Rawlings's not only for her ability to observe the outer layer of things but also for her genius at going deeper: "You turned your inside light on there [*sic*] community life, and it broke like day" (486). Hurston claims that Rawlings is fully aware both of the reality of the life she depicts and also its mythic aspects, that is, her consciousness of the "three layers of life." She finds in Rawlings's work a faithful representation of everyday village life and also a recognition of its cosmic significance. Above all, Hurston notes that Rawlings's ability to understand the workings of the universe allows her to empathize with her characters, particularly her black characters: "You *looked* at them and saw them as they are, instead of slobbering over them as all of the other authors do" (486).

Thus, Rawlings and Hurston shared a deep appreciation of the cultural, mythic, artistic, and human qualities of the communities about which they wrote. Furthermore, Annette Trefzer claims that the two authors kept their focus on community as a means of moving beyond the "rigidly defined" gender and racial roles that they found in the South. Even though both women were staunch individualists, the communities they created in their work became the "basis of self-definition" (69). Nellie McKay describes the process: "Community identity permits the rejection of historically diminishing images of self imposed by the dominant culture; it allows marginalized individuals to embrace alternative selves constructed from positive (and more authentic) images of their own creation" (69).

Trefzer defines the identities that Hurston and Rawlings create in their work as "unstable, slipping, and literally floating" (69). Besides the fact that both women were continually moving from one place to another (Hurston even lived on a houseboat during part of the time she knew Rawlings), they also construct fluid personae in their work. Critics today accuse Hurston of lying—or, rather, embroidering the truth—in *Dust Tracks on a Road* and complain that they can only find "a self in hiding" (Prenshaw 17) in Rawlings's work. Trefzer explains the dynamic: "metaphors particularly of the southern home are inherently fictitious and conflicted because the South signifies both a romanticized, pastoral location *and* an oppressive, exclusionary space" (73).

Complicating the issue of creating an identity in the contemporary South is Hurston's mask wearing. When she calls Rawlings "my sister"— "whether it pleases you or not"—this implied kinship is problematic. Is she trying to create an affinity with Rawlings, the more successful of the two in a mostly white publishing world, or does she feel a genuine, personal connection to her friend? Hurston came out of the Harlem Renaissance culture that was heavily influenced by the mask-wearing minstrel show, according to Ann Douglas in *Terrible Honesty: Mongrel Manhattan in the 1920s*: "Minstrelsy put the fooling techniques of black culture, the 'puttin' on ole massa' routines of mimicry and role-playing developed in the days of slavery, at the heart of American entertainment. Blacks imitating and fooling whites, whites imitating and stealing from blacks, blacks reappropriating and transforming what has been stolen, whites making yet another foray on black styles, and on and on: this *is* American popular culture" (76).

In a culture so invested in doubleness, Hurston's sincerity is ambiguous, but the back-and-forth aspect of doubleness engendered borrowings across the race line during the 1920s. According to Douglas, "Cross-race analogies fostered by cultural proximity and creative rivalry proliferated" (82). Douglas even finds an "expressive mix of romantic imagination and shrewd observation" (86) in F. Scott Fitzgerald's *The Great Gatsby* and Hurston's *Their Eyes Were Watching God*, although "no direct contact" between Fitzgerald and Hurston has ever been found (82). In the case of Rawlings and Hurston, significant parallels can be found in their work (besides the themes mentioned above). Some of their first pieces of literature are remarkably similar. In its style, characterization, and format, Rawlings's "Cracker Chidlings" (1931) is reminiscent of Hurston's "The Eatonville Anthology" (1926). And Hurston's *Seraph on the Suwanee* (1948) seems to hark back to Rawlings's Cracker tales, including "Lord Bill of the Suwannee River" (written in 1931 but published posthumously in 1963).

Unfortunately, with the exception of Trefzer, critics have overlooked Hurston and Rawlings's literary friendship. Barbara Speisman's play *A Tea with Zora and Marjory*, published in 1988, is a romantic reenactment of their friendship. Unfortunately, Speisman did not have access to Rawlings's recently published letters to Norton Baskin, which cast a more nuanced light on racial issues between the two authors.

## Hurston's Life up to 1942

To understand how these issues affected the two authors' friendship, a brief glance back at their backgrounds is in order. Hurston and Rawlings began life in environments that were polar opposites—Rawlings enjoyed a childhood of privilege in the North, while Hurston endured privations as the daughter of a former slave. Hurston was not born in Eatonville, as she claims in *Dust Tracks on a Road*, but in Notasulga, Alabama, on 15 January 1891. She often misrepresented the date of her birth—to 1901, 1903, or 1910—perhaps in order to be thought a child of the new century, to be admitted to high school when she was in her twenties, or to gain an advantage in appearing younger while being older.

Hurston obscured the basic fact of her existence—that her father was from "Over de Big Creek" in Notasulga, a sharecropping former slave who married up. Hurston, instead, was like Athena, born of her father's head, a child of imagination who insisted on creating her own unique identity. As an adult she would become an anthropologist and scientifically study mythology and folktales, but early on she must have had a strong sense of her mythologizing tendencies and believed that a story about her genesis in the first all-black town suited her desire to be a special individual. Her first biographer, Robert Hemenway, calls her "a woman of fierce independence" who "was a complex woman with a high tolerance of contradiction" (5). Her skill in the art of masking effectively disguised her inner life.

Furthermore, Hurston's masking of her birthplace in the Deep

South allows her to make a life of her own choosing in the New South. Thus, in *Dust Tracks* she claims: "I was born in a Negro town. I do not mean by that the black back-side of an average town. Eatonville, Florida, is, and was at the time of my birth, a pure Negro town—charter, mayor, council, town marshal and all" (3). Hurston liked to picture herself as a child of the first incorporated African American community, established by twenty-seven African American males on 18 August 1887. Her father, John Cornelius Hurston, was the minister of one of the two churches in town and served as mayor from 1912 to 1916. In her small town she held a privileged position as the pastor's daughter and felt that she had a special destiny, especially after she was inspired by tales she read in books: "My soul was with the gods and my body in the village" (56).

Hurston's idyllic village life changed forever on 18 September 1904, the day her mother died. At Lucy Hurston's funeral, her family "assembled together for the last time on earth." Two weeks later, thirteen-year-old Zora was forced to pack her bags and leave the only home she had ever known. "With a grief that was more than common," she began a life of wandering from one family member to another, never sinking roots for long in the Florida soil she loved. Her childhood had been idyllic in Eatonville, to which the family had moved a year or so after she was born. In *Dust Tracks*, Hurston writes of her love of nature, of books and learning, and of storytelling. She recalls the Florida landscape: "I was only happy in the woods, and when the ecstatic Florida springtime came strolling from the sea, trance-glorifying the world with its aura." She also remembers her home lovingly as "the center of the world." Yet the bigger world outside always beckoned to her: "It grew upon me that I ought to walk out to the horizon and see what the end of the world was like" (36).

After her mother's death, Hurston was not allowed to explore the world on her own terms; instead, she struggled for her very existence. She calls the years from 1904 to 1914 her "haunted years," because her life was so dismal. Unfortunately, few records exist from this period of her life. She was sent to Jacksonville to attend school with her sister, Sarah; her brothers John and Robert also attended school in the area at the Florida Baptist Academy (later the Florida Memorial College). In

Jacksonville, Hurston learned that she was "a little colored girl" (*Dust Tracks* 94). For as long as she was enrolled in school she received an excellent education, but she probably had to work, most likely as a maid, because her father sometimes did not pay her tuition.

This desperate period ended when Hurston's brother Robert, soon to become a practicing physician, invited her to care for his children in Nashville, Tennessee, in 1912. But eventually Hurston left his home when he expected her to do the household chores and did not allow her to pursue her dream of an education. She ran off to become the personal maid to Miss M., a singer in a Gilbert and Sullivan troupe, probably around 1915. Little is known about Hurston's first direct contact with the theater, but drama would become the great passion of her life. Even though Hurston was to gain her fame as a novelist, her dream had always been to make her mark as a dramatist. Her connection to Miss M.'s troupe ended in Baltimore in 1916, after Hurston had an appendicitis attack. Fortunately, her sister, Sarah, was living in Baltimore, and Hurston stayed with her.

This fateful event gave Hurston the opportunity to attend night school—possibly she falsified her birth date to be admitted. In 1917 she would move on to Morgan Academy. After graduating from Morgan in 1918, she entered Howard University. At long last, Hurston was in a position to actualize her potential and associate with the brilliant minds of her generation. Lorenzo Dow Turner, who wrote *Africanisms in the Gullah Dialect*, taught her African words, and Montgomery Gregory directed her as a member of the Howard Players. Gregory's desire to establish a national Negro theater would become Hurston's lifelong dream, too. Hurston also joined a literary club sponsored by Alain Locke, who encouraged her to publish in Howard University journals. She met other writers known as the "New Negroes" in Georgia Douglas Johnson's literary salon. In the following decade, these writers—Bruce Nugent, Jean Toomer, Alice Dunbar-Nelson, and Jessie Fauset, among others—would become part of the core group of the Harlem Renaissance.

Hurston's literary career began when work she submitted to journals was accepted. In 1924 she sent her second short story, "Drenched in Light," to Charles S. Johnson, the editor of *Opportunity*, a publication of the Urban League. The story was not only published but received second prize in the annual *Opportunity* literary contest. The subject of "Drenched in Light" is Eatonville, which is, according to Hemenway, "her unique subject, and she was encouraged to make it the source of her art" (20). Johnson urged her to move to New York City, and by 1925 she found herself living in Harlem.

At the next *Opportunity* awards banquet, in 1925, Hurston not only won more prizes for her work but met Langston Hughes, Countee Cullen, Carl Van Vechten, Fannie Hurst, and Annie Nathan Meyer—all of whom would support her in the coming decade. Meyer, a founder of Barnard College, would assist Hurston in getting accepted into the college and in being awarded a scholarship. Attending Barnard provided a significant turning point for Hurston. She began to study anthropology with the father of modern anthropology, Franz Boas, who believed in the distinctive culture of African Americans. Boas urged Hurston to do fieldwork in her hometown, in order to preserve her heritage that was slipping away.

In the 1920s, Hurston's literary and scientific interests in anthropology were merging. She used the knowledge of her native community and its people to deepen and complicate her stories. At the same time, she aspired to be "*the* authority on Afro-American folklore" (Hemenway 87), with her main interest in the "Negro farthest down" (*Dust Tracks* 177). But finances were a never-ending problem. In 1927 Hurston accepted the aid of Charlotte Osgood Mason, a wealthy white New York woman who was willing to fund Hurston's folklore expeditions as long as Mason retained control over how the material would be used. This bargain with the devil would eventually cause Hurston to break her academic ties with her respected professors—although she did graduate from Barnard— and, on a psychic level, wear her down because of Mason's controlling nature. On the other hand, with the freedom from academic restraint and method this arrangement afforded her, Hurston was able to follow her unique interests. She became intrigued by hoodoo and traveled to New Orleans to see how it was practiced and to study the life of the priestess Marie Leveau. Hoodoo appealed to Hurston, because women were allowed to play a prominent role in its rituals. Perhaps she simply became her father's daughter, seeking an outlet for her spiritual side.

Around the same time that her relationship with Mason was at a breaking point (Mason severed her contract with Hurston on 31 March 1931) and the country was heading toward the Great Depression, Hurston, desperate for an income, felt that the best vehicle for her work was the theater and that the best type of production was a folk musical based on her memories of Eatonville. She was thrilled when her play *The Great Day* ran for one night at the John Golden Theatre on 27 January 1931. Unfortunately, it was forced to close, because Hurston had no producers or money waiting in the wings to keep the production going. Instead, she took her dream south, to Rollins College in Winter Park, Florida, and staged two productions, *From Sun to Sun* and *All De Live Long Day* (versions of *The Great Day*), in 1933 and 1934. Many people from her hometown of Eatonville acted in these plays; thus her dream of a folk theater was partially realized.

Hurston's association with Rollins College was significant for another reason. Robert Wunsch, the theater director assisting her in the staging of her plays, encouraged Hurston to send her short story "The Gilded Two Bits" to *Story* magazine, which published it in 1933. The story was read by publisher Bertram Lippincott, who wrote Hurston to ask if she had a novel she could submit. Hurston quickly replied affirmatively— and then on 1 July 1933 moved to Sanford, Florida, to write one. She completed *Jonah's Gourd Vine* by September 6 and was evicted from her apartment on the same day she received an acceptance letter for her novel. *Jonah's Gourd Vine* was published in May 1934. The next year Lippincott published Hurston's book of folktales, *Mules and Men*.

Hurston now entered her prime creative period, during which she pursued fiction, drama, and anthropology simultaneously. She was thrilled when she was awarded a Guggenheim Fellowship in March 1936 and was able to travel to Jamaica and Haiti to do anthropological research. While in Haiti she began writing *Their Eyes Were Watching God*, embodying all of her passion for her lover, Percival (Percy) McGuire Punter, into the portrayal of Tea Cake. She completed the book in seven weeks, and it was published on 18 September 1937. She also continued her anthropological studies in voodoo in Haiti and published *Tell My Horse* in 1938.

After this peak period, Hurston still had to struggle to survive. She began working for the Works Progress Administration on 25 April 1938 and contributed folklore and interviews with former slaves to *The Flor-ida Negro*, which was not published at the time. Her job lasted until 1939, when the WPA was dismantled. Hurston was once again forced to search for a vehicle in which to express herself. Her publisher, Bertram Lippincott, suggested that she write her autobiography, and Hurston wrote *Dust Tracks on a Road*, which was published in 1942.

## Rawlings's Life up to 1942

Marjorie Kinnan Rawlings was born on 8 August 1896 in Washington, D.C. Her father was principal examiner in the U.S. Patent Office, but according to Rawlings, "he lived the true life of his mind and heart on his Maryland farm" ("Marjorie Rawlings" 343). Rawlings claimed that she "learned her love of nature" from her father. Her mother's family was from southern Michigan, and she spent her summers on their farm. Living close to the land as she was growing up "planted deep in [her] a love of the soil, the crops, the seasons and a sense of kinship with men and women everywhere who live close to the soil" (343).

Rawlings began writing at an early age and started publishing letters and award-winning short stories in the *Washington Post* when she was fourteen years old. Her father died in 1913, and the family moved to Wisconsin, where Rawlings attended the University of Wisconsin. She thrived in college and pursued drama and writing, often publishing her works in the *Wisconsin Literary Magazine*. She starred in a play titled *Lima Beans* during her junior year. She met and fell in love with Charles Rawlings, and they became engaged during her senior year.

After Rawlings graduated from Wisconsin with honors, she headed to New York City to work for the YWCA. She spent her time writing and trying to get published. When she married Charles Rawlings in 1919, the couple moved briefly to his hometown of Rochester, New York.

When they could not find work they enjoyed there, they moved to Louisville, Kentucky, where Rawlings found a job as a feature writer for the *Louisville Courier-Journal*. She wrote a column titled "Live Women in Louisville." By 1921 the Rawlingses had moved back to Rochester, and Marjorie Rawlings began writing for the *Rochester Evening Journal*. During this time, she composed poetry in a series called "Songs of a

Housewife" and a novel, *Blood of My Blood*, which was published post-humously in 2002.

Although they were gainfully employed as writers, in 1928 Charles and Marjorie Rawlings felt restless and decided to alter dramatically their lives by buying a seventy-two-acre farm in frontier Florida. Rawlings describes the beauty of the land that they found in rural Cross Creek, in the Ocala National Forest, southeast of Gainesville: "This was not the Gold coast of Florida. . . . It was a primitive section off the beaten path, where men hunted and fished and worked small groves and farms for a meager living. . . . And the country was beautiful, with its mysterious swamps, its palms, its great live oaks, dripping gray Spanish moss, its deer and bear and raccoons and panthers and reptiles" ("Marjorie Rawlings" 344).

Marjorie Rawlings's inspiration took off, and she began chronicling the events, people, and nature that surrounded her. She submitted her first creative work, "Cracker Chidlings," to *Scribner's Magazine* in 1930. This series of vignettes, which were not really full-fledged short stories, caught the attention of Maxwell Perkins, the editor of Scribner's great American novelists F. Scott Fitzgerald, Ernest Hemingway, and Thomas Wolfe. From the moment he first read her work, Perkins "realized he had a gem in the rough," according to Rodger Tarr (introduction to *Max and Marjorie* 2). Tarr explains the effect Perkins had on her work: "Early on she had very little sense of audience, or at least of the Scribner audience. She laced her work with a mixture of intellectualism and bawdiness that often defeated her purpose. She always captured essence but seldom fully grasped form. Perkins became her framer" (3).

While they worked on the structure of her stories, Rawlings realized that she had to learn more about the Cracker people whose lives she was about to chronicle. She wanted to range further afield, beyond her Cross Creek neighborhood to the big scrub, an area bounded on the west and north by the Oklawaha River and on the east by the St. Johns River and Lake George. In late August 1931 Rawlings moved in with Piety and Leonard Fiddia, a Cracker family she had befriended in the scrub. From Piety—a "ninety-pound wisp of a white-haired mother, who ploughs" and can kill a rattlesnake—Rawlings learned how to "wash her heavy quilts," take care of domestic chores, and speak certain local phrases.

From Piety's young son Leonard—"a boy as indigenous to the scrub as the deer" (*Max and Marjorie* 40)—Rawlings learned survival skills that were often on the far side of the law. In a 4 November 1931 letter to Perkins, Rawlings describes the pleasures of life in the scrub: "The life in the scrub is peculiarly right. While I was there, I did all the illegal things too; stalked deer with a light at night, out of season, kept the family in squirrels, paddled the boat while my friend dynamited mullet, shot limpkin on the river edge and had to wade waist deep in cypress swamp to get him (if you haven't eaten roast limpkin, you just haven't eaten)" (45).

One of the illegal activities in which Leonard Fiddia was engaged was moonshining. His dangerous brushes with the law and other outlaw 'shiners in the scrub would form "the main thread" of Rawlings's first novel, *South Moon Under*. Rawlings was on hand to observe an incident that would provide background to the novel: "Just the week before I went over to stay, a cousin of my 'shiner friend betrayed him, with two others, to the federal agents, and his still was torn up and burned. I had one experience I would not have missed for a great deal—a discussion of a group of the 'shiners and their friends, of various plans or dealing with the traitor. Nothing definite has been done to him yet . . . but in one way and another they are closing in on him, and some day he will simply disappear" (45).

Rawlings seemed fascinated with the wildness of the country and its people as she exclaimed to Perkins, "The scrub, as a matter of fact, has defeated civilization" (44). The "scanty population" that remained and was almost a dying breed of people is what captured her imagination. She explains the hold that people such as the Fiddias had on her: "I knew they were gentle; honest. I knew that living was precarious, but just how hand-to-mouth it is, surprised me. I was also astonished by the *utter lack of bleakness or despair*, in a group living momentarily on the very edge of starvation and danger" (44).

Rawlings immersed herself in their way of life by doing the "illegal things" that they did to the point that she began to lose a sense of the boundary that had previously existed between her old, sophisticated northern self and her current one: "It is so easy for me to live their life with them, that I am in some danger of losing all sophistication and perspective. I feel hurried sometimes, as though I must get 'written out' in this country within the next few years, because so much is no longer strange or unusual to me" (45). In this statement she is showing the strong empathy she developed for her Cracker friends which she would eventually convey to her fictional characters. Her vision would culminate in *The Yearling*, which powerfully evokes the scrub life she lived with the Fiddias and other scrub friends, including Cal Long and Barney Dillard, who taught her how to hunt and fish, identify plants and animals, and survive in the wild. In the 1930s and early 1940s, Rawlings would make use of this material and write her famous Cross Creek–area works *Golden Apples* (1935) and *Cross Creek* (1942) and her big scrub novels, *South Moon Under* (1933) and *The Yearling* (1938), the last of which won her the 1939 Pulitzer Prize and fans worldwide.

After the publication of *Cross Creek*, Rawlings's life would take a dramatic turn. One of the people featured in the book, Zelma Cason, a census taker and friend, would file a lawsuit in 1943 charging that *Cross Creek* had invaded her "right to privacy." The case would drag on for another five years, after being argued in front of the Florida Supreme Court, and would take a toll on Rawlings's time, energy, and creative work. Although the Florida high court on 9 August 1948 agreed that Cason's privacy had been invaded with the publication of the book, the justices gave Rawlings a pyrrhic victory of sorts, fining her only one dollar plus court costs. In the aftermath of the trial, Rawlings wrote only a few more short stories and articles about Cross Creek, thus completing her cycle of Florida works.

The focus of this book is on the year 1942, when Hurston and Rawlings met and were at the height of their careers. Chapter 1 will chronicle the development of their friendship, based on their letters to each other and other documented evidence of their meetings. Chapter 2 will examine the development of their craft of writing, culminating in the creation of their masterpieces, Hurston's *Their Eyes Were Watching God* (1937) and Rawlings's *The Yearling* (1938). Chapter 3 discusses both authors' attempts to look back on their lives in memoirs—Hurston's *Dust Tracks on a Road* and Rawlings's *Cross Creek*, both published the year they met. And, finally, chapter 4 will discuss the way the two authors influenced each other and touched each other's lives as they both struggled to complete their last creative works.

1

# "Friendship is a mysterious and ocean-bottom thing"

The Hurston-Rawlings Friendship

MARJORIE KINNAN RAWLINGS FIRST acknowledged Zora Neale Hurston's existence a few years before they met, as early as 1939. Rawlings had been reading Hurston's books, and she mentions her name in a lecture titled "Regional Literature of the South" that she delivered at the annual luncheon of the National Council of Teachers of English in New York on 25 November 1939 (the essay was later published in *College English* and *English Journal* in February 1940). In the article, Rawlings disparages the term "regionalist," believing that regional writers' "ultimate artistry is inadequate for a claim to the creation of literature" (278). She may have been self-serving, because at the time she was sometimes dismissed as a "regionalist" and resented all the limitations and gender discrimination that the term implied. Rawlings ends her lecture by considering the novels of three recently published southern female writers—Julia Peterkin, Elizabeth Madox Roberts, and "the negress, Zora Neale Hurston"—and claiming that their books "seem to me very close to literature." Nevertheless, she delivers a disclaimer: "Yet, again, permanence, or relative permanence, is too difficult for me to gauge" (277). Regarding Hurston's work, she explains: "It is the newest book by Zora Neale Hurston, *Moses, Man of the Mountain*, that tempts me to admit her to my own private library of literature. The book is reminiscent of Thomas Mann's great *Joseph in Egypt*. A timeless legend, part of man's priceless literary and spiritual heritage, is here revivified through the luminous negro mind. The book is racial, rather than regional, and I had best avoid a positive judgment on the excuse of irrelevancy to my subject matter" (278).

Rawlings's judgment that Hurston's book can be categorized as "racial" marginalizes it just as much as if she called it "regional." The fact that Rawlings mentions race at all indicates that it is at the back of her mind when she initially regards Hurston and her work. Rawlings further distances herself from Hurston's work by claiming that they do not share the same subject matter. Yet she seems attracted to the vitality of Hurston's "luminous negro mind."

After this initial awareness of Hurston as a writer, there is a question concerning when Rawlings actually met Hurston. Judging from Rawlings's letters to her husband and friends, their first meeting most likely occurred when Hurston invited Rawlings to speak at Florida Normal and Industrial College, a black school in St. Augustine, on 5 July 1942. Rawlings then reciprocated by inviting Hurston to tea at her hotel, the Castle Warden, the next day.

However, Rawlings's longtime African American servant Idella Parker—the author of the memoir *Idella: Marjorie Rawlings' "Perfect Maid"*—claims that the two authors became acquainted as early as the fall of 1940. Parker recounts that she came to work for Rawlings in September 1940 and that Hurston showed up for a visit shortly thereafter. Parker believes that the two authors had met previously at Rollins College, "where they both went from time to time to speak to groups of students" (86). Hurston's hometown of Eatonville is located only a few miles from the campus in Winter Park, and Hurston often visited faculty members there in pursuit of her dramatic and literary projects; thus she may have met Rawlings on one of these visits. Unfortunately, there is no verification in letters or newspaper accounts that they attended or spoke at the same event. Rawlings, who received an honorary doctorate from Rollins in 1939, frequently visited the campus as the honored guest of its president, Hamilton Holt, and participated in the Animated Magazine, a festival of distinguished speakers who publicly discussed their work in front of large audiences (see Reich). Hurston was not on the program with Rawlings on any of the dates that Rawlings spoke, nor was she likely in the predominantly white audience listening to Rawlings.

According to St. Augustine historian David Nolan, a more likely initial meeting may have occurred in St. Augustine through both writers' friendship with Mary Holland, the wife of Spessard Holland, Florida's twenty-eighth governor, who served from 1941 to 1945 (Nolan interview). Rawlings shared the platform with Governor Holland during the 1941 Animated Magazine at Rollins and became a friend of his wife. Hurston also considered Mary Holland one of her most admired friends, and she dedicated *Seraph on the Suwanee* to her (as well as Rawlings). Perhaps Mary Holland introduced the two writers in St. Augustine, and, later, Rawlings invited Hurston to Cross Creek, as Idella Parker reports.

Parker's account of Hurston's first visit to Cross Creek "about 1940" (86) is interesting for the light it sheds on the two women's friendship. On the day of the visit, Rawlings announced to Parker that an author was coming to visit and asked her "to plan something nice for lunch." Parker relates how shocked she was that "The woman was black!" and explains: "And here was Mrs. Rawlings, inviting her in and sitting her down on the porch like she was the queen of England" (86). The two women spent the day together: "I could hear them begin to loosen up and laugh and talk a little louder, and I guessed that Mrs. Rawlings was pouring drinks for them both." As the afternoon wore on, it became obvious to Parker that Hurston "was in no shape to be driving home that day." Parker was further shocked when Rawlings informed her that Hurston would spend the night—and sleep with Idella in the tenant house. Parker records her response: "Imagine this now! Here was a black author who had come to visit Mrs. Rawlings and had been treated like an equal all day long, talking, laughing, and drinking together on the porch for all the world to see. But when it came to spending the night, Zora would be sent out to sleep with the servants. This was not for lack of bedrooms, mind you. Mrs. Rawlings had two empty bedrooms in the house, and no one else staying in either one" (87).

This single detail—that Rawlings sent Hurston to sleep in the servants' quarters—seems to have become definitive in people's perceptions of the two women's relationship. The assumption is that Rawlings was a racist and that Hurston was her victim, a view that John Lowe summarizes in *Jump at the Sun*: "Rawlings didn't mind spending all day with Zora, or even getting drunk with her, but when Hurston spent the night at Cross Creek she had to sleep in the maid's cabin" (335). Trefzer, on the other hand, looks at the incident from another perspective: "This incident, however, may be less a sign of the absence of 'friendship' between Hurston and Rawlings than proof that Hurston knew how to play by the rules of segregation, as her first visit with Rawlings in St. Augustine had shown" (75). In her published letters, Rawlings certainly starts off sounding like a racist, but her views dramatically evolved—possibly due to her association with Hurston.

Although there is no evidence that Rawlings was in any way influenced by the Ku Klux Klan or that she shunned close association with Hurston because of her fear of racial violence, the Klan was active in the small towns of central Florida. Rawlings lived most of the time alone in her Cross Creek farmhouse. Hurston, too, may have wanted to steer clear of any racially charged or misinterpretable situations. In *Southern Exposure*, Florida civil rights activist Stetson Kennedy documents the Klan's criminal activities in Florida during the 1940s, even connecting the Klan's practice of white supremacy to the racism surrounding Hitler's implementation of laws meant to advance the "master race": "In the matters of peonage, feudalism, exploitation, and denial of suffrage to her own citizens, the South is 100 per cent as fascistic as was Nazi Germany. . . . [T]he storm troopers of Southern fascism—the Klan, police, state guardsmen—are preparing for *Der Tag* when they can demonstrate that they can be just as terroristic as the Nazis" (191).

Although neither Rawlings nor Hurston made this connection between the Klan and the Nazis, it is unlikely that either woman wanted to do battle on this political front during wartime, when fear and prejudice ran loose throughout the world; instead, they focused on creating a friendship. The time to do battle would come later. Besides, this was a busy time for both women, who were at the height of their careers. Rawlings visited Eleanor Roosevelt in the White House in April 1941, and on her way back to Florida she stopped in to see Ellen Glasgow in Richmond, Virginia. During the summer a film crew from MGM began filming *The Yearling* in Florida. Although Spencer Tracy was to star in the film, the movie had to be postponed for various reasons. On 27 October 1941, Rawlings married her longtime companion, Norton Baskin, who was getting ready to open their St. Augustine hotel, Castle Warden, which had a penthouse apartment for the newlyweds. After the wedding, Rawlings began commuting the nearly ninety miles between St. Augustine and Cross Creek. When she bought a home on Crescent Beach, south of St. Augustine, it also became part of her commute. Staying in the Castle Warden apartment made her feel like a "wildcat in a cage," she reported in a letter to Ellen Glasgow: "The pull of Cross Creek is still strong and I have to go back every week or two. It would be so sensible to wean myself away from it altogether, but after you've read the book [*Cross Creek*] I think you will understand the almost unreasonably deep roots there" (*Selected Letters* 221).

During this same period, Hurston filed for divorce from her second husband, Albert Price III, in February 1940, although they briefly reconciled. She quit a teaching job at North Carolina College for Negroes (now North Carolina Central University) in Durham in March 1940 and returned to her anthropological research. Hurston spent the spring and summer of 1940 doing research on the "sanctified" churches of South Carolina and making a film about religious practices with anthropologist Jane Belo. When they completed their work, Hurston was anxious by Labor Day to return to New York City, where she could "see and to feel" again, as she reports to Fannie Hurst (*Hurston: A Life in Letters* 461). She was also eager to get back in contact with Percy Punter, so that they could resume their love affair (*Dust Tracks* 261).

During the winter of 1940–41, when Hurston began her autobiography for Bertram Lippincott, she decided to write the memoir in California as a houseguest of her wealthy friend Katharine Edson Mershon, a fellow anthropologist. Hurston was also attracted by the proximity to Hollywood, presumably because she wished to explore film possibilities. According to Carla Kaplan, "Some of her closest friends, such as writers

Marjorie Kinnan Rawlings and Fannie Hurst, saw their writing adapted for very popular movies, and Hurston may have hoped to follow their example" (*Hurston: A Life in Letters* 435). Kaplan reports that several of Hurston's works were reviewed by film studios, but nothing came of their interest. Hurston was hired in October 1941 as a Paramount "story consultant," yet most of her creative work in Hollywood was not on the movies but on her memoir, *Dust Tracks on a Road* (436). After her lack of luck in Hollywood, Hurston eventually moved to St. Augustine in the spring of 1942 and was hired to teach creative writing in summer school at Florida Normal. She also spent her time revising *Dust Tracks on a Road*, which was published in November 1942.

Given Hurston's schedule in 1940, 1941, and 1942, it seems unlikely that she would have met Rawlings in the fall of 1940, as Parker claims. At that time, Hurston was living in New York City and working hard to finish *Dust Tracks on a Road*. On 15 January 1941 she writes Annie Nathan Meyer that she has "put the last word down on my book" (*Hurston: A Life in Letters* 461). A more likely time for the meeting was in the spring of 1942, when Hurston moved back to St. Augustine.

By 5 July 1942 the women had established enough of a relationship for Hurston to invite Rawlings to speak to her class at Florida Normal. Hurston's biographer Hemenway speculates on the visit: "The white woman was so dazzled by her companion that without thinking she invited her to tea at her husband's segregated resort hotel" (296). The tea took place the next day, on 6 July. Besides the eyewitness accounts of Don Wilson and Norton Baskin, Parker and Rawlings also wrote reminiscences. Parker's memory of the event differs from Wilson's and Baskin's. She recalls that "Mrs. Rawlings was excited to see her old friend again." But, in contrast to her earlier visit, "This time when Zora arrived, she came up to the penthouse by the back stairs. She looked poor and tired and broken. It looked like Zora has fallen on some hard times. She didn't stay long, and Mrs. Rawlings was saddened by this visit" (88). Further on in that passage, Parker points out: "The word among the black community was that back in Eatonville Zora had acted so uppity and superior to her own people that they had rejected and shunned her. She had no friends among her own race" (88).

Rawlings's memory of the visit is recorded in a 7 July 1942 letter to fellow Scribner's author and St. Augustine friend, Edith Pope. Curiously, Rawlings addresses her letter to Pope's dog, Patrie, and recounts the visit from the viewpoint of her pointer, Moe. This bizarre narrative viewpoint, which does not occur in any other of Rawlings's letters, may be a way for Rawlings to mask her true feelings about the visit or, at least, to figure out on paper how she felt about the visit. In Moe's words, Rawlings describes the day:

> The Missus had a most interesting caller yesterday, by invitation, and my feelings are rather mixed about it. It was the Florida negress, Zora Neale Hurston, who has done some really superb work. She is at the Florida Normal School and will teach there this winter. She is a lush, fine-looking café au lait woman with a most ingratiating personality, a brilliant mind, and a fundamental wisdom that shames most whites. She puts the full responsibility for negro advancement on the negroes themselves and has no use for the Left Wingers who consider her a traitor, nor for the "advanced" Negroes who belong to what she calls the fur-coat peerage. . . .
>
> The Missus has had quite a jolt and feels rather small. By all her principles, she should accept this woman as a human being and a friend—certainly an attractive member of society acceptable anywhere—and she is a coward. If she were on her own, she would do it. She feels that she cannot hurt her husband in a business way. But her pioneer spirit is itching. (*Selected Letters* 222–24)

In response, Pope laments the fact that she is in Mississippi and cannot attend the get-together. On 20 July 1942 she writes to Rawlings: "It is really sad that the one winter Zorah Neal [*sic*] Hurston is in St. Augustine I am not. I've wanted to meet that woman for years on end, and have even hunted for her name in the Washington phone book with the intention of going to see her. I do think she is remarkable, an impression confirmed by your letter. Gee, I wish I thought I'd get home while she is there" (Edith Pope Papers, University of Florida Libraries).

Pope does not react to Rawlings's ambivalence about race, but Rawlings's letter summarizes her fears about race early in her relationship with Hurston. In contrast to Pope's more accepting attitudes, the fact that she speaks from a dog's viewpoint may show her discomfort with the topic or distancing from her own feelings of shame over her prejudices. Over the next several years, Rawlings would critically examine her racial prejudice, and her views on race would evolve to a more enlightened position, as Anita Tarr explains (A. Tarr 141–42).

In contrast, at this point in their relationship, Hurston apparently did not want to demonstrate any sense of racial difference, as evidenced by a letter she wrote to Rawlings ten months after the tea at Castle Warden. On 16 May 1943, presumably after Rawlings had sent Hurston a copy of *Cross Creek*, Hurston writes her appreciation of the memoir: "Twenty-one guns! I have just read 'Cross Creek' carefully and prayerfully. It is a most remarkable piece of work. You turned your inside light on there [*sic*] community life, and it broke like day. . . . I am at your feet in admiration" (*Hurston: A Life in Letters* 486–88).

Hurston ends the letter by extending an invitation to Rawlings to join her in a journey on Hurston's houseboat, *The Wanago* (i.e., Want to Go): "How I wish that we could explore both the Indian and St. John's [*sic*] river together" (487–88). Hurston's assessment of Rawlings's book may have been heartfelt praise, calculated flattery, or a way of ingratiating herself to Rawlings, who had the kind of mainstream success that Hurston craved. Throughout her life, Hurston followed this pattern of flattering her white patrons, beginning at Barnard College when Fannie Hurst, Annie Nathan Meyer, and, later, Charlotte Osgood Mason gave her financial, social, and emotional support. Mary Helen Washington attributes Hurston's behavior to the fact that she was "fiercely determined to have a career, no matter what or who had to be sacrificed" (14). Therefore, if she had to resort to "un-Hurstonlike" statements or acts, she would do so, as Hurston admits: "So I shall wrassle me up a future or die trying!" (*Hurston: A Life in Letters* 194). But there is no evidence that Hurston was being ingenuous with Rawlings.

About the same time Hurston was cultivating her friendship with Rawlings, she was also corresponding with Tracy L'Engle Angas, a white Florida friend and cousin of author Madeleine L'Engle. Angas was a professional actress who had performed minor roles in Broadway productions, including *Rosanne*, a Negro play cast with white actors. Hurston and Angas originally became acquainted in 1937, when Angas asked

Hurston for permission to do a dramatic reading from *Mules and Men*. According to Frank Orser, Hurston and Angas continued to develop their friendship in the 1940s and probably spent time together. In a letter written in 1943, Hurston, who was living on her boat in Daytona Beach at the time, invites Angas to visit her, saying that the boat is "your second home" (65). In another letter, written in May 1943, Hurston writes to Angas: "I must talk with you to get back my soul" (64). Orser concludes: "The tone of the letters is, in fact, so personal and intimate as to suggest that the two women were the best of friends. . . . This is a bit puzzling, however, since there is nothing else in the known biographies of either woman to indicate how, or whether, such a friendship ever developed. Perhaps, with Hurston's knack for hyperbole and her enthusiasm, or in the desperation of her circumstances, the closeness is simply overstated" (64).

Hurston's relationship with Angas, at least on paper, resembles her connection to Rawlings. Her interactions form a pattern: instant intimacy suggesting shared literary interests, invitations proffered in hopes that they will be reciprocated, offers of work and financial aid. Indeed, in 1945, when Angas had an editorial connection with the *Encyclopedia Americana*, she offered to pay Hurston to write an article on "Negro, American" that would replace an article written by W. E. B. DuBois in 1904. Besides giving her the opportunity to attack DuBois as "the most pleadingest of all the special pleaders" (*Hurston: A Life in Letters* 533), Hurston jumped at the chance to maintain her connection to Angas, particularly since Angas sent her other small paying commissions.

Rawlings did not immediately respond to Hurston's hyperbolic 16 May letter, but she did send it to her editor at Scribner's, Maxwell Perkins, on 11 August 1943. He replied enthusiastically: "Thanks ever so much for letting me read Zora Hurston's letter. She certainly writes good letters, and is obviously a very unusual person. I hope some day you can go on that trip with her [on the *Wanago*]" (Rawlings, *Max and Marjorie* 552). The fact that Rawlings sent Hurston's letter to Perkins indicates that she regarded Hurston as a fellow author worthy of Perkins's notice. Perkins would eventually sign Hurston on as a Scribner's author, but not for four more years. It is unclear why Hurston did not sign a contract with Scribner's at this time. Perkins was a genius and could transform even the roughest manuscript into a best-seller, as he did for two of Rawlings's other friends, Marcia Davenport and Edith Pope. A connection with Scribner's at this time in her career would have been a life-altering experience for Hurston.

Shortly after she sent the letter to Perkins, Rawlings finally wrote back to Hurston. In reply, Hurston sent Rawlings the most disturbing letter she would ever write to her. After receiving Hurston's lavish praise for *Cross Creek*, Rawlings must have replied during the summer of 1943 that she was not able to work because of servant problems (Parker had left Rawlings's employ and had "gone Harlem") and because her husband had enlisted in the American Field Service for ambulance duty on the front lines of battle in Burma. On 21 August 1943, Hurston offers to work as Rawlings's servant:

> How I wish that I were not doing a book too at this time! I would be so glad to come and take everything off your hands until you are through with yours. I know just what you need. You are certainly a genius and need a buffer while you are in labor. Idella is much less intelligent than I took her to be. What a privilege she had! Well, it is inevitable that people like you will waste a lot of jewelry by chunking it into hog pens. Even though I am busy, if it gets too awful, give a whoop and a holler and I will do what I can for you. I really mean that. . . .
>
> Really, now, Miss Rawlings, if you find yourself losing your stride, let me help you out. I know so tragically what it means to be trying to concentrate and being nagged by the necessity of living. Of course yours is not financial as mine was at one time, but still with the scarcity of help in these war days, it might call for all sorts of annoyance to just get fed and bedded. (*Hurston: A Life in Letters* 494–95)

Elizabeth Silverthorne in *Marjorie Kinnan Rawlings: Sojourner at Cross Creek* claims that "Marjorie took her up on the offer and she came and spent ten days" (233). Unfortunately, Silverthorne provides no footnotes, specific evidence, or dates to back up this claim. She based her book, though, on extensive conversations with Norton Baskin, although she has since discarded these transcripts and, in a recent interview, does not recall the details of this episode. She is certain that if Hurston had worked at Rawlings's home, it would have been to help a friend out. During an interview, Rawlings's nearest neighbor, J. T. Glisson, did not recall that such an extended visit took place, nor does Baskin mention it in any of his so-far-published interviews.

To a twenty-first-century reader, Hurston's letter is baffling. On 16 May, Hurston was writing to Rawlings, "You are my sister"; three months later, she is seemingly offering to be Rawlings's servant. Donald Wilson pointed out in an interview with me that Hurston might have believed that the only way Rawlings could have Hurston around on a daily basis was for Hurston to serve Rawlings. On the other hand, Hurston may have been engaging in doublespeak. Hurston's relationship with Rawlings and her circle was possibly more important to Hurston than Hurston's friendship was to Rawlings. Hurston may have ingratiated herself in order to remain on intimate terms with Rawlings. Yet, Hurston also says in the letter that her own work prevents her from helping Rawlings. Thus, simultaneously, she is being supportive of Rawlings in order to remain on a friendly basis or gain access to her circle, while privileging her own work over Rawlings's.

Two days later, on 23 August 1943, Rawlings gives her interpretation of Hurston's offer in a letter to her husband:

> I am in a mellow mood about human beings, for the Negro writer, Zora Neale Hurston, has done one of the most beautiful things I have ever known. After several months, in which she must have thought I had taken offense at her letter about "Cross Creek," I wrote her a good letter. I am ashamed to say that I alibied about taking a river trip with her, telling her I should love to (which is true) but that I was deep in work on a book. I mentioned that I was in trouble as to getting the work done with all my energy free for it, as Idella had "gone Harlem." I said that though I put no high value on my work, still I had thought Idella felt she shared in it in giving me an unirked background, and that surely there was nothing menial in her work, since the wives of countless creative workers of one sort and another did exactly the same things for their husbands and were glad to participate in that way. I said that I had felt, evidently mistakenly, that in treating and considering

Idella as a friend, in sharing my books with her, talking with her, I gave her something she would not ordinarily get. (*The Private Marjorie* 114)

Rawlings then gives her reaction to Hurston's offer, unaware of her own racist overtones:

I shed tears over the woman's offer. She is an artist in her own right, and if ever the "nigger" was going to come out, it would presumably be in one who had gone as high professionally as she has. She and Dr. [George Washington] Carver seem monumental to me. To transcend the humiliation of their position and being at the peak themselves, to have such graciousness—. Such bigness. I feel so small, thinking of my alibi to her. When she and I have finished our present books, I shall take the trip with her if it costs me the lawsuit and you your business, not, God knows, in any spirit of condescension but with a desire to learn and to know. Her offer settles in my mind all doubts I have had about throwing myself into the fight for an honest chance for the Negro. The mass of people, black or white, is always bound to be the hoi polloi. The rare, choice individual is the one who carries the torch, and nothing must stand in the way of such an individual. And of course, when the individual is big enough, as she is, and as Dr. Carver was, any Deep South, obstructionism, any Jewish-radical "fight for rights," is a candle before a great wind. (114–15)

Rawlings is seemingly unaware of how racist her use of "nigger" is in this frank letter to her husband. She unwittingly reveals all of her ambivalences, both toward an African American woman helping her and toward an artist on her professional level. Just because Rawlings can talk to the educated Parker about her work, Rawlings assumes that Parker values Rawlings's work as highly as Rawlings does. Yet this letter contains hints of Rawlings's change of heart regarding African American human rights. She claims that Hurston's generous offer "settles in my mind all doubts I have had about throwing myself into the fight for an honest chance for the Negro." Over the course of the decade, Rawlings would write and act in support of these rights.

In his introduction to *The Private Marjorie*, Rodger Tarr discusses in depth the evolution of Rawlings's views on race. "On the subject of race," he admits, "Rawlings is an enigma. She tried so hard publicly to change the face of America, yet in private she routinely employed racially charged stereotype and slur" (4–5). Tarr claims, though, that there was "definite love, however paternalistic," between Rawlings and her black servants. Black women such as Martha Mickens "became a part of Rawlings's own education," and her complicated relationships with them "open[ed] up a whole new world of white-black relationships in the otherwise staunchly segregated Cross Creek" (5). Tarr goes so far as to say that Rawlings, in her appreciation of black culture, even "became a part of that black culture" (5).

Hurston seemed to be the catalyst that moved Rawlings to be more open to black culture. In a 19 October 1943 letter to Edith Pope, Rawlings explains her willingness to be an advocate for black human rights: "Did I write you that Zora Neale Hurston wrote me of her distress and disgust at Idella's leaving, and knowing that I was trying to get to work on a book, offered—though she is working on a book of her own—to come and take over until I finished my book? It is one of the biggest things I have ever known a human being to do. It made me ready to go—all for the Negro race" (Edith Pope Papers, University of Florida Libraries).

Complicating and stalling Rawlings's evolution at this time was her infamous "invasion of privacy" lawsuit, which she was occupied with during the 1940s. Zelma Cason, a former friend, sued Rawlings for defamation of character for Rawlings's portrayal of her in *Cross Creek*. The case ended up before the Florida Supreme Court, but not before it cost Rawlings large amounts of money and countless hours of worry. While the case was in limbo, Rawlings was fearful of losing the lawsuit by attracting notice and demonstrating for African American rights in racist Florida of the 1940s, even though the case had no racial overtones.

In December 1943, after exchanging Christmas greetings with Hurston, Rawlings's ideals were tested when Hurston decided to pay an unexpected visit. In a 22 December 1943 letter to Baskin, Rawlings writes about the visit: "I have just had a most interesting experience—one that I knew was coming sooner or later—that I had been dreading—and once it happened, there was no more dread—I am referring to an overnight visit of Zora Neale Hurston!" (*The Private Marjorie* 208). She had long suspected that Hurston would drive over from Daytona to renew their friendship. Rawlings had precipitated the visit by sending Hurston a Christmas card and, thinking of Hurston "alone on her houseboat," offered to send her "oranges and pecans." Rawlings describes her note: "As it came out, my note had sounded terribly depressed and blue, and I had spoken of making no progress on my book, etc.—and she had decided maybe she could help me or give me a lift, and had dropped her work and driven clear over here just to try to cheer me up" (209).

Rawlings explains her reaction when Hurston turned up on her doorstep: "Well, I had the most mixed emotions. I was so touched by her doing it, as I was touched by her offer to do my housekeeping while I worked—and it was supper-time, and it was night-time and bed-time—and dat old debbil prejudice fair stuck a needle in me. I was ashamed, and I was worried, and I thought this would probably be the evening Mrs. Glisson would come up to ask me something, and the word would go out, and I would lose the law-suit!" (209).

As Rawlings was pondering what to do, her servants, Martha and Sissie Mickens, solved her dilemma:

Meantime, Martha and Sissie had fallen *fatuously* in love with Zora—and Zora herself had arranged things with such modest tact that I felt like a dog for having any qualms. Martha came over to say that she had supper ready for Zora. I said no, I wanted her to have supper with me. And I thought, "Watchman, what of the night?"—and Zora had already been invited by Martha to spend the night there, and had taken her bags over there, and was taking it for granted that she would sleep there—and if I was a bitch about it, Zora would never have blinked an eyelash. It was all so quietly and gracefully done to spare me any embarrassment, if I proved the sort who needed sparing! And I thought of the tenant house already crowded to the rafters, and my empty house, and I thought, damn it, now is the time for all good men to come to the aid of a moral principle! So I said I didn't want to be selfish or disappoint Martha, but I had so much more room, and would

Jack please bring her bags over here to the back guest room. And I have never in my life been so glad that I was not a coward. I had to hurdle an awfully wide ditch! I was amazed to find that my own prejudices were so deep. It has always surprised me that my thinking is so Southern. But I felt that if I ever was to prove my humanitarian and moral beliefs, even if it cost me the lawsuit I must do it then. (209)

The visit must have succeeded in drawing the women closer together. For Rawlings, it marked a turning point in her thinking on race relations: "Well, from spending that time with Zora, who is a nigger, who is an artist, who is big and wonderful, I have advanced a long way, and she helped me in a way that she never thought of. She is entirely at home in both the white and the negro world, and any citizen of the cosmos should be so at home, and I am way ahead by the experience. We had a fine time, and by the time she left an hour ago, I had gone a long way" (209–10).

A troubling detail in this letter is that Rawlings freely uses the same racial slur to describe Hurston that she uses with her servants, seemingly unconscious of any negative connotations that this pejorative word conjures up. Hurston herself in her work does not seem particularly disturbed by it either. Hurston uses the word "nigger" ten times in *Seraph on the Suwanee*. In a 3 September 1947 letter to her Scribner's editor, Burroughs Mitchell, Hurston writes: "I am conscious that the use of 'nigger' in the text will offend some Negro readers. However, I am objective in my observations, and I know, as they know honestly, that the heroine would have certainly used that word. However, as a publisher, the discretion is yours" (*Hurston: A Life in Letters* 555).

Hurston knew that her white friend Carl Van Vechten had published a novel in 1926 titled *Nigger Heaven* and that its title had received a lot of criticism from black male authors. Hurston defended his right to use that word for his title, according to Carla Kaplan (*Hurston: A Life in Letters* 555).

Rawlings admits, though, that her new openness and generosity about race have taken a psychic toll. During the night Hurston spent in her home, Rawlings had a nightmare, as she reports to her husband:

In the nightmare, I was taking a stand, and had gone to a negro football game where "high whites" were to be, and I was going with Negroes as a moral gesture. And it was going to cause me trouble in the lawsuit, and was going to make a pariah of me, and I hated it, but the die was cast. And when I reached the boxes, and a Negro came out and fervently welcomed me and I felt quite ruined, lo and behold, you [Baskin] were suddenly by my side, and were shaking hands with the Negro, and I had the most wonderful feeling of your standing by me. . . . And I woke up. (*The Private Marjorie* 210)

Rawlings enters the public arena in her dream, and she is forced to make a "moral gesture" in front of an audience of both whites and blacks. Her fear comes out, namely, that her relationship with Hurston will have a negative impact on her "invasion of privacy" trial. In fact, a week later, in a 29 December 1943 letter to her husband, Rawlings admits that the case has "done a good deal to shred my nerves" (*The Private Marjorie* 217). When the mail brings a copy of Cason's brief for the appeal to the state supreme court, Rawlings admits to her husband: "I was right in my fears about Zora! But I think my shame is still secret" (217). Obviously, Rawlings is feeling vulnerable about her decision to do the right thing, but her dream indicates that she is reassured that her husband will support her.

During Hurston's visit the conversation between the two women must have touched on race relations, because Rawlings was surprised to learn that Hurston was not an advocate of special treatment for blacks. "Zora is much more conservative about the 'Negro question' than I," Rawlings recounts. "She feels that it is up to the Negroes to prove themselves as human beings, but I feel that a fight must be made, human nature being as selfish as it is" (*The Private Marjorie* 210). Hurston had already explained her position in *Dust Tracks on a Road*. At the end of the chapter dealing with race, she states her view that blacks cannot be lumped together in one group labeled "Negro": "I maintain that I have been a Negro three times—a Negro baby, a Negro girl and a Negro woman. Still, if you have received no clear cut impression of what the Negro in America is like, then you are in the same place with me. There is no *The*

*Negro* here. Our lives are so diversified, internal attitudes so varied, appearances and capabilities so different, that there is no possible classification so catholic that it will cover us all, except My people! My people!" (237).

Throughout her lifetime, Hurston received much criticism, particularly from black male authors, for not being more of an activist for black civil rights. It is not surprising that they were critical in the 1940s when Hurston was quoted as saying "The Jim Crow system works" in a February 1943 interview published in the *New York World-Telegram*. Thus it is ironic that just when Rawlings appears to be ready to make the leap toward greater involvement in the struggle, Hurston is reluctant to encourage her forward. Hurston, of course, is a product of the all-black community of Eatonville and was raised with a sense of entitlement that comes from being the mayor's daughter. She always felt that she was the equal of anyone; yet she was fully aware of the social conditions surrounding her legacy as the daughter not only of the mayor but also of a former slave.

After this high point in intimacy and understanding, there is no evidence indicating why the friendship between Hurston and Rawlings lapsed over the next five years. Both authors were struggling with physical, emotional, and spiritual concerns, and perhaps they did not have the time or energy to pursue their relationship. The war also played a role. Rawlings's husband enlisted as an ambulance driver in the American Field Service in July 1943 and was sent to India until October 1944. Rawlings complained to Maxwell Perkins on 29 March 1944: "I am afraid that I won't be able to write until Norton is safe home, or if that worst happens, for a year or two after" (*Max and Marjorie* 562). Rawlings turned her attention to writing nearly daily letters to her husband (now published in *The Private Marjorie: The Love Letters of Marjorie Kinnan Rawlings to Norton R. Baskin*, edited by Rodger Tarr). She also devoted much of her attention during the war years to writing letters to service people. Tarr notes that "She often received more than one hundred letters per week, and to answer them—work that she found debilitating—she had to employ secretaries to help her" (*The Private Marjorie* 17). Hurston, too, was affected by the war. She served on the Recreation in War project and spoke to segregated groups of GIs stationed around

Florida in 1943. She also increasingly turned her attention outward from her literary work to politics. By 1946 she was living in New York and assisting Grant Reynolds in his congressional campaign against Adam Clayton Powell Jr. She also worked on a community child-care program in Harlem.

In addition, both women's personal lives were in turmoil during the mid 1940s. Rawlings suffered from being separated from her husband during the war and was involved in a costly lawsuit. Hurston's life, too, was in continual upheaval as she moved back and forth between Florida and New York City, and between her Florida houseboats, *Wanago* and *Sun Tan*. She found time to marry and divorce James Howell Pitts of Cleveland in 1944. Increasingly, her focus turned to Honduras. In 1944 she was fascinated by British gold miner Reginald Brett's accounts of Mayan ruins in Honduras near the Patuca River. She tried to raise money for an exploratory trip by applying for grants to the Guggenheim Foundation and the Library of Congress, but both institutions rejected her applications.

Hurston and Rawlings also struggled with their writing. Rawlings tells of the agonizing ten-year struggle to write her next novel, *The Sojourner* (which wouldn't be published until 1953). Hurston couldn't get her manuscripts approved for publication either. She wrote a novel about Eatonville, filling it with stories from *Mule Bone* and *Polk County*, but it was rejected by her publisher, Lippincott. She then threw herself into researching a study of the life and times of Herod the Great, which she would be obsessed with until her death and would elicit no interest from publishers.

The winter of 1946–47 was the low point for both authors. Hurston fell into a deep depression due to the rejection of her novel and lack of money to support her anthropological trip to Honduras. Rawlings was devastated by the turn her *Cross Creek* trial had taken. In 1946 the circuit court at Gainesville found her innocent of invading the privacy of Zelma Cason, whom she had characterized in *Cross Creek* as "an ageless spinster resembling an angry and efficient canary" (56). Cason immediately appealed the verdict to the Florida Supreme Court. Once again, Rawlings's time, energy, and money were consumed in continuing the fight. The state supreme court a year later reversed the earlier decision and fined Rawlings one dollar plus court costs. Rawlings felt that she was fighting this battle on behalf of all authors who valued freedom of expression. Whether the trial destroyed her feeling of being at home in Cross Creek is not known, but the same year the verdict from the state supreme court was handed down, she bought a farmhouse in Van Hornesville, New York, and made southern Michigan the setting of *The Sojourner.*

Rawlings experienced another devastating setback on 17 June 1947, when her beloved editor, Maxwell Perkins, died suddenly of pneumonia after two days of illness. On 9 July she wrote to her friend Bernice Gilkyson: "It was startling to realize . . . how much we wrote *for* him, and certainly with his judgment constantly in mind. I dream about him often and wake up in tears" (*Selected Letters* 300). The sad irony of Perkins's death is that shortly before he died, he signed Hurston to a Scribner's contract for her next novel. On 16 April he had written to Rawlings: "By the way, we have just taken an option on Zora Hurston's next novel. All I had read of hers was that autobiographical book, but she came in, and gave me the impression of somebody so full of life and emotion and intelligence that whatever she did should be good. She roused up the whole office by the vitality of her presence" (*Max and Marjorie* 609). Rawlings responded on 30 April: "I am delighted that you may publish Zora Neale Hurston's next book. I feel that she has a very great talent. You really should read her 'Moses, Man of the Mountain.' She has not only the Negro gift of rhythm and imagination, but she is proud of her blood and her people, and presents her stories from the Negro point of view. I am very fond of her. And will you send me her address? I have been wanting to write her, but didn't know where she was" (609).

This letter leads us to wonder why Hurston had not signed a contract with Scribner's much earlier. If Hurston had signed a contract with Scribner's in 1943 and had been able to work with Perkins for the next four years, her writing career may have taken a dramatically different turn. Rawlings certainly benefited from her association with Perkins. They wrote voluminous letters to each other, analyzing Rawlings's work endlessly. Rawlings knew how much Perkins's guidance would mean to Hurston's career and must have recommended that Perkins take her on as one of his writers; therefore, it is a mystery why it didn't happen sooner. Even the advance money was a shot in the arm for Hurston; it gave her the means to make her dream trip to Honduras come true. She set sail on 4 May 1947 "with high hopes that her adventure was about to begin" (Hemenway 304).

Six weeks later, Perkins was dead and Hurston had to make her own way in her career, although she continued to work with her new editor at Scribner's, Burroughs Mitchell. She was able to publish her final novel, *Seraph on the Suwanee*. Hemenway calls it "an unsuccessful work of art" (314), mainly because Hurston "turned away from the resources that had previously sustained and inspired her art. . . . The folklore that had graced Eatonville and provoked Hurston's celebration of black people now comes from the mouths of southern whites" (315). Hemenway claims that this new direction may have come from Hurston's desire to show that "there was cross-cultural borrowing of folklore in the South" (315), but it may also have come from her desire to emulate Rawlings's commercial success with *The Yearling* and *Cross Creek*. Hurston had Hollywood aspirations and may have been impressed by the fact that Rawlings's *The Yearling* was being filmed in central Florida in the mid-1940s (the film was released in 1946, starring Gregory Peck and Jane Wyman).

While Hurston was trying to establish herself in a white publishing world, Rawlings in early 1948, according to Tarr, continued to struggle with her racism: "her recognition of her own racist tendencies and those of her friends plagued her" (introduction to *The Private Marjorie* 511). She argued frequently on the issue, including with the governor of Florida. Rawlings and Hurston may have met during this period, as a 4 March 1948 letter to Phil May, Rawlings's longtime lawyer and friend, indicates. Rawlings tells May that Hurston "is due in sometime over the weekend" (Phil May Papers, University of Florida Libraries).

In April 1948, Rawlings made an important breakthrough in her views on race by speaking at Fisk University, an all-black institution, and staying with its president. Making use of interviews with Norton Baskin, Silverthorne describes Rawlings's visit:

> She turned back her honorarium to the Fisk University scholarship fund and paid her own expenses for the train trip. In Nashville she

stayed in the home of the university president, Charles S. Johnson. This was a public gesture of support for racial integration: Johnson was the first black president of Fisk, which had always had a mixed faculty. She met many blacks with "brilliant minds" and "charming personalities" on this trip. As usual she insisted on speaking informally and welcomed opportunities to talk with the students in small gatherings. (287)

Hurston's battles in 1948, on the other hand, were more on an epic scale. On 14 September 1948 she was wrongly accused of sodomy by a ten-year-old boy and two of his friends and was indicted on 1 October. Like Rawlings in the energy-sapping, mind-consuming "invasion of privacy" trial, Hurston became obsessed with clearing her name and considered the situation mind-boggling: "The thing is too fantastic, too evil, too far from reality for me to conceive of it," she wrote on 30 October 1948 to her friend Carl Van Vechten and his wife, Fania Marinoff (*Hurston: A Life in Letters* 570). She was further distressed because "a Negro who works down in the courts secured the matter and went around peddling it to papers. That is the blow that knocked me loose from all that I have ever looked to and cherished" (571). Hurston was pilloried in the black press; the 23 October 1948 issue of the *Baltimore Afro-American* published a front-page story titled "Boys, 10, accuse Zora." The subtitle is even more shocking: "Did She Want 'Knowing and Doing' Kind of Love?"—a sly reference to Hurston's recently published *Seraph on the Suwanee*. Hurston called the article a "sluice of filth" and told Van Vechten that the shock led her to contemplate suicide: "I have resolved to die. It will take a few days for me to set my affairs in order, and then I will go" (573). She concludes with an opinion about her race: "My race has seen fit to destroy me without reason, and with the vilest tools conceived of by man so far" (572). Rawlings heard about Hurston's despair and wrote to Van Vechten: "Charlie Scribner reported that our Zora had been in trouble on a 'mild sex charge.' This is idiotic. Sex is never mild." She signed the letter, "Cousin Marjorie" (*Selected Letters* 325).

By 18 November 1948, each of the children had confessed or confirmed the fact that they had been engaging in homosexual acts and wanted to displace their guilt onto adults nearby, including a janitor and

Hurston. This testimony, combined with the fact that Hurston's passport proved that she was out of the country at the time the alleged actions occurred, caused the case to be dismissed on 14 March 1949. The trial cost Hurston, according to Carla Kaplan, "both her peace of mind and the book she was working on at the end of the decade, a novel entitled *The Lives of Barney Turk*" (*Hurston: A Life in Letters* 448).

It took Hurston a long time to recover. A year later, in the fall of 1949, she reports to her Scribner's editor, Burroughs Mitchell: "I feel that I have come to myself at last. I can even endure the sight of a Negro, which I thought once I could never do again" (undated letter, fall 1949, Scribner Archives, Princeton). She was grateful to her publisher and the other friends who believed in her and stood by her side during her ordeal. In an undated letter in the fall or winter of 1948, she profusely thanks Rawlings, who had sent Hurston "a kind and loving letter" the previous spring. Rawlings must have urged Hurston to keep her spirits up, for Hurston replies: "I am not so sure that I have done my best, but I tried. I need not tell you that my goal still eludes me. I am in despair because it keeps ever ahead of me" (*Hurston: A Life in Letters* 575). Rawlings must also have sent Hurston money, because Hurston thanks her for it: "Naturally, I am praying that [*Seraph on the Suwanee*] will have a big sale so that I can return the sum that you so generously loanded [*sic*] me. Oh, my dear, so much has happened to me since that time. I have had to go through a long, long, dark tunnel to come out to the light again. But I had the feeling all the time that you believed in me and that I had better git up and git or you would feel let down" (577). Hurston signs the letter, "With faithful feelings."

Hurston's spirits improved to the extent that she was able to send Rawlings and her husband a colorful Christmas card with the hand-drawn image of a burning log and the handwritten message "With ardor and fire I wish you a Merry Olde Christmas and a happy New Year" on 22 December 1948. Apparently, Rawlings had earlier sent Hurston her reaction to *Seraph on the Suwanee*, because Hurston begins by saying, "A long letter follows, but I must say here how much your two letters did for me" (*Hurston: A Life in Letters* 577). Rawlings must have remarked on the similarities between black and white dialect in the book, because Hurston reflects on whether the whites learned their language from the blacks or vice versa. She concludes that "Negroes introduced into N. America spoke *no* English at all, and learned from the whites" (577). After her signature, Hurston adds a postscript: "Had a lovely *long* letter from Mrs. Spessard Holland. Isn't she *wonderful*? I admire you two above all other women.—Love, Zora" (578).

For some reason, their relationship lapsed again for the next four years. Perhaps Hurston was so humiliated by the sex-charges incident and the necessity of asking her friends for money that she could not resume her relationships on the same footing as before. Or maybe the difficulties of daily life, ill health, and lack of financial resources interfered with the continuity of friendship. Both women were tormented by their inability to complete their next novels. After *Seraph on the Suwanee*, Hurston was never to publish another novel, though she tried for thirteen years; Rawlings struggled for a decade on *The Sojourner*, finally publishing it in the year of her death.

Fortunately, Rawlings and Hurston had an opportunity to renew their friendship just before Rawlings's death. Hurston must have written Rawlings a letter in April 1952. At the time, Hurston was happily living in a rented house in Eau Gallie, Florida, as she writes to a friend: "I am in this little town, growing a garden when I get tired of the typewriter, and winning bak [*sic*] my health" (*Hurston: A Life in Letters* 679). Recognizing that much time had passed and feeling uncertain of the status of their relationship, Hurston addresses Rawlings as "Miss Rawlings." In a letter dated 6 January 1952, Rawlings indignantly responds to the formality: "Zora, my dear, And where do you get this 'Miss Rawlings' stuff? I am Marjorie and you know it." Showing further that they are out of touch with each other, Rawlings remarks, after commenting on Hurston's interest in politics and support of Robert Taft, "I cannot share your enthusiasm for Taft. I don't know what the answer is but sure to God 'tain't him." In another example of their growing estrangement, Rawlings retorts, when asked about her latest book, "Again, what, under Jonah's Gourd Vine, are you talking about when you spoke back in April of 'my latest book'?" She had apologized earlier for not responding sooner to Hurston's letter with the excuse, "I have been and am still sweating out perhaps too difficult a book for my abilities."

Rawlings closes the letter with an invitation:

Now you are at Belle Glade and I am at Cross Creek and we are both working like Lucifer trying to keep from getting kicked out [of] heaven, and I shall not be going South in the State, but if you happen to come prowling further North, do stop by at least for overnight or even longer. It might do us both good to compare notes from hell.
I have so much to tell you.
    With love,

Marjorie Rawlings
(unpublished letter, University of Florida Libraries)

Sadly, Rawlings may never have had a chance to tell Hurston all of her news. This letter was the last piece of correspondence between the two women. When Rawlings died on 14 December 1953, it would take a year and a half for Hurston to acknowledge in a letter the painful fact. Her response on 13 June 1955 to their common friend Mary Holland shows her grief:

Dear, dear, dear Miss Mary:
You will never know how happy the arrival of your delayed letter made me! My soul was reaching out to you. I was so depressed by the death of Marjorie Kinnan Rawlings, first because I am deprived of the warmth of the association, and secondly because I feel that I failed her in her last extremity. She wrote me, and Burroughs Mitchell, who was editor to us both at Scribners, wrote me that she was ill. I wrote her that I would be there as soon as I could, but everything went bad for me at that time. My car, like the old one-horse shay, just fell to pieces, and there I was with no transportation, and no means to replace it, and could not bear to admit it to her lest she feel sorry for me. Next thing I knew was the announcement of her death. (*Hurston: A Life in Letters* 728)

Hurston ends the letter with an account of her own struggles in writing a novel about Herod the Great, a project that would dominate her until her own death on 28 January 1960.

## Hurston's and Rawlings's Views on Friendship

On the surface, Hurston's and Rawlings's disparate socioeconomic and racial backgrounds would seem to hinder a friendship between the upper-middle-class northern woman and the daughter of an Alabama slave. Yet the two women bonded on an artistic level, because they had the same goal in life. In an era when it was difficult for women to be treated as equal with men, Hurston and Rawlings sought solidarity in each other as they aspired to reach the same level of recognition as their contemporary male counterparts in American literature. Through her close association with Perkins, Rawlings knew firsthand of the quality of attention that Hemingway, Fitzgerald, and Wolfe received at Scribner's and from the rest of the world. Perkins's letters to Rawlings are full of gossip and information about the other three. Hoping to make her feel part of the group, he asks her to check on Fitzgerald when she is passing through Asheville, North Carolina, and encourages her to go deep-sea fishing with Hemingway off of Bimini. Nevertheless, Rawlings often complains in her letters to Perkins that her work cannot compare to theirs, and she never truly felt part of their inner circles.

Rawlings, instead, sought to create her own band of authors close to home. In St. Augustine she considered Edith Taylor Pope her "protégée," according to Tarr (*The Private Marjorie* 15). She referred Pope to Perkins, and he helped transform her disorganized first manuscript into the best-selling novel *Colcorton* (1944). Novelist Marsha Davenport, the former campaign manager for Wendell Willkie, was another of Rawlings's close friends with whom she shared many literary discussions. Rawlings and her St. Augustine friends took their calling as writers seriously. Rawlings must have immediately recognized a kindred spirit when she met Hurston in 1942. It is not surprising, therefore, that the two would develop a lifelong friendship based on these common aspirations.

What is surprising is that two authors can be friends in the first place, according to Matthew Bruccoli in *Fitzgerald and Hemingway*: "The mortality rate of literary friendships is high. Writers tend to be bad risks as friends—probably for much the same reasons that they are bad matrimonial risks. They expend the best parts of themselves in their work. Moreover, literary ambition has a way of turning into literary competition; if fame is the spur, envy may be a concomitant" (3). As a famous example of a dysfunctional two-author friendship, Bruccoli claims that later in life, Hemingway was trying to get back at Fitzgerald in *A Moveable Feast*, by casting aspersions on Fitzgerald's reputation and masculinity, in order to secure his own place in the canon of American literature. As their common editor, Perkins may even have encouraged the rivalry. In an 18 March 1948 letter to Arthur Mizener, Rawlings writes: "Consciously or unconsciously, our magnificent mutual friend and editor, Maxwell Perkins, played off his authors against one another. He knew the stimulation to a writer of knowing what other writers were both doing and failing to do" (*Selected Letters* 308).

Even though Rawlings and Hurston dealt with parallel subjects—namely, life and death in small Florida villages that were eighty miles apart—their interactions with each other do not appear to have been competitive in nature. Even when Hurston intruded on Rawlings's territory—the world of white Florida Crackers—by publishing her own novel about the Florida Crackers, *Seraph on the Suwanee*, Rawlings never indicated that she minded. In her letters to Hurston, she was always gracious, supportive, and warm.

But, in her letters to her husband, Norton Baskin, Rawlings grappled with the racial complications underlying her friendship with Hurston. Clouding the issue, Hurston, for her part, often seemed to wear the mask that she donned when dealing with more socially powerful whites. Hurston's early friendships with rich, successful white women while she was a student at Barnard set the tone for her dealings with powerful white women whom she met later in life.

Hurston's views on race have baffled critics since she first began writing. Throughout her life, she received a firestorm of criticism from black male authors, in particular, for not being politically conscious enough. They felt that the folk world she presented was not relevant to the social, economic, and political issues of the twentieth century. Delia Konzett in *Ethnic Modernisms* tells how Hurston and the younger members of the Harlem Renaissance, including Langston Hughes and Wallace Thurman, split from the great black male tradition inspired by W. E. B. DuBois: "Provocatively calling themselves the 'Niggerati,' they instead turned radically to the black folk tradition for inspiration[,] unlike DuBois and

Locke, for example, who associated it with a crude or primitive aesthetics in need of literary refinement" (71).

Unfortunately, Hurston became associated in many people's minds only with one type of black folk tradition, namely, the folksy one that she sometimes portrays of her Eatonville hometown. In reality, nearly every work she produced looks at race from a different perspective; her stories take place in Harlem, in south Florida, in the Caribbean, in Cracker Florida; her anthropological research leads her to New Orleans, Haiti, and other countries of the Caribbean. In all of these locales, she looked with an open mind at each culture she found. She was multicultural before her time, as Konzett notes: "Her portrayal of black culture inflected by various regions . . . breaks down its homogeneous appearance and thereby questions the stereotypical binaries of a black and white American society" (74). As a result, Hurston cannot be pinned down as presenting an ethnocentric, fixed view on racial issues, nor can she herself be pinned down with a fixed identity. Konzett points out that, for Hurston, "race becomes a complicated cultural construction rife with contradictions and multiplicities. . . . The multipositional shape and migrating characteristics of race necessitate that Zora become an actor with many masks, negotiating an essentially displaced and dynamic identity that is always in the process of transforming itself" (84).

A woman who is able to wear "many masks" would also prove a challenge to her friends. Rawlings was undoubtedly intrigued by Hurston's contradictions regarding race, but these very contradictions undoubtedly broke down barriers, which, in turn, opened Rawlings's mind to new possibilities of connection.

Fortunately, Hurston's and Rawlings's views on friendship were straightforward. In their letters to each other and to other correspondents, they show that they valued friendship, kept in touch with their friends, and always offered love and support. Rawlings wrote voluminous letters to her husband, to Maxwell Perkins, and to thousands of service people during the war. She maintained close ties to the friends of her youth, such as Beatrice McNeill; her Cross Creek and backwoods Florida friends, such as J. T. Glisson and Leonard Fiddia; her Florida friends, such as Edith Pope, Marcia Davenport, Hamilton Holt, Clifford Lyons, Ida Tarrant, Dessie Smith Prescott, and Phil May; her literary friends, such as Ellen Glasgow, Margaret Mitchell, James Branch Cabell, Robert Frost, Norman Berg, Charles and Julia Scribner, Sigrid Undset, and Carl Van Vechten; and her famous friends, such as Wendell Willkie, Owen D. Young, and Eleanor Roosevelt. She also delighted in her close association with F. Scott Fitzgerald, Ernest Hemingway, Martha Gellhorn, and Thomas Wolfe.

In a similar manner, Hurston remained close to the Eatonville friends of her mother, such as Armetta Jones and Mathilda Moseley; her lifelong New York friends, including Fannie Hirst, Annie Nathan Meyer, Ruth Benedict, Jane Belo, Carl Van Vechten, Ethel Waters, Amy Spingarn, Walter White, James Weldon Johnson, and Burroughs Mitchell; her Rollins College friends, including Hamilton Holt, Bob Wunsch, and Edwin Odgood Grover; and other Florida friends, including Stetson Kennedy, Katherine Tracy L'Engle, Mary Holland, Carita Doggett Corse, Helen Worden Erskine, and Jean Parker Waterbury.

In conclusion, both women believed in friendship as an ideal. Hurston, in fact, writes a paean to her friends in an excised chapter of *Dust Tracks on a Road*. In this chapter, titled "The Inside Light—Being a Salute to Friendship," Hurston claims she is colorblind when it comes to the people she chooses to be her friends. She describes what they mean to her: "Friendship is a mysterious and ocean-bottom thing. Who can know the outer ranges of it?" (321). She admits that she could have been a better friend, and she blames herself for falling short of her ideal: "I keep seeing new heights and depths of possibilities which ought to be reached, only to be frustrated by the press of life, which is no friend to grace. I have my loyalties and my unselfish acts to my credit, but I feel the lack of perfection in them, and it leaves a hunger in me" (308).

Hurston and Rawlings's relationship may have fallen short of perfection, but it was a positive force for both of them. Despite the racial, economic, and social barriers between them, they maintained a cordial friendship throughout their lives.

# 2

## "Thinking in heirogliphics"

Mastering the Craft of Writing

**Z**ORA NEALE HURSTON AND MARJORIE KINNAN RAWLINGS wrote books that celebrated small central Florida villages that were about eighty miles apart. Eatonville is located in Orlando, next door to the mainly upscale, small towns of Maitland and Winter Park, and is noted for being the first incorporated all-black community, founded in 1887. Cross Creek, further north, near the Ocala National Forest, in Rawlings's day was a small collection of Cracker and black families struggling to make ends meet. Rawlings also ranges a little further afield in her stories, describing the nearby scrub country around Salt Springs and its Cracker inhabitants. Both authors' works are strongly associated with these rural communities; yet neither woman was born into the communities about which she writes. Hurston was born in Notasulga, Alabama, on 15 January 1891; Rawlings was born in Washington, D.C., on 8 August 1896. They chose to write about their adopted communities—rather than their birthplaces—for remarkably similar reasons. On the one hand, it is easy to enumerate all the obvious differences between the two women, that is, race, social standing, economic means, domestic arrangements, and so forth; on the other hand, it is fascinating how they converge.

Hurston explains what she has in common with Rawlings in a 16 May 1943 letter. After mentioning that both of them "look at plants and animals and people" in the same way, Hurston praises Rawlings: "*You* catch the thing as it is. You note the 'picture-talk' that is something of a linguistic heirogliphics [*sic*]. I am tickled to death with you, Sugar. . . . You were thinking in heirogliphics your ownself" (*Hurston: A Life in Letters* 486). Hurston's use of the term "heirogliphics" is not surprising, because she used it earlier in "Characteristics of Negro Expression" in order to define the way the "Negro . . . add[s] action" to a word "to make it do." She gives as an example using the word "chop-axe": "the speaker has in his mind the picture of the object in use. Action. Everything illustrated. So we can say the white man thinks in a written language and the Negro thinks in hieroglyphics" (830–31). As a trained anthropologist, Hurston was used to thinking of hidden meanings to words behind cultural practices. In this case, she is referring not only to Rawlings's ability to capture the exact cadences of Cracker speech but also to her ability to present the reader with deeper symbolic meanings. Hurston, too, was also a genius at accurately recording the language of metaphors and similes—conveying deeper meanings—that were commonly used in her community.

## Hurston's Works through *Their Eyes Were Watching God*

Hurston became a writer once she reconnected with the African American communities of central Florida in early 1928 and learned how to make her characters "move in reality." She did not have a high-class editor at a major publishing house to give her constant support and advice, as Rawlings had in Maxwell Perkins for sixteen years. Instead, Hurston was forced to rely on her wits and personal charm in order to survive. As early as 17 October 1925, she confides to one of her white patrons, Annie Nathan Meyer, a novelist and founder of Barnard College, how difficult her struggle has been: "I have been my sole support since I was 13 years old. You will appreciate the tremendous struggle necessary for me to merely live to say nothing of educating myself. . . . I've taken some tremendous losses and survived terrific shocks. . . . being pounded so often on the anvil of life I am growing less resilient. physical [*sic*] suffering unnerves me now" (*Hurston: A Life in Letters* 67).

Hurston also had to endure racial prejudice, though she seemingly made light of it. When she writes to Meyer that her white classmates are urging her to attend the junior prom at the Ritz-Carlton and plan on exchanging dances with her if she brings "a man as light" as herself (*Hurston: A Life in Letters* 71), Meyer discourages her on the "grounds that it would be racially inappropriate to do so," according to Carla Kaplan (71 n. 3). Hurston dons her mask and responds with a lighthearted pun: "No doubt you are right about the Prom. But even if things were different, I could not go. Paying 12.50 plus a new frock and shoes and a wrap and all the other things necessary is not my idea of a good time. I am not that 'Ritzy' yet" (72).

The way Hurston bridged the huge gap between Barnard College and Eatonville was, first, through the short stories she was beginning to write about Eatonville and which she submitted to *Opportunity*, the literary journal of the Urban League; and second, by studying anthropology at Columbia University with the famed professor Franz Boas. When she arrived at Barnard in 1925, Hurston's initial career choice was writing, as she notes in her "Record of Freshman Interest": "I have had some small success as a writer and wish above all to succeed at it. Either teaching or social work will be interesting but consolation prizes" (qtd. in Hemenway 21). Robert Hemenway notes that although "anthropology and art are not incompatible vocations," they require "different uses of personal experience" (21). During this early period in Hurston's development of a self-identity, anthropology gave her, according to Hemenway, "the relatively rare opportunity to confront her culture both emotionally and analytically, both as a subject and as object. She had lived Afro-American folklore before she knew that such a thing existed as a scientific concept or had special value" (21–22).

Although her Eatonville stories were winning prizes in the *Opportunity* writing contests in 1925 and 1926, Boas's sway was more compelling. Boas was able to secure for Hurston a considerable amount of financial stability through a grant of fourteen hundred dollars that Hurston received from the Association for the Study of Negro Life and History in

1927. Hurston's project was to return to the South to collect folklore, following Boas's encouragement to focus her intellectual interests on researching African American cultural remnants.

Besides the significant amounts of money that Boas was able to steer toward Hurston, his biggest impact on the development of her self-identity was through the teaching of his core concepts, namely, that race does not explain the differences that exist between communities, that it is environment that shapes individuals and their groups. Viewed as a "friend of the Negro," Boas was a scholar whose theories of racial equality helped to "uplift the race," according to Lee Baker (40). Boas was so well regarded in the outside world that he appeared on the cover of the May 1936 issue of *Time* magazine. The cover article refers to Boas's most famous study, *The Mind of Primitive Man*, as "the Magna Charta of self respect for the 'lower races'" and goes on to note: "Boas observed that nowhere on earth was there such a thing as a pure race, and that the term 'race' was vague and approximate at best"; furthermore, Boas doubts that there are any "superior races" (qtd. in Baker 42). Anyone who believes in the inferiority or superiority of races is full of "Nordic Nonsense," in Boas's opinion (42). Two years later, on 10 December 1938, Boas led 1,284 scientists from 167 universities in signing a "Scientists' Manifesto" denouncing Nazi theories of race. The goal of the manifesto was "to counteract the vicious, pseudo scientific activity of so-called scientists who try to prove the close relation between racial descent and mental character" (43). Although Boas's anti-Nazi activity was still in the future at the time Hurston was his student in the 1920s, he had formulated his views about race much earlier.

Boas theorized that each culture has its own style, one that is created by the "genius of the people" (*Volksgeist*), a kind of "mental operator" that acts "to assimilate newly borrowed traits by imprinting a style upon them, and to fashion invented traits according to the culture's style" (Verdon 440). Furthermore, the *Volksgeist* "does not 'arrange,' organize, regulate the social organism's multifarious activities; *it more or less creates stylistic inventories*" (442). Certain individuals in the group can function as "text carriers" of the *Volksgeist*; the words of texts they write or speak reflect "the collective mindset of a people who produced a culture" (443). The texts, according to Michel Verdon, are "the outward, 'object-ive' surface manifestations of something internal, yet never grasped, for Boas did not analyze his texts from a cultural point of view" (443). Boas believed in "letting the natives speak" without any interference from the anthropologist. In Verdon's view, though, cultural texts *"call for interpretations*, either on the part of the narrator or on that of the ethnographer," and "Boas avoided such interpretations" (443).

Boas's theories helped spark not only Hurston's intellectual curiosity but also the Harlem Renaissance. Susan Hegeman claims that his work, which emphasized that "African Americans were fully capable of becoming valued members of American society *irrespective of* their race," was instrumental in creating a "type of thinking" that was "important to the development of the Harlem Renaissance," namely, that "black Americans possessed a particular cultural heritage, identity, and destiny" (473). In *Harlem Renaissance*, Nathan Huggins explains how this cultural heritage was "contradictory to the main thrusts of the American tradition":

> There was none of the austerity and anguished conscience of the Puritan fathers, none of the flighty idealism of the transcendentalists, nowhere Benjamin Franklin's dicta—temperance, industry, frugality, chastity—nor Ralph Waldo Emerson's "self-reliance." Indeed, one might look in vain for that secularized Protestant Ethic, Social Darwinism. These compulsive (some would say, anal) traits of American character seem absent from the black metropolis. For the popular mind, Harlem was associated with spiritual and emotional enthusiasm (some would say, soul), indulgence, play, passion, and lust. (85)

After the ravages of World War I, this "spiritual and emotional enthusiasm" was exactly what the world needed. Huggins points out that the postwar "disenchantment with civilization" was the direct result of "mass warfare, the trenches, the gas, the weapons of the Great War [which] exposed the ugly brutality that lurked beneath the surface of genteel manners" (88). It is no wonder that artists, intellectuals, and the common person turned to primitivism as a means of tapping into the "pure and essential" qualities of human life. In Huggins's view, "European intellectuals, particularly the French, had discovered the sophistication of African culture." Postimpressionist and cubist artists were influenced by African styles, which were free of the trappings and artifice of civilization (88). As a result, according to Huggins, Americans found Harlem "a tonic and a release" (89). Paul Morand, a French journalist, found it "the only relief from the relentless engine of America" (90).

As an African American, Hurston found her spiritual home in Harlem, as a mecca of like-minded people. But her feelings for the "primitive" were not the same as white Americans.' She was not seeking release, rebellion, or therapy by going to Harlem. Nor were her views the same as her forebears, such as W. E. B. DuBois and Alain Locke. She and the younger black artists of the Harlem Renaissance—calling themselves the "Niggerati"—turned "radically to the black folk tradition for inspiration unlike DuBois and Locke, for example, who associate it with a crude or primitive aesthetics in need of literary refinement," according to Delia Konzett (71). When Hurston and her fellow young black authors published *Fire!!* in 1926, they broke with *The New Negro* mentality of assimilation and progress by presenting what Langston Hughes calls "those elements within the race which are still too potent for easy assimilation" and which the elites want "hidden until they no longer exist" (qtd. in Lewis 193–94). In *The Big Sea*, Hughes further describes the purpose of this new approach: "the idea being that it would burn up a lot of the old, dead, conventional Negro-white ideas of the past, *épater le bourgeois* into a realization of the existence of the younger Negro writers and artists" (183).

Though armed with knowledge from her brilliant mentor, Hurston was still forced to earn money to survive. Through Harlem Renaissance contacts such as Locke and Hughes, she met their patron Charlotte Osgood Mason, a wealthy lover of African American art and artists. A former anthropologist herself, Mason offered Hurston two hundred dollars a month to return to Florida and gather all the folktales and songs she could find. According to her contract with Mason, signed on 8 December 1927, Hurston was to "seek out, compile and collect all information possible, both written and oral, concerning the music, poetry, folk-lore, literature, hoodoo, conjure, manifestations of art and kindred subjects" among her research subjects, which were southern blacks (Alain Locke Papers, Howard University).

Initially, Hurston, who called Mason "Godmother" and believed there was "a psychic bond" between them, described her duties in exalted terms: "I must tell the tales, sing the songs, do the dances, and repeat the raucous sayings and doings of the Negro farthest down. [Mason] is altogether in sympathy with them, because she says truthfully they are utterly sincere in living" (*Dust Tracks* 177). Later in her five-year relationship with Mason, when Hurston realized that she did not own the intellectual property she was gathering, she rebelled at her inability to turn her rich material into art. She felt that Mason was treating her like a primitive child, like someone who had to be controlled and could not be trusted. Another one of Mason's protégées, Louise Thompson, labeled Mason a "racist" and claimed that she was "indulging in fantasies of Negroes" (Hemenway 107). Mason may also have practiced gender discrimination, because she did not hold her male authors to the same restrictions on their intellectual property.

No matter how bitter Hurston was at the end of her contract with Mason, she did acquire the same valuable quality that enriched both her and Rawlings's stories—empathy with her characters and their lot in life. Thus, when Hurston went into the field for the first time and set up camp at the Everglades Cypress Lumber Company in Loughman, Florida, she knew she was going in search of the genius of the people. At first she had difficulty communicating with the workers, because "The glamour of Barnard College was still upon [her]" and she was talking to the people in "Barnardese" (*Dust Tracks* 174–75). Using this approach, she did not find enough material "to make a flea a waltzing jacket" (175). Hurston must have noticed the vast gulf that lay between her Barnard world and the jook joints and work camps that housed "family men, fugitive murderers, honest workers, knife-wielding good-time girls, Christian mothers, hard-living gamblers, and jackleg preachers," according to Hemenway (111). To gain their confidence, she lowers herself to their level and tells them a fib: "I was also a fugitive from justice, 'bootlegging.' They were hot behind me in Jacksonville and they wanted me in Miami. So I was hiding out. That sounded reasonable. Bootleggers always have cars. I was taken in" (*Mules and Men* 61). She joins in the dancing at the jook joints and exchanges her $12.74 dress from Macy's for a $1.98 mail-order dress (63).

Besides the fact that Hurston gathered a lifetime's supply of anthropological material in Loughman, she also met Big Sweet, who not only provided a role model for her female heroines, such as Janie Crawford in *Their Eyes Were Watching God*, but also taught Hurston about the use of language in the African American community. In *Mules and Men* and *Dust Tracks on the Road*, Hurston portrays Big Sweet as a larger-than-life personality. She is a big woman, and during a brawl one night she saves Hurston's life when a jealous woman attacks Hurston with a knife. Big Sweet dominates the community not only with her physical prowess but also with her facility with language. Hurston describes her "specifying" abilities when she sees Big Sweet in action for the first time: "She was really giving the particulars. She was giving a 'reading,' a word borrowed from the fortune-tellers. She was giving her opponent lurid data and bringing him up to date on his ancestry, his looks, smell, gait, clothes, and his route through Hell in the hereafter" (*Dust Tracks* 186).

Big Sweet even helped Hurston with her anthropological investigations in the community: "Big Sweet helped me to collect material in a big way. She had no idea what I wanted with it, but if I wanted it, she meant to see to it that I got it. She pointed out people who knew songs and stories. She wouldn't stand for balkiness on their part. We held two lying contests, story-telling contests to you, and Big Sweet passed on who rated the prizes" (*Dust Tracks* 188–89).

By March 1927, Hurston recognized that she was doing immeasurably valuable work, as she wrote to Langston Hughes: "I am getting inside of Negro art and lore. I am beginning to *see* really and when you join me I shall point things out and see if you see them as I do. . . . Langston this is going to be *big*. Most gorgeous possibilities are showing themselves constantly" (*Hurston: A Life in Letters* 114). In April, Hurston sent Hughes her rules of composition, which would later be revised and published as "Characteristics of Negro Expression." She tried to entice him into transforming the material she had gathered into "the *real* Negro art theatre," writing on 12 April: "Well, I shall, or rather *we* shall act out the folk tales, however short, with the abrupt angularity and naivete of the primitive 'bama nigger. Just that with naive settings. What do you think?" (116). She even offered to give him most of the credit if only he would join her: "I am perfectly willing to be 40 to your 60 since you are always so much more practical than I. But I *know* it is going to be *Glori-*

*ous*! A really new departure in the drama" (117). She tells Hughes that she is becoming one with her subjects: "I am truly dedicated to the work at hand and so I am not even writing, but living every moment with the people" (113). She believes that "she would demonstrate that 'the greatest cultural wealth of the continent' lay in the Eatonvilles and Polk Counties of the black South" (Hemenway 112).

Most of the material Hurston gathered in 1928 was incorporated into *Mules and Men*, published in 1935. Long before its publication, Hurston had begun to push against the scientific restraints that anthropological study was imposing on her. Although she would continue to do research and propose field expeditions, her literary writings became more and more of a creative outlet for her talents. Hurston's turn toward literature had many reasons. The first involves her intellectual inheritance from Franz Boas. Boas's belief in "letting the natives speak" without any interpretation or psychological probing on the part of the ethnographer may have dampened Hurston's spirits when she realized that her folk subjects had so much more to offer of their culture; she may have felt stifled being only their recorder.

Second, Hurston had already committed "academic suicide" (according to Hemenway) in 1927 by publishing a plagiarized article on Cudjo Lewis titled "Cudjo's Own Story of the Last African Slaver" in the *Journal of Negro History*. In 1972, William Stewart discovered Hurston's plagiarism of Emma Langdon Roche's *Historic Sketches of the Old South* (Hemenway 96–97). If Boas had discovered the academic dishonesty in Hurston's work, it would have been humiliating to her and ended her career. On the other hand, Hurston's relationship with Boas may have reached its end point in any case. When Hurston called him "Papa Franz" at a party, he retorted: "Of course Zora is my daughter. Certainly! Just one of my missteps, that's all" (Douglas 284). Hurston may have wanted to get out of this uncomfortable oedipal relationship any way she could, even at the expense of her academic integrity.

Third, Hurston regretted having signed a contract with Mrs. Mason. Because Mason technically "owned" the material and could control how it was to be used, Hurston had to hide the gems she had found in the field. Her letters to Hughes are full of admonitions to keep her findings secret. On 12 April 1928 she writes him about her latest inspiration—an expansion of "The Eatonville Anthology"—which must remain hidden from Mason: "I can *really* write a Village Anthology now, but I am wary about mentioning it to Godmother for fear she will think I am shirking but *boy* I think [I] could lay 'em something now. I told you I must not publish without her consent" (*Hurston: A Life in Letters* 115). In 1929, when Hurston proposed writing a play with Hughes titled "Jook," which would be full of "all of the songs and gags" she had, she warned him: "I know that G[odmother] would never consent for me to do so, so you will have to take it all in your name" (Hemenway 127). According to Ann Douglas, Mason was afraid that any commercialization of the folklore would be a "prostitution of Hurston's authentic black material" (284).

Fourth, as Hurston became a more knowledgeable anthropologist and gained experience in the field, her research began to have an impact on her own life. Hemenway notes how Hurston changed after she returned from her hoodoo expedition to New Orleans: "Alan Lomax, collecting folksongs with her in 1935, remembers her as guarded and mysterious about her conjure experiences, maybe even a little frightened by them; the New Orleans ceremonies marked her for the rest of her life" (123).

Once Hurston had broken the ties to Mason and her mentors at Columbia, she was free to express her connection with her Eatonville folk in any way she wished. Building on early stories such as "The Eatonville Anthology" (1926), written before her arrangement with Mason, Hurston went on to tell the story of her parents' lives in *Jonah's Gourd Vine* (1934) and of her own in *Their Eyes Were Watching God* (1937). Both novels combine elements of the folk experience Hurston had acquired growing up in Eatonville and in her anthropological research—"the ability to turn the inside light on community"—with the peaceful understanding of "the universe and its laws." Her crowning achievement in getting the mix right is *Their Eyes Were Watching God*.

"The Eatonville Anthology"

Boas's theories on the *Volksgeist* are played out in Hurston's early, most overtly anthropological story, "The Eatonville Anthology," published in 1926 in the *Messenger* while Hurston was still a student at Barnard. The "Anthology," with its connotations of the author's taking an overview and then picking out the most representative items, certainly functions as an inventory of the culture. In fact, it is reminiscent of the raw documentary footage that Hurston would shoot with Jane Belo in South Carolina in the spring of 1940. This silent footage, located in the Margaret Mead Film Collection at the Library of Congress, consists of eight clips showing scenes of people at work and at play. It begins with children playing games, perhaps outside their school; then Hurston shifts gears and films workers logging and distilling sugarcane; she also shows women lounging on their porches at home; and, finally, she ends by filming a baptism in a lake or river. The clips cover all the cultural loci in the community—that is, school, church, workplace, playground, and home—and are filmed from an anthropologist's perspective.

Like Hurston's anthropological footage, "The Eatonville Anthology" covers all communal bases. The fourteen vignettes are not in chronological order; they are a collage of items arranged haphazardly. The fragmented structure of the "Anthology" is modernist in nature, requiring the reader to make the connections and form a coherent whole of Eatonville in his or her mind. The story is similar to other fragmented pictures of community life written during this era, such as Edgar Lee Masters's *Spoon River Anthology* (1915), Sherwood Anderson's *Winesburg, Ohio* (1919), Hemingway's *In Our Time* (1924), and Faulkner's Yoknapatawpha stories. Even though the "The Eatonville Anthology" has "no central narrative line," John Lowe in *Jump at the Sun* believes that it "signals a real advance in Hurston's craft, merging elements of fiction, folklore, and humor in an economic narrative shorthand" (66).

Unfortunately, when the reader begins to assemble the bits and pieces of story fragments, the overall portrait of Eatonville is not completely favorable. Konzett concurs that the "Anthology" is filled with an "underlying critical exposure of destructive communal behavior, such as domestic violence, alcoholism, and prostitution" (101). It begins with "The Pleading Woman," Mrs. Tony Roberts, "who goes door to door begging for things" (813). The cyclical nature of her begging—"The next day, it commences all over"—suggests mental illness. In the next story, "Turpentine Love," once again, mental illness is implied in the description of Jim Merchant's wife, who is "subject to fits" (814). She is supposedly cured by "a dose of turpentine" in her eye. In the untitled third story, Becky Moore also seems ill. She has had "eleven children of assorted colors and sizes" (814) with an assortment of men. The other women in the town won't allow their children to play with hers, because they are "afraid that [her profligacy] is catching" (814).

Other stories center on domestic violence and deception. In the untitled ninth story, Mrs. Jody Clarke, "a soft-looking, middle-aged woman, whose bust and stomach are always holding a get-together" (817), is engaged in a cycle of abuse and reconciliation with her husband. When she makes a mistake in her husband's store, he yells at her. He "used to beat her in the store when he was a young man," but now that he is older, "He can wait until he goes home." Nevertheless, when his wife is away from him at church, she "somehow always misses her husband" (817). In the next story, Mrs. McDuffy also gets a beating from her husband for shouting "her determination" in church. Mr. McDuffy argues that she does it to "slur" him, out of "spite," so he figures that he can hit her, because "his fist was just as hard as her head" (818).

In "Pants and Cal'line," Cal'line Potts seeks revenge when her husband courts another woman. She puts up with his shenanigans for a long time until she reaches the breaking point and then takes off after him and his paramour with an ax. Unfortunately, the story breaks off. Hemenway suggests that a printing error created this abrupt ending without a denouement (69), and, indeed, other errors abound. (For example, Oviedo is spelled "Oneido" in another story). On the other hand, Lowe speculates that because the characters carry the names of Hurston's actual aunt and uncle, "She may also have been unwilling to go further with this tale from her own family at this early stage in her career" (69).

In "The Head of the Nail," a wronged wife, Laura Crooms, goes further and wrecks havoc on her husband's lover, Daisy Taylor, "the town vamp." Daisy taunts Laura in front of the men hanging out by the store by making "goo-goo eyes" at her and challenging her to battle: "If she ain't a heavy hip-ted Mama enough to keep him, she don't need to come crying to me" (821). "Timid" Laura takes up the challenge—and an ax handle—by attacking Daisy on the head. Unfortunately, Daisy had been using shingle nails to hold her hair in place, which prompts one of the men to remark, "I was just looking to see if Laura had been lucky enough to hit one of those nails on the head and drive it in" (822). The wry narrator tells us that since this incident Daisy has moved on to Orlando:

"There in a wider sphere, perhaps, her talents as a vamp were appreciated" (822).

The "Anthology" closes with a Brer Rabbit story about a time "before the stars fell" and when "all the animals used to talk just like people" (824). Mr. Dog falls in love with Miss Coon and wants to impress her with his singing. Brer Rabbit tricks Mr. Dog, who wants to get his "voice sweetened," and splits his tongue in two with a knife. Hurston closes the story with a childish rhyme: "Stepped on a tin, mah story ends" (825).

By ending with a Brer Rabbit story, Hurston connects her work to the old southern tradition of storytelling and suggests that the world she has created in these vignettes is timeless, unchanging, hermetic, and untouched by contemporary events. In *The Black Atlantic: Modernity and Double Consciousness*, Paul Gilroy claims that Hurston saw the folk as "custodians of an essentially invariant, anti-historical notion of black particularity" (91). Konzett claims that the "hermetic" type of black community portrayed in *Mules and Men* (and the "Anthology" appears to fall into this category) "give[s] the reader the misleading impression that black folk culture is foreign, exotic, and ultimately disconnected rather than marginalized from the mainstream American perspective" (100). Konzett explains further: "Poverty, ignorance, and disenfranchisement become seemingly unchanging ontological conditions, characterizing the black community as having no recourse to civic and social agency in the larger context of America's sociopolitical landscape. For all their vitality, charm, and independence, Hurston's characters display a political complacency that unwittingly upholds the Southern feudal order, with its social stagnation and white supremacist outlook" (100–101).

Part of the responsibility for this portrait lies with the wry narrator, who picks up on people's foibles. The narrator seemingly straddles the two cultures, namely, the one that he or she is observing and the one from which the narrator is speaking. In a sense, this narrator may be looking at the community from a white reader's viewpoint—and critiquing it. None of the Eatonville residents in the "Anthology" would fit into white, mainstream America. Old Man Anderson, for example, is "different from us citybred folks" (815), because he has never seen a train. Brazzle is the "biggest liar in the world" and tries to make people believe that he saw a doctor "cut open a woman, remove everything . . . and replaced the organs so expertly that she was up and about her work in a couple of weeks" (817). In "Double-Shuffle," the narrator paints a portrait of the town as backward, out of step with the times: "Back in the good old days before the World War, things were very simple in Eatonville. People didn't fox-trot" (818); instead, the townspeople put on a "break-down," in which they do an old-fashioned "grand march."

The residents of Eatonville identified this narrator as Hurston her-self and resented her portrayal of them as backward and degenerate. In my interviews with Eatonville residents who knew Hurston, Harriet Moseley, whose great-great-uncle was Joe Clark, the prototype for Jody Clarke in "The Eatonville Anthology" (and for Jody Starks in *Their Eyes Were Watching God*), revealed the townspeople's feelings concerning their fictional depiction: "everyone was mad at her . . . all the citizens around here. She would do all her writing up at Joe Clark's store and she would talk about the citizens. Instead of using fictional names, she would use their ordinary names. My godfather got highly mad with her, because she used his name in one of her books" (Lillios 26). Moseley's godfather, Ellis Jones, became so angry that he threatened Hurston with a gun, but Hurston "jumped up and left. She ran in the house, got her bag, and left. If she hadn't, he was going to kill her," according to Mo-seley (26). Eatonville's centennial brochure (1887–1987) also mentions the townspeople's antipathy: "With no attempt to insult or degrade her friends and neighbors, she lost faith and goodwill of most all who knew her. . . . Zora's novel 'Jonah's Gourd Vine'—depicted daily life in Eaton-ville, calling names and happenings—local citizens objected, they dis-liked her" ("Town of Eatonville" 37).

Jimmie Lee Harrell, an Eatonville resident born in 1905, points out that the other people in the community "didn't have much schooling" and were envious because "Zora was well educated." She explains: "The people who were living here at the time weren't making too much of their lives. I think they were just jealous. But they don't talk like they hated her or nothing" (Lillios 25).

In these early stories, Hurston seems to be testing her material, and she may have "stretched" the truth in some instances. Konzett argues that once Hurston created this type of black community, she was ready to move on and "portray black folk culture with more flexibility" and variety (101). Indeed, Hurston's subsequent depictions of black culture, such as *Moses, Man of the Mountain, Seraph on the Suwanee,* and her unfinished work on Herod the Great, present very different perspectives on race, gender, and community. Her books on Moses and Herod expanded the discussion of race to the African diaspora.

## Jonah's Gourd Vine

Hurston's technique of broadening perspective to include more spiritual (in this case, African) elements, creating an overall, unifying metaphor in her work, and deepening characterization begins with her first novel, *Jonah's Gourd Vine.* The novel shows the migration of characters from their closed-off communities in the Old South to the New South, which was Florida at the turn of the century. Furthermore, Hurston extends the discussion of race in Eatonville to include African remnants that still existed within the culture. Lowe provides the most perceptive comment about the plot of the novel, which concerns the social and spiritual life of the black minister John Pearson: "John's tragedy lies not only in the separation of his body and soul but also in the sundering of his life from his African heritage" (147). Compared to the one-dimensional folk depicted in "The Eatonville Anthology," John Pearson is much more psychologically developed. He is the first in a line of epic male heroes, such as Moses and Herod, who will preoccupy Hurston for the rest of her writing career. These characters are empire builders, leaders of their communities, full of charisma, power, and attraction to women—but they also possess fatal flaws.

Even though Hurston brought African elements into the story, John Pearson is firmly grounded in Hurston's life in Alabama and Florida. The novel is basically the story of Hurston's parents' courtship and marriage, which began in her birthplace of Notasulga, Alabama, and moved to Eatonville, Florida. Regarding the origins of the book, Hurston claims that she did not want John's story to center on race; she wanted to write about the psychological and spiritual underpinnings of a real man: "While I was in the research field in 1929, the idea of 'Jonah's Gourd Vine' came to me. . . . What I wanted to tell was a story about a man, and from what I had read and heard, Negroes were supposed to write about the Race Problem. I was and am thoroughly sick of the subject. My interest lies in what makes a man or a woman do such-and-so, regardless of his color" (*Dust Tracks* 206).

Hurston reaffirmed her intention to focus only on the manhood of her protagonist rather than his life as a black man in a letter to James Weldon Johnson on 16 April 1934: "I have tried to present a Negro, preacher who is neither funny nor an imitation Puritan ram-rod in pants. Just the human being and poet that he must be to succeed in a Negro pulpit" (*Hurston: A Life in Letters* 298). She had a model right in front of her— her father. As Lowe notes, "Hurston began her novelistic career by appropriating the voice of her *earthly* father, the preacher John Hurston" (86). The original title for *Jonah's Gourd Vine*, *Big Nigger*, shows her ambivalence toward her subject. Lowe explains: "'Big Nigger' . . . would have signaled a double message to the black audience, for they would realize the term meant one thing to whites (someone uppity or to be feared) and another to blacks" (87). Hurston had called her father by this name behind his back because of his "well-cut broadcloth, Stetson hats, handmade alligator-skin shoes and walking-stick" (*Dust Tracks* 114). Lowe relates this name to the leading metaphor of the book, Jonah's gourd vine, because of the envy John stirred up in his community: "John's enemies in the book are always trying to 'pull him down' and 'chop him down' by punishing his pride, as does Jonah's gourd vine" (88).

In some ways, Hurston was able to empathize with her father and get into his mind-set, because they shared many characteristics. As an artist, she may even have sought to emulate his oratory as a preacher and his power as a founding father in the community. Although Hurston loved the fact that she was her "Mama's child," she may have resembled her father even more. Not only did they share a similarity in physical features—she admits that she looks "more like [her father] than any child in the house" (*Dust Tracks* 28)—but they seemed to share inner compulsions. When she realizes that she has an innate desire "to wander," she links this quality to her father: "Some children are just bound to take after their fathers in spite of women's prayers" (32).

Other aspects they shared included multiple marriages or partners, preaching as a calling, and interest in spiritual matters. While her father served as moderator of the Macedonia Baptist Church in Eatonville for many years, Hurston was initiated as a hoodoo priestess. Hoodoo was a religion that allowed women to take positions of power, unlike the Baptist Church of her father. Lowe makes a connection between Hurston's and her father's interest in religion, calling Hurston a griot, which he then defines: "A griot frequently inherits his father's role, and as a sacral/social/scientific teller of tales—and, most significantly, her father's tale—Hurston signifies that she alone of her siblings has been bequeathed the prophetic/narrative mantle and voice" (93). Hurston was not interested in organized religion, but she was fascinated with its storytelling aspects. Hurston claimed that her father not only had a facility with words as a preacher but was also one of the best storytellers at Joe Clark's store. She also inherited her father's desire for something better in life. He had moved his wife and eight children out of the Old South of Alabama to the New South of Eatonville, because, as Hurston reports in *Dust Tracks*, "he began to want things. Plantation life began to irk and bind him. His over-the-creek existence was finished. What else was there for a man like him?" (15). Likewise, Hurston never gave up on trying to find her main chance as she moved from writing to anthropology to theater and even teaching.

In *Dust Tracks*, Hurston finds much to admire about her father. She portrays him as an epic, masculine force of nature, striding into Eatonville: "Into this burly, boiling, hard-hitting, rugged-individualistic setting walked one day a tall, heavy-muscled mulatto who resolved to put down roots" (12). She continues: "he had a build on him that made you look. A stud-looking buck like that would have brought a big price in slavery time" (13). Beyond the physical, she looks more deeply into his nature: "I know that I did love him in a way, and that I admired many things about him. He had a poetry about him that I loved. That had made him a successful preacher" (91).

Despite his poetic nature, he could also lash out at her. In *Dust Tracks* she lists the insults her father rained upon her, from the moment of her birth to his request when her mother died that her school in Jacksonville adopt her. When Hurston was born, her father was so disappointed that she was a girl that he threatened to slit his throat. As Hurston relates: "one girl was enough. . . . I don't think he ever got over the trick that I played on him by getting born a girl. . . . He was nice about it in a way. He didn't tie me in a sack and drop me in the lake, as he probably felt like doing" (27–28). In another childhood incident, at the dinner table before Christmas, her father angrily rejects her Christmas wish for a horse: "It's a sin and a shame! Lemme tell you something right now, my young lady; you ain't white. Riding horse! Always trying to wear de big hat! I don't know how you got in this family nohow. You ain't like none of de rest of my young 'uns" (38).

In her visions in *Dust Tracks*, Hurston prophesies her future in terms of her father's rejection of her: "I knew my fate. I knew that I would be an orphan and homeless. I knew that while I was still helpless, that the comforting circle of my family would be broken, and that I would have to wander cold and friendless until I had served my time" (57). Spiritually, her father never really supported her. Whereas her mother had always urged her to "jump at de sun," her father tried to "squinch her spirit." In his defense, her father justified his treatment based on the harsh reality of the times: "It did not do for Negroes to have too much spirit. He was always threatening to break mine or kill me in the attempt. . . . He predicted dire things for me. The white folks were not going to stand for it. I was going to be hung before I got grown. Somebody was going to blow me down for my sassy tongue" (21).

Hurston's complicated family dynamic, reflecting the harsh realities of post–Civil War life in the South, is played out in *Jonah's Gourd Vine*. It begins in Notasulga, Alabama, with the story of John Pearson's childhood abuse at the hands of his stepfather, Ned Crittenden. As the story opens, Ned is berating sixteen-year-old John for staring at white passersby from the door of the family's cabin: "Yo' brazen ways wid dese white folks is gwinter git you lynched one uh dese days" (2). Ned yells at John, bringing up the fact that his father was likely the white owner of the plantation: "Yo' mammy mought think youse uh lump uh gold 'cause you got uh li'l' white folks color in yo' face, but Ah'll stomp yo' guts out and dat quick!" (2). Ned's wife, Amy, sticks up for her son and confronts Ned: "anytime you tries tuh knock any dese chillun 'bout dey head wid sticks and rocks, Ah'll be right dere tuh back dey fallin.' Ahm dey mama" (3).

Ned reveals that he is jealous because John receives special treatment due to his light skin color: "John is de house-nigger. Ole Marsa always kep' de yaller niggers in de house and give 'em uh job totin' silver dishes and goblets tuh de table. Us black niggers is de ones s'posed tuh ketch de wind and de weather" (4). Amy responds that she wants a better life for her children than the one Ned had experienced as a slave. "You growed up in slavery time," she explains. "When Old Massa wuz drivin' you in de rain and in de col'—he wasn't don' it tuh he'p you 'long. He wuz lookin' out for hisself. . . . but dese heah chillun is diffunt from us" (5). Amy then laments the fact that the legacy of slavery has caused men like Ned to fail as fathers: "We black folks don't love our chillun. We couldn't do it when we wuz in slavery. We borned 'em but dat didn't make 'em ourn. Dey b'longed tuh Old Massa" (5). But then she reminds him that a new era has dawned: "But we's free folks now. De big bell done rung! Us chillun is ourn" (5). Ned then admits that he has "bound John over tuh Cap'n Mimms," a cruel, white landowner who has "whipped niggers nigh tuh death." Amy retorts: "Dis heah bindin' over ain't nothin' but uh 'nother way uh puttin' us folks back intuh slavery" (7). John ends up escaping Mimms's clutches and seeking work with Alf Pearson, his presumptive father.

This opening sequence illuminates the oppressive situation of African American life after the Civil War, particularly centering on the rancorous relationship between the sexes. Novelist and feminist Toni Bade Bambara explains: "One of the most characteristic features of our community is the antagonism between men and women" (qtd. in Patterson x). This antagonism appears in much of Hurston's work: John Pearson in *Jonah's Gourd Vine* continues the abusive cycle begun by his stepfather and mistreats his wife, Lucy; Jody and Tea Cake emotionally abuse Janie Crawford in *Their Eyes Were Watching God*; Sykes terrorizes his wife, Delia Jones, with a rattlesnake in "Sweat."

In *Rituals of Blood*, Orlando Patterson blames the institution of slavery for uprooting blacks from their ancestral homes in Africa and shattering their customs, which centered on tribal and family unity. Such a disruption undermined their sense of identity and, in the case of males, undercut their masculinity: "the single greatest focus of ethnic domination was the relentless effort to emasculate the Afro-American male in every conceivable way and at every turn" (xiii). According to Patterson, slavery "was most virulent in its devastation of the roles of father and husband. . . . Hence, the status and role of husband could not exist under slavery, since it meant having independent rights in another person and, in both the U.S. South and West Africa, some authority over her.

Fatherhood could also not exist, since this meant owning one's children, having parental power and authority over them. Both infringed upon the power of the master and were therefore denied in law and made meaningless in practice" (27).

Fatherhood was at best a "marginal role" for African American men, Patterson claims. It was not a "base of self-actualization" but rather "a site of shame and humiliation" (21) Marriage also carried the taint of slavery. Patterson notes that African American male violence toward women was a compensatory mechanism for their own emasculation by slave owners (37). Ann Patton Malone uncovered many "reports of domestic violence in planters' records involving slave men against their wives" and blames this violence on the "overwhelming sense of powerlessness and impotence which threatened the male's concept of his manhood and fatherhood" (229).

Ned is a perfect example of a male whose sense of identity is shattered by the institution of slavery and who is unable to pick up the pieces in his postslavery life. His stepson, on the other hand, tries to forge a new identity and sense of manhood when he moves to Florida and discovers, while working at a railroad camp, that he has a facility with words. One day he imitates the preacher's sermon, and his friend Blue remarks: "You kin mark folks. . . . Dass jes' lak dat preacher fuh de world. Pity you ain't preachin' yo'self" (107). Blue also tells John that there is a "whole town uh nothin' but colored folks" nearby, and John eagerly moves there with his family. After attending a Covenant meeting and leading the singing of the song "He's a Battle-Axe in de Time Uh Trouble," John comes to the realization that he is meant to serve God. As he tells the congregation: "Brothers and Sisters, Ah rise befo' yuh tuhday tuh tell yuh, God done called me tuh preach" (111). The irony of John's awakening to his calling, which the narrator makes us realize, is that at bottom he is an artist, not a man of God. Because he can move people with his words, John thinks he is a preacher, but Hurston in "The Characteristics of Negro Expression" claims that this ability is typical of the black pastor: "Whatever the Negro does of his own volition he embellishes. His religious service is for the greater part excellent prose poetry. Both prayers and sermons are tooled and polished until they are true works of art. The supplication is forgotten in the frenzy of creation" (834).

Related to John's seductiveness with words and images is his attractiveness to women. Lowe makes the connection between the two, writing that his "artistic aspect feeds into his other self, the lover" (120). Unfortunately, John's wife stands in the way of the free reign of his passions. She tempers these passions and, for a time, helps him maintain a balance in his life. But, with his slapping of her and her subsequent death, nothing can save him from his passionate nature or his disgraceful behavior. Lowe also makes the point that with Lucy's death, Hurston's empathy with her father figure ends and shifts to the side of her mother (125). The key scene that illustrates this point occurs when Lucy is dying (Hurston also describes this movingly in chapter 6 of *Dust Tracks*). Even though he is a Christian minister, John insists on imposing hoodoo practices as Lucy lies dying. Lucy's last wish is that these practices—covering the clock and mirror, taking the pillow beneath her head—not be carried out. In *Mules and Men*, Hurston goes into great detail regarding the meaning of these practices, which are derived from the "Ewe-speaking peoples" of West Africa: "The spirit newly released from the body is likely to be destructive. This is why a cloth is thrown over the face of a clock in the death chamber and the looking glass is covered over. The clock will never run again, nor will the mirror ever cast any more reflections if they are not covered so that the spirit cannot see them" (229). Indeed, once Lucy dies, her spirit—in the form of a wind that is "howling, barking, and whining until the break of day"—seemingly rises up to attack John. He is so terrified that he "huddle[s] beneath his bed-covers shaking and afraid" (*Jonah's Gourd Vine* 133). Like the gourd vine of the title, he has been struck down not only for his barbarous treatment of Lucy throughout her life but also for betraying his calling as a Christian minister.

Hurston is not necessarily condemning John because he goes against Christianity, but she is commenting on the worm that eats away at his integrity, honor, and trustworthiness. In a letter to Carl Van Vechten, Hurston explains the symbolism of the gourd vine (from Jonah 4:6–10) and how John is eaten away from within: "You see the prophet of God sat up under a gourd vine that had grown up in one night. But a cut worm came along and cut it down. Great and sudden growth. One act of malice and it is withered and gone. The book of a thousand million leaves was closed" (*Hurston: A Life in Letters* 291).

John perishes when the car he is driving is hit by a train. In contrast to the living, green symbolism of the growing vine, John is struck down—just like Hurston's father—by a machine and dies a violent death: "The engine struck the car squarely and hurled it about like a toy. John was thrown out and lay perfectly still" (200). At his funeral an anonymous preacher turns away from Christianity and, instead, preaches "a barbaric requiem poem" (201). He tells how in heaven John's mourners beat on the "O-go-doe, the ancient drum," which is the "voice of Death." They shun "Kata-Kumba, the drum of triumph, that speaks of great ancestors and glorious wars" (202). All that is heard is the "voice of Death—that promises nothing, that speaks with tears only, and of the past" (202). The book ends like Macbeth's famous speech about the brevity and poignancy of life—"it is a tale / Told by an idiot, full of sound and fury / Signifying nothing." John is, finally, "the poor player / That struts and frets his hour upon the stage." In the end, not even his African gods can save him. The "voice of Death" wins over the "drum of triumph."

## Their Eyes Were Watching God

In *Their Eyes Were Watching God*, Hurston begins almost at the point where *Jonah's Gourd Vine* ends, that is, at the founding of Eatonville. But then she shifts the action further south to the area around Lake Okeechobee. By moving the setting to the "muck," her characters encounter a new environment, free of all influences—from white, mainstream America and from what Mary Katherine Wainwright calls "the folkloric ethos" of small, all-black towns like Eatonville (234). The muck is filled with a different type of population, namely, transient blacks who come from the Caribbean. This setting functions as a sort of underworld—intensified by the deadly hurricane—that the heroine, Janie Crawford, must experience in order to be transformed and gain self-awareness.

In contrast to *Jonah's Gourd Vine*, this novel contains fewer personal details from the author's own life. Hurston bases the story on the life of Joseph E. Clark (Hurston added the "e" at the end of his name), the founder of Eatonville, whose store was the center of communal life. Born in 1859 in Covington, Georgia, Clark married Julia Hightower, a Blackfoot Indian, in the early 1870s, and together they had three daughters. In a family memoir titled *Joseph E. Clark*, the oldest daughter, Mattie, recalls one of her mother's outstanding features: "My mother had the most beautiful hair you have ever seen. It was so long, that she could sit on it" (32). This detail would become significant in the novel; Janie's hair is featured as symbolic of her beauty and individuality. In the early 1880s, Clark moved his family to Florida in order to work in Josiah Eaton's orange groves. His wife died a year or two later, and Clark soon married his second wife, Martha. In a memoir about the Clark family history, Olga Fenton Mitchell and Gloria Fenton Magbie in *The Life and Times of Joseph E. Clark* recount their grandmother Mattie's description of Martha Clark's "meanness" that, eventually, drove Mattie away from Eatonville; she was never to see her father again. But there is no hint in the memoir that Clark was abusive. Eatonville historian Frank Otey writes: "The mean-spirited character of 'Clarke' with an 'e' does not equate with the real 'Clark' . . . who helped establish, guide and supported a women's lodge, 'Household of Ruth'" (67). In fact, Hurston's mother was a member of the Household of Ruth, a benevolent church society. When I asked Harriet Moseley, Clark's great-great-niece, if there was any family history related to Clark's beating of Martha, she indignantly denied this allegation (Lillios 26).

Hurston was less interested in Clark's personal life than in his public life in Eatonville and his career as a founding father and empire builder. On 17 July 1885 he joined his boss, Josiah Eaton, in signing the incorporation papers for the creation of the town of Maitland, next door to Eatonville. Clark even served one year as the town marshal under Eaton's leadership as the first mayor. During this period, Eaton sold land to Clark, in order to create an all-black town, and another white landowner, Lewis Lawrence, gave him twelve acres (plus ten acres to found the St. Lawrence AME Church). The centennial booklet of the town of Eatonville discusses the underlying reason for the drive to create an all-black town: "It appears that the all-white community of Maitland found the Blacks and the area they inhabited to be somewhat 'unsightly' and wanted them to move to another area" ("Town of Eatonville" 18). By 1889, Clark was not only elected mayor but also served as business manager of the town newspaper, the *Eatonville Speaker*, from 1888 to 1890; ran the town post office, established in 1889; and owned a general store called Clark & Co., Dealers in Staple—and—Fancy. He died in 1911.

The information we have about Joe Clark is sketchy at best. Hurston knew Clark from when she moved to Eatonville as a small child in the 1890s until 1904 when her mother died and she moved away. She undoubtedly saw him when she returned to town for brief visits until 1911, when Clark died. Because Clark was so much older, Hurston could not have known many intimate details about his life. Instead, he was a convenient target onto which she could project her feelings about the town and its people. For example, Clark especially becomes a target when Hurston discusses love in the novel. Although little is known about Clark's love life—beyond the fact that his first wife had beautiful hair and his second wife was mean—Hurston injects her own love life into the novel. When she wrote the novel in Haiti in late 1936, she was recovering from a devastating love affair with Percy Punter. She admits her feelings in the chapter "Love" in *Dust Tracks*: "I tried to embalm all the tenderness of my passion for him in 'Their Eyes Were Watching God'" (260). Even though Punter was twenty-one years her junior, Hurston "did not just fall in love. I made a parachute jump" (252). Her affair with Punter was "the real love affair of my life" (255), but it could not last given her primary commitment to her career. When Punter asked her to give up her work and marry him, she fled New York, but she suffered greatly in the breakup that followed. She admits in *Dust Tracks* that they hit each other: "No broken bones, you understand, and no black eyes" (257). But their fighting signified the end: "For always a blow to my body had infuriated me beyond measure" (257), and Hurston left to save herself.

Before she could deal with the subject of love's transformative power, Hurston needed a structure for her ideas and feelings. She came up with the three-husband format, starring Logan Killicks, the farmer with sixty acres and a mule; Jody Starks, the Joe Clark figure, who founds a town; and Tea Cake, the free spirit. Jon Woodson argues that Hurston was highly influenced by Jens Peter Jacobsen's novel *Marie Grubbe* and that the structure, characterization, some imagery, and wording in *Their Eyes Were Watching God* are remarkably similar to those in *Marie Grubbe*, which was first published in 1876 (and reached Harlem in translation in 1917). Woodson points out that the "novel was brought to the attention of Hurston's circle by Nella Larsen," who mentions it in a letter published in *Opportunity* in 1926. Woodson says: "It is likely that Hurston took violent opposition to the novel, which she found offensive because of the portrayal of its female protagonist. According to my reading, Hurston chose to respond to the book by creating her own novel, in which she tried to create a more suitable female heroine" (620). According to Woodson, Jacobsen's novel centers on a "woman of extraordinary beauty" who marries a son of the king of Denmark, Frederick the Third, but then runs off with the husband of her oldest sister; she then marries a "prosperous farmer"; and, finally, she falls in love with a farmworker, marrying beneath her station and tending a ferry and an inn for the rest of her life. Other similarities abound, such as the use of direct and indirect discourse, "a synchronic view from a timeless perspective," a recounting of the protagonist's story at the end of the novel, and parallel images, such as the fish net at the end of *Their Eyes* (in Jacobsen's novel, a passage reads: "Over all the earth there was a net of invisible threads binding soul to soul, threads stronger than life, stronger than death" [qtd. in Woodson 97]).

In *Their Eyes Were Watching God*, Hurston takes these disparate elements—the history of Eatonville, the story of Joe Clark, her love affair with Percy Punter, the possible "borrowing" of themes from *Marie Grubbe*—and mixes them together to create a novel uniquely her own. She adds a symbolic dimension, centering on the cosmic meaning of the hurricane as the transformative power in the novel.

Eatonville in *Their Eyes* is much the same static, hermetic locale as it is in "The Eatonville Anthology" and *Jonah's Gourd Vine*. People have not changed; they sit in front of Joe Clarke's store and pass the time of day. When the heroine, Janie Crawford, walks by, they sit "in judgment" and "hope that she might fall to their level some day" (2). Janie has dutifully followed the script that her grandmother Nanny laid out for her by marrying a man of property, Logan Killicks. Nanny, a former slave, wishes she had had the same opportunities that Janie will have in life. She wistfully says, "Ah wanted to preach a great sermon about colored women sittin' on high, but they wasn't no pulpit for me" (15). "On high," for Nanny, means the power and property that a good position signifies. For this reason, she pushes Janie towards Killicks, who owns sixty acres.

But after submitting to Killicks's rule and becoming like his servant in the fields, Janie seizes the first opportunity to escape when she sees Jody Starks, "a citified, stylish dressed man," coming down the road. He tries to woo her by promising to put her on a pedestal: "A pretty doll-baby lak you is made to sit on de front porch and rock and fan yo'self and eat p'taters dat other folks plant just special for you" (28). Janie is thrilled by Jody's plans to start a new life in Eatonville, where he soon establishes his store and gets himself elected mayor. When the townspeople celebrate his election, they ask Janie to speak "uh few words uh encouragement," but Jody cuts them off: "mah wife don't know nothin' 'bout no speech-makin.' Ah never married her for nothin' lak dat. She's uh woman and her place is in de home" (40–41).

Janie's spirit is suffocated under the weight of this heavily patriar-chal society. Ann duCille in *The Coupling Convention* points out the hopelessness of Janie's position in this world: "It is, however, not mere men who oppress in this novel but ideology—the ponderous presence of an overarching system of patriarchal domination" (120). The Eatonville that Hurston creates in the novel is not only oppressive because of its patriarchy but is also static and unchangeable because of race. Hazel Carby argues in "The Politics of Fiction, Anthropology, and the Folk" that Hurston presents "a representation of 'Negroness' as an unchang-ing, essential entity, an essence so distilled that it is an aesthetic position of blackness" (77). But, duCille's and Carby's views refer to only half of Hurston's portrait of gender and race in the story.

When Janie meets Tea Cake and moves with him to the muck, ev-erything suddenly changes. She enters a world of flux and potentiality. Janie is wide-eyed when she sees it for the first time: "To Janie's strange eyes, everything in the Everglades was big and new. Big Lake Okechobee [*sic*], big beans, big cane, big weeds, big everything. Weeds that did well to grow waist high up the state were eight and often ten feet tall down there. Ground so rich that everything went wild. . . . People wild too" (123). According to Konzett, critics have misread Hurston because they have seen the ethnocentric Eatonville as the main black community in her novels. Carby, for example, does not take into account "Hurston's references to foreign cultural influences (particularly Caribbean) and the different patterns of migration in Florida," which are southward.

Konzett concludes: "In the end, *Their Eyes* emphasizes the cross-cultural and transnational characteristics of Florida, demonstrating that modern social, demographic, and cultural changes occur differently in various regions across the United States" (89).

When Janie and Tea Cake migrate south, they enter the cross-cultural world that Konzett describes. Many transient, undocumented black workers from the Caribbean, particularly from the Bahamas, worked in the fertile fields that surrounded Lake Okeechobee in the 1920s. Just before the fateful hurricane strikes, Hurston mentions how all the different groups have blended together to form a new type of black community vastly different from her mythic Eatonville: "Since Tea Cake and Janie had friended with the Bahaman workers in the 'Glades, they, the 'Saws,' had been gradually drawn into the American crowd" (146).

Janie takes full part in these revelries and often stays up so late at the "fire dances" that "Tea Cake would not let her go with him to the field. He wanted her to get her rest" (146). She has taken on the characteristics of her place—"Everything went wild. People went wild too." Janie has thoroughly shed her Eatonville skin and revels in the freedom to speak her mind and take part as an equal in all the communal activities: "Only here, she could listen and laugh and even talk some herself if she wanted to. She got so she could tell big stories herself from listening to the rest" (128). She has embedded herself in this free-spirited community, and her personality blossoms. When they are not working, the people play games, dance, gamble, and tell stories, and "people seldom got mad, because everything was done for a laugh" (128). What the muck lacks, though, is balance and a means for Janie to grow spiritually. If everything is done for a laugh, it is also done on the surface of things.

Only an act of God as powerful as a hurricane can upset the balance once again, uprooting Janie from her complacent, pleasure-centered lifestyle and bringing her to a new self-awareness. The storm as a metaphor has always been symbolic of creation, destruction, and regeneration, because it involves the mingling together of the four elements. By uniting air (wind), water (rain), and fire (rays of light in the eye of the storm), all of which disturb the fourth element, earth, the hurricane symbolizes cosmic synergy. Primitive peoples such as early native Americans worshiped the hurricane as a "deity of the winds and waters, and also of the heavens" (Cirlot 147–48).

Hurston's hurricane was also real. Her portrait of the "monstropolous beast" in *Their Eyes* was most likely colored by three specific hurricanes in 1928, 1929, and 1935. Lowe has noticed this correspondence and believes that Hurston combined aspects of all three in her novel. The hurricane that Hurston experienced firsthand occurred in 1929, when she was in Nassau, the Bahamas. She reports its impact in *Dust Tracks*: "I lived through that terrible five-day hurricane of 1929. It was horrible in its intensity and duration. I saw dead people washing around on the streets when it was over. You could smell the stench from dead animals as well. More than three hundred houses were blown down in the city of Nassau alone" (195).

Hurston did not experience the 1928 and 1935 hurricanes firsthand, but they also played a role in the creation of the storm in *Their Eyes*. Hurston was in New York, waiting for the publication of *Mules and Men*, when the 1935 hurricane struck Florida. It was the strongest hurricane in recorded history, a category 5 storm that swept through the keys. It had sustained winds of 200 miles an hour, with gusts up to 250 (Gannon 92), and was so forceful that the sky lit up, ignited by particles of sand hitting each other to create electric sparks. Four hundred and eight people died in this storm.

The 1928 hurricane was also one of the most powerful on record and one of the worst natural disasters in U.S. history. The Red Cross reported in 1929 that 1,810 people lost their lives; three quarters of those were black, many of them undocumented Bahaman transient workers (Will 127). This hurricane, a category 4, with sustained winds of 155 miles per hour, devastated Puerto Rico before it entered the United States at West Palm Beach. The swirling winds created a tidal-wave effect in Lake Okeechobee, which had only soft mud dikes to hold back the raging waters of ten to fifteen feet that soon broke down the dikes and flooded the surrounding countryside. Unfortunate people such as Janie and Tea Cake, who are waiting for "the sun to get friendly again," are doomed. Tea Cake's and Janie's awareness of danger is probably dimmed by the fire dancing and storytelling that is going on in their house during the storm. When Muck-Boy gets up to dance, he goes "crazy through the feet" and "dance[s] himself and everybody else crazy" (149). Lowe sees these activities as a diversion the group uses to build solidarity in the face of the impending storm: "The combination of the hilarious John de

Conquer stories and snippets of bawdy dozens lines helps the figures gird up their loins against cosmic forces. John, a traditional and daring figure, frequently gambles with God and the Devil; similarly, the defiance of the dozens humor seems directed against a malevolently approaching storm. A beneficent Culture attempts to ward off a threatening Nature" (188).

During their revelries, Janie and Tea Cake stop and are awestruck when the storm's fury reaches its height. Janie, too, searches for God and finds him appropriately in the eye of the storm. The brief cessation of winds gives her a moment to contemplate her fate; indeed, the eye of the storm represents the void through "one may pass out of the world of space and time into spacelessness and timelessness" (Cirlot 148). Janie, for the first time in the novel, senses God's presence as she and Tea Cake wait out the storm's fury: "The wind came back with triple fury, and put out the light for the last time. They sat in company with the others in other shanties, their eyes straining against crude walls and their souls asking if He meant to measure their puny might against His. They seemed to be staring at the dark, but their eyes were watching God" (151).

Janie comes in touch with God as the creator of earthly disturbances and the maker of destinies. Yet Hurston does not develop this theme further, nor does she extend Janie's spiritual development in a religious sense. Lowe sees the hurricane as a plot device, typical of other storm-centered books: "Most of the hurricane-genre books routinely use the storm as Hurston does, placing it at the end of the book to bring the narrative to an exciting conclusion" (203).

The storm also forces Janie to evolve beyond her relationship with Tea Cake after he dies a horrible death brought on by rabies and Janie's desperate attempt to shoot him before he kills her. By moving to the muck with him, Janie releases her life "to the uncertainties and potential chaos of the uncultivated, untamed swamp, where love and death linger side by side" (Gates 193). She not only feels the depths of passion with Tea Cake but also sees the dark side of human nature when he is bitten by the rabid dog. Tea Cake's rabies and death destroy Janie's old way of life. The hurricane and the earlier image of the pear tree stand as polar opposites, as metaphors for Janie's developing concept of self. The pear tree represents fertility and rootedness. Only the force of the storm can uproot a tree, that is, the stability of her life with Tea Cake.

Feminist critics, though, see Tea Cake not so much as a stabilizing factor but as a domineering force in the relationship. DuCille notes that the culture is to blame for his dominance, whereas Deborah Plant believes that once Tea Cake is dead, Janie is "freed from external, patriarchal control. No longer entrapped by gender roles and expectations, [Hurston] and Janie can follow wherever the inside urge leads" (*Every Tub* 173). DuCille agrees that Janie is "largely without community" at the end of the novel, but she still feels that "female subjectivity does not win out over patriarchal ideology" (*Coupling Convention* 121). Instead, she feels that Janie will still be trapped, because of her "propensity for manipulating reality, for conflating dream and truth, for accepting others' horizons," which "stifles women's self-realization" ("Intricate Fabric" 147).

Hurston's introduction and conclusion to the novel illustrate duCille's point. The problem with women, the narrator claims at the beginning, is that they "forget all those things they don't want to remember, and remember everything they don't want to forget. The dream is the truth. Then they act and do things accordingly" (1). At the end, Janie is lost in her fantasies of the dead Tea Cake. Her last memories of him "commenced to sing a sobbing sigh out of every corner in the room," until Tea Cake's image comes "prancing around her." She tells herself, "Of course he wasn't dead," proving duCille's point that Janie is "manipulating reality"; yet the key words—"his memory made pictures of love and light against the wall" (184)—suggest that Janie has opted out of patriarchal society altogether. She has transformed the horrible experience into a spiritual one. And love is the transforming agent, as Hurston describes the experience of falling in love in *Dust Tracks*: "it seems to be the unknown country from which no traveler ever returns. What seems to be a returning pilgrim is another person born" (265). Tea Cake's memory, even the "day of the gun, and the bloody body," has now become the grist on which her creative imagination can work; her imaginary world has now commenced to sing. As Houston Baker points out, Janie has become "a storyteller and blues singer par excellence" (59). No longer her nightmare, Tea Cake is now her inspiration. Janie's state of mind—"Here was peace"—indicates that she has passed out of the eye of the storm into the timeless world of art.

## Rawlings's Works through *The Yearling*

Rawlings did not arrive in Florida with a facility for using "heiroglyph-ics"; she had to acquire it through careful observation. When she first visited Florida in 1928, she was still a journalist with aspirations of be-coming a novelist. In fact, she moved to Florida in order to make a fresh start as a novelist. Rawlings first became aware of the attractions of north-central Florida while on vacation with her first husband, Charles Rawlings. They were visiting Charles's brothers, Jimmy and Wray, who ran a gas station and a real estate business in Island Grove, near Ocala. As they explored the region, Marjorie and Charles fell in love with the beauty of the landscape and felt, as fledgling writers, that they could write their great novels if only they could buy some property in the area and settle down among the Cracker people who populated the woods. A few months later, Charles's brothers found a seventy-two-acre farm at Cross Creek—complete with a farmhouse, barn, tenant house, and equipment—and the young couple eagerly bought it.

Elizabeth Silverthorne in *Marjorie Kinnan Rawlings: Sojourner at Cross Creek* romanticizes their decision:

> The half-wild remoteness and mystery of the Scrub fascinated Marjorie as did the simplicity of the people's daily lives. She and Chuck were charmed by the natural beauty of the area, the rivers and the lakes with floating islands, the tall palms and great live oaks dripping with Spanish moss, and the fragrant orange groves,
>
> "Let's sell everything and move South!" she said to him. "How we could write!" (55)

This scenario describing Rawlings's decision to transform her life may or may not be accurate, but Rawlings certainly dedicated herself to captur-ing the magical and mythic qualities of the place.

When Rawlings carefully observed this landscape and the Cracker in-dividuals who inhabited it, she discovered not only her calling as a writer, as Rodger Tarr notes, but also her subject matter: "Once she committed herself to the Crackers whose stark lives enriched her literary soul, and once she was *en rapport*, as she called it, with her black help, Rawlings found her literary voice" (introduction to *The Private Marjorie* 2).

Rawlings did not discover this voice the moment she set foot on

Florida soil. She had to learn and hone her craft by trial and error until she was lucky enough to come under the guidance of her gifted editor at Scribner's, Maxwell Perkins. Together they constructed a Cross Creek of the imagination that reflects not only what they considered the "truth" of the place but also their own personalities and values. Today we would say that they are simply superimposing their own vision or even fantasy of Cross Creek onto the landscape. In "The Death of the Author," Roland Barthes argues that anything, even a landscape or a nation, can be read as a text: "a text consists of multiple writings, issuing from several cultures and entering into dialogue with each other" (12). He believes that the reader of the "text" authors it: "there is one place where this multiplicity is collected, united, and this place is not the author . . . but the reader . . . the unity of a text is not in its origin, it is in its destination . . . the reader is a man . . . who holds gathered into a single field all the paths of which the text is constituted" (12). In other words, each reader will have his or her own version of the text, in this case, Cross Creek.

J. T. Glisson acknowledges this concept in the introduction to his book *The Creek*. As Rawlings's nearest neighbor, Glisson was twelve years old when Rawlings was writing *The Yearling*. He is the person still alive who knew her best:

> When I was a young'un, Cross Creek was a small island of humanity in a sea of forests. We were a handful of independent, ornery Cracker families (white natives of Georgia and Florida) with the exception of a writer from up north and one extended black family. Thanks to the swamps and hammocks of north central Florida we were able to maintain our isolation for a half-century after motels and signboards spread across the rest of the state. . . .
>
> It is still impossible for me to separate the place from the people who lived there because surviving necessitated taking on the ways of nature. . . .
>
> There was no electricity, telephones, or central heat. With the exception of our resident writer, Marjorie Kinnan Rawlings, the entire community derived some or all of its living from fishing (illegally, in the opinion of outsiders) and hunting frogs and alligators. We made our own rules and settled our differences within the community. (2)

This is the Cross Creek that Glisson remembers, but he points out that Rawlings created a "second Cross Creek when she wrote a book by that name that described her vision of us in our world." Despite Rawlings's manipulation of reality, Glisson approves of her portrait of Cross Creek: "Her book is beautifully and eloquently written, and in my view could not be improved upon. I am truly grateful for her gift of *Cross Creek* as well as her novels that preserve her view of the time and place that is still my image of home" (2). Nevertheless, Glisson points out that there are multiple Cross Creeks, including the one portrayed in the movie of the same name and the imaginary landscapes created in the imaginations of all the people who have read Rawlings's books, seen the movie, or visited the farmhouse, which is now designated a National Historic Landmark.

## "Cracker Chidlings"

When she first arrived in Florida, Rawlings had no such view of Cross Creek and began jotting down random incidents or character sketches as they occurred. By 1930, after residing at the Creek for two years, she gathered together the tales, the portraits of her Cross Creek neighbors, and detailed descriptions of landscape and titled the collection "Cracker Chidlings." "Chidlings," which is the vernacular for "chitterlings" (also known as "chitlins" or "chittlins"), refers to the small intestines of pigs or other animals that are boiled or fried for food. Upper-class southern society regards this food as offal, but it helped slaves survive when their masters gave it to them as waste products of animals they had slaughtered. Thus it is an apt metaphor for people and events that are marginalized yet which matter in a substantive sense.

Rawlings sent "Cracker Chidlings" to *Scribner's*, which bought it on 11 March 1930 and published the vignettes in February 1931. The eight "chidlings" in the collection show Rawlings's transition from journalist to author. She faithfully records details concerning the setting and characters; in addition, she poeticizes the language and adds meaning and irony to the seemingly random events. Thus she relates in one "chidling" how 'Shiner Tim's wife "works every run with Tim," because—given their illicit activity of making and selling bootleg liquor—"A car with a woman ain't so noticeable-like" (33). In another sketch, Miney Whitman stages

"Thespian antics" for a new youth in town. The naive young man is lured to Crackerneck Road in search of "a ravishingly beautiful bad girl," only to find the scrub coming to life: "From hundred of yards around emerge male youths, slapping their thighs and laughing like hell" (36). In "The Preacher Has His Fun," the new Methodist preacher suddenly quits: "He simply gave up the whole town as a bad job" (37). In his last sermon he tells his flock, "I go to prepare a place for you. Where I am, there ye may be also" (38). The townspeople, feeling guilty that they had not "supported him properly," later learn that he has become the chaplain at "Raiford, the State penitentiary."

The final "chidling" hints that the Cracker lifestyle is ephemeral and on its way to disappearing. In "The Silver River," Colonel Buxton, a "Kentucky gentleman," tricks Widow Hopkins into selling her land, which includes river rights along the Silver River and Silver Springs itself. The narrator explains: "Like most lovely things, it has caused much squabbling among men" (39). Later, he meets his match when a Cracker youth rises to become Judge Atkinson after studying "law by a fat-wood fire to good purpose." Atkinson discovers that Buxton had been careless about proving title to the land and plots to snatch it away from him. He informs Buxton: "I have already stole the Silver River. There is just one difference between you and me. You stole it from a poor widow woman and I stole it from a Goddam rascal" (40).

The publication of "Cracker Chidlings," meant to be "raw" and "true sketches of the Cracker folk in the still pioneer heart of Florida" (qtd. in Silverthorne 59), raised a firestorm of protest. The editor of the *Ocala Evening Star* labeled Rawlings's work "Literary Chitterlings" and attacked Rawlings for not portraying the authentic life of the Florida Crackers. He guessed that she had spent time in the Cumberlands and was "palming off material collected" there as "Florida life" (Rawlings, *Uncollected Writings* 253). In a letter to the editor published on 2 February 1931, Rawlings fiercely defended herself: "I have not visited the Cumberland mountains. . . . The Florida frontier—unfortunately fast-vanishing—has been my first experience of the kind, and my cracker friends and acquaintances have come into my life with all the freshness of new material" (253). She further emphasizes to him her accuracy: "My dear sir, my sketches are so true, that I have softened them, not colored them, for fear that if they came to the chance attention of the subjects—all within a forty-mile radius of my home—offense would be taken at my frankness where none was intended" (254).

As a portent of what was to come, offense was taken by the mother of one of her subjects. In the chidling titled "The Preacher Has His Fun," Rawlings begins by writing that "Harry Barnes and a handful more have given their town a bad name" (37). The new preacher who is coming to the town is warned that he is going "to a town full of niggers." The critic adds, "Yes—but you'll find they have white skins" (37). Harry Barnes's mother objected to the portrayal of her son as a town misfit and "stalked up and down the road" in front of Rawlings's house "threatening to come in and give Marjorie a horsewhipping," according to Silverthorne (61). Ironically, Zelma Cason was the one who made peace between the two women.

Although Rawlings fiercely defended her freedom of speech and did not care about "hurting people's feelings" (*Max and Marjorie* 105), she recognized that this early work was "straight journalism," "almost non-fiction" (446). In retrospect, eight years later when she was considering including "Cracker Chidlings" in a collection of short stories, she admits to Perkins in a 27 February 1940 letter: "They give me, myself, a terribly embarrassed feeling. They have no pretense at artistry. They are only regional studies, saying, 'Aren't these people amusing!' If I had never progressed beyond 'Cracker Chidlings' in my use of the Florida material, I could make no claim to being a creative writer" (446). Nevertheless, the stories were an early testing ground of her material, allowing her to sketch out an entire community—she originally proposed titling the work "Cracker Town"—and to explore the "village psychology" (41).

"Jacob's Ladder"

When Rawlings sent her next Cross Creek story, "Jacob's Ladder," to *Scribner's Magazine,* her work came to the attention of Maxwell Perkins for the first time. In his first letter to Rawlings, on 19 November 1930, Perkins praises her portrayal of the Florida Crackers, who, he notes, have "always been looked upon as a low people." He explains what has attracted him to Rawlings's writing: "One great quality in what you have written is that you enable the reader to see them from a new point of view, by which he can sympathize with them." The reader can understand "the nature of these . . . people, identifies himself with one or the other of them, and shares their experiences" (Rawlings, *Max and Marjorie* 28). Perkins, an astute reader of modern American literature and a shaper of the great novels written by his authors, was able to assess Rawlings's potential genius in her early stories. The quality he most appreciates in her work is her empathy with her characters (which is the same quality that Hurston praises in Rawlings's work in her 1943 letter). Rawlings, in her response to Perkins dated 24 December 1930, explains her purpose in writing "Jacob's Ladder": "You see, I began with my mind full of the power of this environment—and after all, from the human if not the cosmic point of view, the courage of these people is more important" (34).

As can be seen by the previous quotation, Rawlings sees the destiny of her Cracker characters intertwined with the power of nature. In "Jacob's Ladder" it is "the high winds" of September—the hurricanes—that will change the lives of the main characters, Florry and Mart, forever. They meet at a dance, and even though she is shy and "rabbity," she feels an immediate connection with him: "Suddenly, the girl knew that this man was not a stranger. He was like herself. More, he was a part of herself. She was a part of him" (46). They go their separate ways that night even though "High winds were coming." Florry has a premonition that the winds would "sweep across her, move her on. When they were gone, she would not be in this place" (48). When she awakes the next morning, she finds herself in the middle of a hurricane. In the "lull of the gale," Mart appears and talks her into fleeing from her abusive father—reasoning that "All two of us so kind o' rabbity" (52)—and making a new life with him.

Unfortunately, their new life together is a desperate struggle for survival as Mart tries his luck with farmwork, fishing, illegal trapping, and "shining." They wander from the piney woods to the seashore to the scrub and to the hammock. Nothing works out for the young couple. They are devastated when Florry gives birth to "a puny boy-child" who cannot survive, because she is too fragile to nurse and care for him. Their lowest point comes when Mart gets into trouble with the law because of his debts and has to give up his traps, which are the source of his livelihood. Mart explains his plight: "Hit ain't like I was a sorry thing wouldn't do a man's work nor a day's work, neither. . . . You knows I've scratched like a hound dog at a gopher hole. Nor I ain't been pertickler what 'twas done, fishin' or trappin' or 'shinin' or sich." He concludes: "There ain't nothin' left to try. There ain't no'eres left to go. Us been a-climbin' ol' Jacob's ladder thouten no end to it" (100). After hearing the biblical reference, Florry recognizes that Mart is spiritually defeated: "He's like to had the chidlin's beat out of him" (100). She talks him into returning to her home in the piney woods. They trek for miles across the Florida terrain, arriving, finally, at Florry's father's home, in the midst of a hurricane. After they survive the hurricane, Florry finally feels she has come full circle and is home at last.

Rawlings struggled with the ending of "Jacob's Ladder" and vacillated between three versions. Her first inclination was to make the story tragic and end with Florry, "if not defeated by 'the high winds of change,' at least with her last shred of security swept from under her by them. The ultimate violence had been done to her" (Rawlings, *Max and Marjorie* 30). Rawlings's conception of Florida fully encompasses this dark side. In "Florida: A Land of Contrasts," written in 1944, Rawlings defines Florida as a mix of good and bad elements: "Florida is kindly. It is also repellent. It is beautiful and also ugly. . . . Florida began and has continued as a combination of man's dreams and man's greediness" (*Uncollected Writings* 302–3).

Rawlings's second proposed ending would take Florry "a step beyond the present one": "She could be shown, unchanged, with nothing more than she has ever had—her courage—between her gaunt body and the cyclic sweep of natural violence which is the background of this life. She could be shown living like a rabbit in the brush, as it were, self-sufficing, building her own security out of her fearlessness, making her own isolated nest" (*Max and Marjorie* 30). Rawlings rejected this ending as "anti-climax" and, finally, considered a third, in which "there is no point to be made in annihilating both [Florry and Mart]." She explains:

> Florry's instinct would naturally draw her back, in a circle, to the one sure thing she knew—the clearing in the piney-woods, the patch of ground her father owned. I would want to keep the summer of heat, much as I have it. It is one of the things here to be

fought. The close of the summer would find Mart at the end of the tether. Florry, who has followed him unquestioning, leaving behind at each move something precious to her, would be moved in her wisdom to lead Mart back to what she knows of permanence. (*Max and Marjorie* 33)

Florry's father is shocked by their return, but he is no longer an "ancient menace" and they are no longer "aliens, or trespassers, or outcasts." The story ends as it begins, with a hurricane: "The seasonal hurricane would be impending. The two would be subject, as they have ever been, as they must always be, to the danger of the elements; but the human factor would be solved" (*Max and Marjorie* 33).

Perkins responded immediately on 29 November 1930 to Rawlings's dilemma by advocating the third ending. He argued that if she were to write an unhappy ending, in which the reader "comes to see Mart as nothing but a miserable Cracker," she would break "the right conception which the reader has hitherto had" of the characters (*Max and Marjorie* 29). An ending in which Florry and Mart "find a permanent resting place" would be more "artistically" pleasing to the reader, Perkins argues. He rejects Rawlings's "tragic" view of life and presents his own philosophy of how life should be portrayed in fiction: "Our great aim is to intensify the human element in the story by strengthening the interest in the characters, and by bringing out the individuality of the characters, so that it will be a story of two people primarily, and only in an underlying sense a story of two Crackers with the sociological significance" (33–34).

It is unclear to whom Perkins is referring when he writes "Our." Does he mean Scribner's, or does he include Rawlings in the circle of gifted authors whose work he is trying to shape? The latter seems more plausible, as a 1934 letter from F. Scott Fitzgerald to Perkins indicates. Writing about Hemingway, Wolfe, and himself, Fitzgerald remarks: "What family resemblance there is between we three as writers is the attempt that crops up in our fiction from time to time to recapture the exact feel of a moment in time and space exemplified by people rather than things" (Bruccoli 11). Perkins not only nurtures this "family resemblance" in his three male authors but also tries to instill it in Rawlings's work. He urges Rawlings to deepen the character of Florry in "Jacob's Ladder": "One expects at the start that Florry at least, will more completely transcend typicality, that her individuality would make her more of a *character* in her own right than she is, apart from her value as a representative of the Florida Cracker" (*Max and Marjorie* 25).

Again and again in her novels, Rawlings shows that she has learned this lesson well by referring to the touchstone of character that Perkins values in fiction. In an 18 November 1932 letter to Perkins, she affirms that her goal in writing is to portray the "cosmic conflict of man in general struggling against an obscure law and destiny" (*Max and Marjorie* 73). Perkins knew that readers would become attracted to Rawlings's sense of empathy with her characters if she emphasized their courageous spirit in overcoming adversity. This feeling of empathy was an integral part of his Yankee upbringing. In a letter he wrote to Rawlings long after they had established their close, personal friendship, Perkins explains how he acquired his values and how they had been inculcated into his way of thinking. In a 26 July 1940 letter, he tells Rawlings that he was raised with a "deep sense of responsibility" toward others. "Duty" and "service" were valued more than material success. His Yankee relatives and acquaintances "soft pedaled wealth," even though they may have had servants working for them (463).

Beyond the feeling of empathy with her characters' struggles against the elements as depicted in her fiction, Rawlings also had an uncanny ability to record their patterns of speech, which was the other aspect that Hurston admired in her work. Rawlings's first husband, Charles Rawlings, notes in an interview on 21 November 1970 how Rawlings developed her literary voice:

> I think in certain respects she's a great writer. I think her ear is a great, great ear. I think it's greater than Hemingway's. I think her ability to listen to a cracker conversation to go in and depict it, suggest the nuances, suggest the touches that were necessary to make it come into perfect light and to reject the rest, was absolutely miraculous. It's a joy to read her dialogue, especially her cracker dialogue. . . . To say that it's a joy to read Marjorie is a tribute to her. (unpublished interview, University of Florida Libraries)

As her first husband notes, Rawlings possessed the ability to capture the nuances of Cracker speech, yet she was attacked by the local *Ocala*

*Evening Star* in its 30 January 1931 issue not only for her depiction of the reality of Cracker life in Florida in her story "Cracker Chidlings" but also for "palming off material collected in the Cumberlands, where she must have visited, as Florida life" (*Uncollected Writings* 253). In her rebuttal letter, Rawlings denies that she had ever visited the Cumberlands and suggests, instead, that the editors of the *Ocala Evening Star* are unable to accept the realistic portrait that she is painting in her work: "A bald fact somehow affrights them: they long to swathe it in comforting illusions" (254). Rawlings rigorously defends her accuracy, by saying, "my sketches are so true, that I have softened them, not colored them, for fear that if they came to the chance attention of the subjects—all within a forty-mile radius of my home—offense would be taken at my frankness where none was intended" (254). Ironically, ten years later, in her book *Cross Creek*, offense would be taken by Zelma Cason.

In addition, in her rebuttal letter to the *Evening Star*, Rawlings defends her use of Cracker dialect, which she says she has "studiously" recorded: "Perhaps my newness in this country gives a pristine quality to the oddities of speech that come to my ears" (*Uncollected Writings* 254). She also defends the descriptions of her fictional characters by claiming that she has a sympathetic connection to them: "These people are to me all that is delightful. . . . Before they have been quite swallowed up, let us know and enjoy these picturesque people, pioneer remains. They are much more vital than you and I" (254–55). A few months later, this controversy reached the pages of the *Miami Herald* (9 April 1931), which strongly defended Rawlings's right to artistic freedom. The *Herald* pointed out what would become the hallmark of Rawlings's fiction: "the compassion of a woman's great heart" (*Uncollected Writings* 253 n. 1).

The debate in the *Ocala Evening Star* about the reality of her fiction would rankle Rawlings for years. Regarding her work on *South Moon Under* and *Golden Apples*, published after "Jacob's Ladder," she would endlessly query Perkins about the "truthfulness" of her work. While writing *Golden Apples* she tells Perkins: "The truth is the most difficult thing in the world to get at, and I have always felt that the closest approach to truth is the greatest kindness" (*Max and Marjorie* 155). She felt that she had a tendency, in her pursuit of truth, to veer into melodrama: "My great fear is that what should and could be authentic drama, becomes melodrama, without reality. I like to write in a series of dramatic scenes, building each chapter up to its own little climax. If it works, it gives the emotional intensity I want to achieve above everything else. If it doesn't work—we might as well tear up the manuscript and be done with it" (165).

She then quotes Henry James, whose *Art of the Novel* she had been reading at the time: "the question here was that of producing the maximum of intensity with the minimum of strain" (*Max and Marjorie* 165). Perkins advises her not to take James "too seriously" and offers the following encouragement: "I think you have a right diagnosis of your own weaknesses in the matter of writing a novel, but I think you exaggerate them very much, and that knowing them, you will also know how to correct them" (167). Rawlings would eventually achieve her goal when she composed *The Yearling*. By then, she had become a master writer, one who had discovered the "whole secret of fiction": "When the people written about move in reality before our eyes, touch us, then anything they do becomes vivid and important" (284).

### South Moon Under

In the meantime, in 1931, Rawlings's training ground, leading up to the triumph of *The Yearling*, was her struggle to write her first two novels, *South Moon Under* and *Golden Apples*. *South Moon Under* is based on Rawlings's experiences in the scrub country in the Ocala National Forest, near Salt Springs, Florida, when she lived with Piety Fiddia and Piety's son, Leonard. She would later use this same setting and transfer some of Leonard's characteristics to Jody in *The Yearling*.

*South Moon Under* is the story of "the man Lantry," who in the opening pages of the novel resettles his wife and five children twenty-five miles away from their home. They make a new home in the scrub country, a "unique" habitat whose growth "repelled all human living": "The soil was a tawny sand, from whose parched infertility there reared, indifferent to water, so dense a growth of scrub pine—the Southern spruce—that the effect of the massed thin trunks was of a limitless, canopied stockade. It seemed impenetrable" (2). There is a mystery surrounding Lantry that the reader cannot fathom: Why would he seek to live in this most inhabitable region, risking his family's lives? His daughter Piety is aware "how narrow a margin Lantry escaped disaster with his crops."

The narrator explains: "There was something about the most fertile field that was beyond control. A man could work himself to skin and bones, so that there was no flesh left on him to make sweat in the sun, and a crop would get away from him. There was something about all living that was uncertain" (36).

After several years, his wife dies and Lantry finally reveals his secret to Piety—years earlier he had been a 'shiner who killed a federal officer in an altercation. He has been on the run ever since; thus his fear explains his mad desire to live in isolation in the scrub. Ironically, he dies with his secret intact, but his destiny is lived out by his grandson, Lant, a good man who is forced to carry on the family tradition and 'shine for a living. Lant also has to deal with his own fears due to the fact that he is involved in a love triangle with his cousin Cleve; both men love Kezzie, a girl of spirit. Cleve, in a fit of anger, informs the federal agents that Lant has a still, which the agents destroy in a raid. One day, Lant discovers that Cleve is still tracking him in the woods with a rifle. Fear takes hold of Lant: "All his life, he knew now, he had been afraid of something. He had drunk a fear in his mother's milk. . . . A fear pulsed in his veins like poison. . . . He was blind with fear. Danger was a remembered danger, remembered in his bones and in his blood" (326). Lant realizes that he is powerless in the grip of the forces of nature: "Neither river nor swamp nor hammock nor impenetrable scrub could save a man from the ultimate interference. There was no safety. There was no retreat. Forces beyond his control, beyond his sight and hearing, took him in their vast senseless hands when they were ready. The whole earth must move as the sun and moon and an obscure law directed—even the earth, planet-ridden and tormented" (327).

Rawlings explains Lant's fear in terms of the novel's main symbol of south-moon-under: "The people are conscious at all times of the position of the sun and moon and stars and wind. They *feel* the moon under the earth—south-moon-under" (46). According to Bellman: "[Rawlings] ascribe[s] the situation to the forces of nature, which lie entirely beyond human control. Specifically, the cause goes back to the position of the moon at the time—south-moon-under—that is, the moon riding high on the other side of the earth, and powerful enough to affect some of the small woodland creatures" (31).

The novel ends with Cleve's widow, Kezzy, joining her life with Lant's, in spite of her knowledge of the murder. Yet, Lant now must live with the family curse and fears for the rest of his life that he will be captured and imprisoned for his criminal act.

### Golden Apples

After the positive reviews that greeted the publication of *South Moon Under* ("it glows with the breath of life," the *New York Times* reviewer raved; F. Scott Fitzgerald called it "a beautiful book" [R. Tarr, introduction to *Max and Marjorie* 6]), Rawlings's second novel, *Golden Apples*, likewise received "favorable" reviews, according to Perkins (7), although a few critics were negative. *Time* magazine called it a "dull melodrama," and the *Nation* claimed that the novel is "given over to the staples of petty fiction" and is "trite and quite harmless" (Bellman 42). Even today, some critics find it hard to say anything positive about the book. Bellman says that the novel "fails to capture our imagination" and faults Rawlings for her "painful literary naïveté, a glaring lack of dimensionality" (43); and Gordon Bigelow calls it "an ill-starred book from the beginning" (17). No critic was as harsh as Rawlings herself, who labeled the novel "interesting trash instead of literature" when discussing it with Perkins and blamed him for not forcing her to rewrite it; "you should have bullied me and shamed me further," she complains (*Max and Marjorie* 225).

Yet *Golden Apples* is a novel that remains undervalued. Tarr notes in his introduction to *Max and Marjorie* (21) that Perkins compared Rawlings to Faulkner while praising the novel: "It is is a very fine book, and I have it greatly at heart" (209). It is also a novel that Rawlings felt she had to write. After the success of *South Moon Under*, Perkins urged her to continue to chronicle Cracker Florida and write a story about a boy and his fawn, but Rawlings put him off. She was fascinated with relating a tale about an Englishman, Richard Tordell, who emigrates from his native England to the scrubland near Cross Creek. A secret family scandal—his father's new wife had tried to seduce him and, when he rebuffed her, accused him of attacking her—causes his father to banish him to the family's Florida estate. When he arrives on his property deep in the north-central Florida scrub, Tordell finds a poor Cracker sister and brother, Allie and Luke Brinley, squatting in his house and working his land. Realizing that they can be of use to him, he hires them to care for his house and fields. Luke takes his job seriously and convinces Richard that the wild orange trees on his estate, through careful cultivation and grafting, can be developed into a productive grove. Luke tells the local physician, Dr. Albury, about his plans, and he is soon sent to Camilla Van Dyne, a "hard-riding, hard-drinking woman" who owns flourishing orange groves across the lake. Luke's task requires that he be absent for a couple of weeks, and in the interim Allie and Richard strike up an affair, which eventually ends badly when Allie dies in childbirth. At the end of the novel, Richard seeks solace from Dr. Albury and Camilla, who befriend him and try to draw him into their way of life.

Rawlings ran into difficulties when she tried to integrate these two disparate worlds in the novel or, at least, make them equally believable. The result was a failure, according to Rodger Tarr, because she "was out of her element": "She was writing about an Englishman she could know only from a distance. Gone was the intensity of observation she displayed so well in her Cracker stories" (introduction to *Max and Marjorie* 6). Her goal in writing had always been to tell the truth, but the problem is that with *Golden Apples*, Rawlings felt she was veering "*off-key*, into a queer plane that is without reality" (*Max and Marjorie* 155; her emphasis). In her letter to Perkins she admits that she is powerless to edit herself when she is in this plane: "I simply do not know how or why I do it. My only hope is that I have become reasonably able at least to recognize it once it has happened. If I can ever figure out what it is I do, and why, I feel I will be capable of going ahead with my writing[,] speaking in general. Perhaps I just let a haze of words, of imperfect conceptions, carry me along, without focussing sharply and accurately enough. I simply don't know" (155).

Later in her career, and after Perkins's death in 1947, Rawlings would return to explore this queer plane further in what she calls her "queer stories" published in the *New Yorker* in the late 1940s. But while she was composing *Golden Apples* she admits that she cannot handle this non-Cracker material and berates herself for her melodramatic treatment of Tordell and the landed gentry that circles around Camilla Van Dyne and Claude Albury, Dr. Albury's son, who is pursuing a largely unrequited love affair with Camilla. Perkins agrees that Rawlings's treatment of Camilla and her circle is "too romantic" and gives Rawlings suggestions for how to tone her writing down. He admonishes her: "the spirit and quality of the life you picture in Camilla's house and thereabouts, does do an injury to your motives. It is romantic. The treatment of the other part [i.e., the Cracker world of the Brinleys] is not romantic, and neither is your natural writing in your stories, or in 'South Moon'" (*Max and Marjorie* 172).

Rawlings's difficulty was that she was, perhaps unconsciously, at cross-purposes with Perkins. He was urging her in *Golden Apples* to replicate the success she had had with *South Moon Under* and to continue creating uplifting tales with Cracker characters. She had been willing to follow his dictates; as she tells him, "I like to see people bucking something solid, instead of their own neuroses" (*Max and Marjorie* 346). Yet Rawlings also wanted to craft her story more like the work of the authors she admired—F. Scott Fitzgerald and Ernest Hemingway. When she was working on *Golden Apples*, Fitzgerald was finishing *Tender Is the Night* and Hemingway, *Death in the Afternoon*. In a letter to Perkins dated 6 October 1932, Rawlings writes that she has just finished reading *Death in the Afternoon* and "find[s] it quite insane and entirely stirring": "It is one of those books on which you can see the mark of an inner compulsion in the writer. This seems to make, not necessarily for a finished artistry, even in the hands of so true an artist as Hemingway, but for a terrific vitality. I could wish that he had not felt it necessary to apologize for his style and his subject. When he puts aside his self-consciousness and lets go, he moves me as profoundly as anyone, including himself, has done in a long time" (59–60).

In letters to Perkins, Rawlings often discusses her attempts to emulate Hemingway's "rule-of-restraint," which "impressed [her] greatly" (83). Hemingway employs this restraint to good effect in *Death in the Afternoon* when he is describing "the emotional and spiritual climax of death in bull-fighting." After reading the book, Rawlings feels that she "can share with him an overpowering cosmic excitement" (61), as she explains to Perkins: "Hemingway, damn his soul, makes everything he writes terrifically exciting (and incidentally makes all us second-raters seem positively adolescent) by the seemingly simple expedient of the iceberg principle—three-fourths of the substance under the surface. He comes closer that way to retaining the magic of the original, unexpressed idea or emotion, which is always more stirring than any words. But just try and do it!" (115).

Throughout the composition of *Golden Apples*, Rawlings compares her work to Hemingway's and harshly criticizes her inability to strike the right tone. She is fearful that she cannot be as gritty as Hemingway. He is able, through his "bomb-shell intrusions of obscenity" to shock the bourgeoisie, whereas she is horrified when her own work meets with the approval of her "virgin aunt." Rawlings longs for "anything to drive away the fluttering hands and the genteel, ecstatic voices" of people like her aunt who praise her work (*Max and Marjorie* 196).

Besides being as gritty as Hemingway, Rawlings also aspires to delve deeper into reality and her characters' psyches, as Fitzgerald does in *Tender Is the Night*. In an 11 February 1934 letter to Perkins, she writes:

> I thought, beginning to read it after I had written you, that Fitzgerald had filled the contract I was setting up for myself—a book disturbing, bitter and beautiful. I am totally unable to analyze the almost over-powering effect that some of his passages create—some of them about quite trivial people and dealing with trivial situations. There is something terrifying about it when it happens, and the closest I can come to understanding it is to think that he does, successfully at such times, what I want to do—that is, visualizes people not in their immediate setting, from the human point of view—but in time and space—almost, you might say, with the divine detachment. The effect is very weird when he does it with unimportant people moving in a superficial and sophisticated setting. (*Max and Marjorie* 140)

In her initial conception of *Golden Apples*, in a 31 March 1931 letter to Perkins, Rawlings says she wants to emphasize elements that are "disturbing" and "beautiful" in Tordell's sad journey to his new home in the Florida scrub near the River Styx, an actual small river a few miles from Rawlings's home in Cross Creek: "There took shape in my mind one of these young men, to whom, coming into this jungle hammock, an embittered exile, the strange small river would indeed seem another Styx, transporting him from life into death. To his nature as I conceived it, this country would be intolerable. This region is beautiful, but it is not pretty.

It is like a beautiful woman capable of a deep evil and a great treachery. Back of the lushness is something stark and sinister" (*Max and Marjorie* 37). Rawlings attempts to heighten the dark mystery at the heart of her characters' psyches, much as Fitzgerald does in *Tender Is the Night*, by creating epiphanic moments in the narrative that move beyond detailed descriptions. One of the turning points in *Golden Apples* comes when Tordell, in a stupor brought on by a malaria fever and alcohol, stumbles out of his house and into the fields. He recalls the "dusk of English lanes," which have "an orderliness, a beneficence, so that one went to them for peace and comfort," unlike the scrub, which is "a venomous tangle, evil and oppressive." He feels "smothered," because "there was nothing beyond, neither beauty nor peace." Yet he refuses to lose himself in tender nostalgia for England, because "in all love, inherent, was betrayal." He continues to wander in the hammock: "At times his vision blurred, so that palms and pines seemed to telescope one into another" (87). He finally stumbles to all fours beside a stream. There he discovers a sleeping black girl, Rhea, who is naked except for a white magnolia petal that has "drifted down and lay inverted over one breast." Tordell notes that the girl smells of the earth: "The rich sweetness of crushed blackberries rose from her body." For the first time in his new Florida life, he lets go of his repressions and awakens sensually. The view of the girl increases the "pulsation in his head . . . until he thought he would burst. . . . His sight blurred." Rhea's body "dissolved into a black velvet curtain that fell before him, shutting all light from his eyes." He sinks forward until "the dark earth met him" (88).

Rawlings's construction of this scene—that is, with the landscape transforming into an otherworldly entity that envelops the characters— is reminiscent of Fitzgerald's transformation of the Mediterranean into a mythical place. When Nicole and Dick Diver entertain their friends in *Tender Is the Night*, they "create a sense of being alone with each other in the dark universe" and their magical presence makes them "warm and glow and expand" in the eyes of their guests (34). Even though the Florida scrub is a world apart from Fitzgerald's glittering Riviera setting in *Tender Is the Night*, Rawlings still strives for the same effect—to create "a study in the relativity of beauty" (*Max and Marjorie* 38).

The "half-wit" Rhea is the last woman on earth that the aristocratic Englishman would deem beautiful. Tordell, in fact, has "never seen a black woman" (81). Nevertheless, Rawlings describes Tordell's erotic view of her lying asleep with the white magnolia petal covering her black breast as a "gorgeous picture" (*Max and Marjorie* 184). Not having the "faintest desire to be pornographic or nauseating," Rawlings feels that the scene is necessary in order "to give Tordell a completely be-mired condition from which to rise," as she explains in a December 1934 letter to Perkins: "Nothing else could so suggest heat and blackness and muck and fever. It is the low point of his spiritual life" (179). The fact that Rawlings makes the black girl the symbol of degradation (and, it can be argued, the start of Tordell's redemption) and the "stark and sinister" element behind the "lushness" of the landscape suggests a racist or, at least, a narrow view of black fictional characters (reflecting the reality of her age and before her race awareness expands due to her relationship with Hurston). But Rawlings's focus at this point is on Tordell's evolution from his physical (implied) union with the black girl to his spiritual union with his land at the end of the novel. After his orange grove survives the Big Freeze of 1895 and springs into life again, Tordell feels a oneness with the earth: "It seemed to him that the inviolable pulse of the earth beat upward through his veins like sap. . . . He joined himself to the earth, and because the earth itself was a little part of a farther universe, he joined himself through it to the stars, and in the union was his ecstasy" (351).

Even though she finished *Golden Apples* on an uplifting note, Rawlings was dissatisfied with its ending. She regretted having Tordell achieve union with the land, as she explains to Perkins in a 5–6 November 1935 letter: "Why Tordell is not completely successful, I do not know. I understood him thoroughly. It comes to me sometimes that I violated the truth in having him achieve unity with his background. I am almost afraid that his basic character was such that defeat was inevitable for him; perhaps with understanding. I think it might have been better to do as I first planned; have him go down in his despair; probably into death; with a glimmer of vision before him. Letting Luke express the soundness of union with the particular land" (*Max and Marjorie* 231–32). In this passage, Rawlings implies that she feels more in tune with a darker, more complicated view of human nature that Tordell embodies—and which she admires in the works of Hemingway and Fitzgerald. Allowing Tordell only a "glimmer of vision" would ally him with Dick Diver as he departs the Riviera, blessing the beach in a papal cross, or with Gatsby's (rather, Nick Carraway's) tragic awareness at the moment of his death. But Rawlings abandons this type of ambiguous ending, because it is not what her readers expect of her; nor does it fit in with the cosmic awareness that Perkins advises her to use in all of her works. By acceding to Perkins's wishes, Rawlings was able to go on and write *The Yearling*, thus achieving great critical and popular success. Yet she was forced to give up a part of her imagination, because it did not fit into the niche that she felt Perkins had carved out for her. In a revealing letter dated 20 January 1934, Rawlings tells Perkins that she has begun to "box" herself, because she is aware that the "personal angle tends to embarrass" Perkins, who likes his "writers to be neatly boxed in their workshops" (*Max and Marjorie* 137). Perkins is not offended by Rawlings's comment and replies that he is, after all, "a Yankee on both sides of [his] family" and that "personal angles" do embarrass him (138).

It is no surprise that Perkins had no time to delve into Rawlings's personal angles in the mid-1930s, since he was dealing with three of the most psychologically challenging authors in all of American literature. When she writes to him on 3 March 1933 that she is ready to move beyond the Cracker world that had brought her such success with *South Moon Under*, he basically ignores her comment that there will be "No more Crackers. I have two or three humorous short things in mind, but no more Cracker novels. I gave as accurate a picture as possible of a way of life and a group of people—so that's that" (95). In his response, Perkins discusses her British contract for *South Moon Under* and favorable reviews that "express the opinion that these are good people who live a good life in a good place" (96). With down-to-earth comments such as these, Perkins keeps her emotionally on track to write her greatest work, *The Yearling*.

## The Yearling

Rawlings's genius at capturing what Hurston admires most in her work—that is, "the three layers of life" and her comprehension of nature's "heirogliphics"—culminates with the publication of *The Yearling*. Rawlings put aside the divided consciousness that frustrated her writing process in *Golden Apples* and immersed herself in the Cracker world of the Penny Baxter family. In the novel, she depicts the twelve-year-old Jody Baxter with empathy as he traverses the borderlands between childhood and adulthood with his pet deer as a companion. The suggestion that Rawlings write this novel as a children's book came from Perkins (*Max and Marjorie* 114, 116). Such a book, he wrote, would "require very little plot.—Its interest would simply be that of character and that of the peculiar & adventurous life" (116). Rawlings was receptive to the suggestion, because she felt she had "nothing to say for mature people along the South-Moon-Under line" (127). By the time she finally sat down to write the novel in 1936 (its progress was interrupted by the composition of *Golden Apples*, published in 1934), Rawlings changed the original focus from "a story for boys" to "a story *about* a boy—a brief and tragic idyll of boyhood" (233). She had now developed a grander conception of the work and planned to add mythic, universal dimensions to the novel that would transcend the juvenile category.

She began the composition process, though, by grounding the story in reality. First, she sought out Cracker hunters and storytellers to enrich her knowledge of the scrub area near Salt Springs, where she planned to set her novel. She choose her setting carefully, based on its primeval quality and its distance from civilization: "The location [known as "Pat's Island"] is one of the strangest and most beautiful places I have ever seen," she enthuses to Perkins (*Max and Marjorie* 234). She even lived in the scrub with her hunter friends and their families for short periods of time. As early as 4 October 1933, she wrote to Perkins about a visit she made to her old friend Cal Long, a hunter. She also spent time with Barney Dillard, who took her on two bear hunts that became the basis of the hunt for old Slewfoot in *The Yearling* (*Cross Creek* 301). In a letter to Perkins dated 31 July 1936, she describes Dillard as "a perfectly marvelous old pioneer living on the St. Johns river . . . a famous 'bad man,' but honorable and respected" (*Max and Marjorie* 250). Long and Dillard gave her a context for her novel by providing invaluable "anecdotes, hunting incidents, people" (250) that she would not have been able to find on her own.

Rawlings met by happenstance the second person, Dale Wills, who helped to ground her story in reality. When she was deep into writing the story, she felt the need to find a place where she could "do some troublesome writing" without distractions. She located a cabin at Banner Elk,

North Carolina, and spent two months writing there in the fall of 1936. Her portrait of Jody was inspired by her friendship with twelve-year-old Dale Wills, who was living in the nearby Grandfather Home for Children and did small chores for her. Bellman describes the impact of Wills on Rawlings's imagination: "Something about the boy—his strength of character, his wistful expression, his unique manner, perhaps—made a profound impression on her" (58). Wills also inspired her story "A Mother in Mannville," published in the *Saturday Evening Post* on 12 December 1936, and the six-part novelette *Mountain Prelude*, published in the *Post* from 26 April to 31 May 1947 (see Gilmer).

Rawlings was drawn to children on the cusp of adulthood, because of an experience that she had had when she was young. She recalls a particular day that inspired *The Yearling*:

> One of those April days so beautiful you want to reach out and hold it so it will not move on and die. I was standing under a tree. The sun shone through the leaves and a soft breeze caused the light and shadow around me to shift and change. There was a stillness. A stillness that was like the stillness the day Father died [in 1913, when she was sixteen]. And with it came a feeling of ecstasy and regret—a lifting sensation but tinged with sadness. It was a definite premonition of maturity. . . . Then, when I moved to Florida, the full significance of that premonition of maturity came to me, and I wrote "The Yearling." (Evans 18)

Elizabeth Silverthorne claims that Rawlings ultimately found the experience painful when she wedded the feeling to a particular child: "At Cross Creek, in the mountains of North Carolina, and eventually at Van Hornesville, New York, there was usually some neighborhood boy she especially befriended, and once she told a friend, 'There's always some damned little boy to break your heart'" (180). Nevertheless, Rawlings continued to cultivate her friendships with young people. J. T. Glisson in *The Creek* and Ernest Bass in his memoirs have recounted their close friendships with Rawlings and her fine treatment of them when they were young. Glisson, the son of next-door neighbor Tom Glisson, who figured so prominently in *Cross Creek*, had a conversation with Rawlings in which she discouraged him from thinking that he was the prototype for young Jody (he was twelve years old when she was writing the novel) in order to allow him to grow up as his own person (Glisson interview). Rawlings's fascination with youth is similar to Wordsworth's sentiment in "Ode: Intimations of Immortality": "Heaven lies about us in our infancy! / Shades of the prison-house begin to close / Upon the growing Boy" (309). She seems in her work to be attracted to the purity and clarity of vision that children have, as is evident in the justification she gives Perkins for choosing to make Jody Baxter twelve years old: "I want it through his eyes before the age of puberty brings in any of the other factors to confuse the simplicity of viewpoint" (*Max and Marjorie* 251).

Beyond the influence of the Cracker people and landscape around her, Rawlings may have been creatively inspired by the time she spent with Hemingway. Rawlings admired his writing and listened eagerly to all the updates Perkins provided of the more famous author. In June 1936, when *The Yearling* was gestating in her mind, Rawlings went on a "big-game fishing trip" to Bimini with a group of friends that included Hemingway. She had "an unbelievably good time," as she later relates to Perkins. She adored Hemingway as soon as she met him. She had expected "a fire-spitting ogre"; instead, "a most lovable, nervous and sensitive person took my hand in a big gentle paw and remarked that he was a great admirer of my work" (*Max and Marjorie* 244–45). Beyond the personal connection (which continued well into the next decade, as long as Hemingway returned to Florida), Rawlings was fascinated by Hemingway's larger-than-life personality and the stories that seemed to surround his every move. She was also impressed by his sportsmanship, noting that on the day that Rawlings left the boat, "he battled six hours and fifty minutes with a 514-lb. tuna" (245). His mastery of nature and his fortitude on the trail of big game—"he is so vast, so virile"— mirrors Penny Baxter's skill at hunting Slewfoot. Rawlings tells Perkins that Hemingway is gifted with the artist's rare vision into the essence of things but that he "must be afraid of lifting before [the random society people swirling around him] the curtain that veils the beauty that should be exposed only to reverent eyes" (246). Rawlings carried home with her not only some of Hemingway's spirit but also the magic of the moment she found in Bimini, as she raves to Perkins: "Bimini caught at my throat the way the scrub does. The struggle there for existence is terrific" (246).

When Rawlings sat down to write *The Yearling*, she planned to create the novel on a deeper scale than originally conceived in order to encompass other dimensions beyond the everyday and embody her "cosmic awareness." *The Yearling* begins on an April afternoon, when Jody is building a flutter-mill: "It always delights him. Everything for him is young and safe, and the world is good and beautiful" (*Max and Marjorie* 279). At the end of the story, when his mother forces him to kill Flag, his pet deer, his entire world is turned upside down. He cannot comprehend that she wants him to act out of necessity, because the deer is destroying the precious crops that provide their livelihood. He looks on her decision as a profound disappointment: "His own mother has betrayed him. There is no safety any more. Life itself has impinged on him with its harshness and its necessities and its treachery. Then a curtain is lifted, and for a moment he has an understanding of the unavoidable treachery of all life; of the things that force people to betray" (279). It is this exact moment of Jody's awareness that Rawlings wishes to explore and comprehend in the novel.

Rawlings's technique for analyzing this pivotal moment involves casting the story into the realm of fairy tale. On a symbolic level, the story resembles "Hansel and Gretel," with Ma Baxter filling the role of the evil stepmother. Ora, the killjoy mother, has always disapproved of Jody's "ramblin,'" whereas Penny, the indulgent parent, promises to keep Jody's ramblings a secret between them, saying: "Most women-folks cain't see for their lives, how a man loves so to ramble. I never let on you wasn't here" (10). Later, at the story's climax, when Ma decides that Flag must be destroyed, her wrath takes on a sinister air. Jody flees into the scrub after the yearling dies, but this time he is no longer "addled with April" (14); instead, he must face the nightmare world of starvation, which his mother had always feared and which now threatens his very existence.

"Hansel and Gretel" is a particularly apt fairy tale for Rawlings to choose, because it centers on children's hunger and survival in the woods. In the fairy tale, the evil stepmother forces her husband twice to send her children into the forest to die when they run out of food to eat. Jody, too, runs away into the scrub after his mother attempts to kill Flag in order to preserve the family's food supply. Bruno Bettelheim in *The Uses of Enchantment* points out that Hansel and Gretel are at an age when they must adopt more independent roles in life; yet they are reluctant to change. According to Bettelheim: "The mother represents the source of all food to the children, so it is she who . . . is experienced as abandoning them, as if in a wilderness. It is the child's anxiety and deep disappointment when Mother is no longer willing to meet all his oral demands which leads him to believe that suddenly mother has become unloving, selfish, rejecting" (159). When Hansel and Gretel are abandoned in the woods by their parents, the gingerbread house highlights their greediness. As Bettelheim notes, "Carried away by their uncontrollable craving, the children think nothing of destroying what should give shelter and safety" (160). They prove their ability to eat their parents "out of house and home, a fear which they had projected onto their parents as the reason for their desertion" (161). Thus the children's "unrestrained giving in to gluttony" is their "regression to the earliest 'heavenly' state of being—when on the mother's breast one lived symbiotically off her," doing away "with all individuation and independence" (161). According to Bettelheim, "Rather than expecting everything good to come from the parents, the older child needs to be able to make some contribution to the emotional well-being of himself and his family" (165). The fairy tale's "main thrust" is "a warning against regression, and an encouragement of growth toward a higher plane of psychological and intellectual existence" (165).

Later, when she wrote *Cross Creek*, Rawlings makes a connection to Hansel and Gretel by comparing her orange grove to an enchanted forest that brings about transformation: "This is the essence of an ancient and secret magic. It goes back, perhaps, to the fairytales of childhood, to Hansel and Gretel . . . to all the half-luminous places that pleased the imagination as a child. It may go back still further, to racial Druid memories, to an atavistic sense of safety and delight in an open forest. And after long years of spiritual homelessness, of nostalgia, here is that mystic loveliness of childhood again. Here is home. An old thread, long tangled, comes straight again" (*Cross Creek* 16).

Yet, home is an elusive property and can be a fictional construct, too. According to Rosemary George in *The Politics of Home*, "fictionality" is its "intrinsic attribute" (11). Rawlings's narrative takes Jody out of his self-enclosed home in the scrub, where he has been allowed to create a fantasy world centered on Flag, and forces him out beyond its boundaries into the outside world. Jody's great danger in growing up has been his propensity to distort reality to suit his fantasies.

Because Jody grew up in the scrub as an only child, it is not odd that he would create a fantasy world. Although he participates in the bloody reality of the slaying of old Slewfoot, he prefers to reside in his own spectral world. When he enters the woods surrounding his home, he imagines that he sees Spaniards in red capes and shining helmets. In this sense, his imaginary world has both emotional and physical effects: "Jody tingled, and the hair stirred on the back of his neck. It was like seeing Spaniards. It was as though phantoms, dark and shadowy, and not men and women, had passed before him" (91). The people he encounters are not the conquistadores of the Spanish past but poor, disenfranchised Minorcans. To Jody, the Minorcans are symbols of Florida's distant, romantic past. In reality, they are a harsh reminder of life on Florida's frontier and the cruelty of Dr. Andrew Turnball, who had transported their ancestors to work as indentured servants—that is, slaves—on his plantation in New Smyrna Beach in the 1760s. They were so mistreated that they sought to escape their servitude by fleeing through the woods.

Jody's soul mate, the boy of nature, Fodder-wing, also believes in the mythical, mystical Spaniards and is himself a symbol of this otherworldly realm. When Jody looks at his best friend, Fodder-wing's face is "luminous," whereas his body is "humped and twisted." The narrator often compares Fodder-wing to animals, whom he befriends and loves: his body "move[s] in a series of contortions, like a wounded ape"; his "body [is] no more unnatural to him than the body of a chameleon or a 'possum"; he tries to "float from the roof-tree of the barn as gently as any bird" (50). Fodder-wing's experiment in flying from the barn— which adds "a few broken bones further to contort the hunch-backed frame"—is a metaphor for his desire to live in a fantasy world of his own making. Jody has a sympathetic, "secret understanding" of the "crippled boy's longing for flight; for lightness; for a moment's freedom from his body, earth-bound and bent and stumbling" (50–51). In order to grow up, though, Jody must see the inherent dangers in launching off the roof of a barn and residing too long in this imaginary domain.

When Fodder-wing suddenly dies, Jody is bereft, particularly since the death is unexpected and its cause is unknown. Fodder-wing's brother, Buck, tells Jody: "One minute he was breathin.' The next minute he jest wa'n't. Like as if you blowed out a candle" (202). Jody arrives at the For- resters' home after Fodder-wing has died, but he takes part in the wake before the funeral. As he sits beside his friend's body, the dark spirits, instead of the light, now haunt him: "Something sat in a far dark cor- ner of the room and it was the same thing that had prowled the scrub the night his father had been bitten" (209–10). The thing, of course, is death. Jody hallucinates as he stares death in the face: "When the flame flickered, it seemed that Fodder-wing's eyelids fluttered. A light breeze stirred through the room. The sheet seemed to lift, as though Fodder-wing were breathing" (210). Jody then imagines that his friend has turned into one of those spirits that haunt the woods: "Fodder-wing was stumbling about outside in the bushes, with the raccoon at his heels. In a moment he would come into the house with his rocking gait, and Jody would hear his voice" (210). With Fodder-wing's death, Jody real- izes that nature is filled not only with living creatures but with death as well. Still, he romanticizes the event.

It is only when he runs away from home at the end of the novel that Jody finally learns his lesson. For the first time, he confronts the dreadful reality of starvation: "This, then, was hunger. . . . The thing was terrify- ing. It had a great maw to envelop him and claws that raked across his vitals" (418). Once again it is April; a year has passed since the story be- gan, and his transformation is complete: "He had been out in the world, and the world was a troubled dream, fluid and desolate" (422). In the past, his inability to control Flag's natural craving for corn sprouts and cowpeas paralleled his own appetite for fantasies. Their greediness is reminiscent of Hansel and Gretel's, and, as in the fairy tale, the mother is the symbol of the harsh reality that the safety of home is an illusion. The mother has to shoot the deer in order to force her son to grow up. Jody must learn to separate fantasies from reality not only to become an adult but also to survive in the Florida scrub. He can no longer deceive himself that he can domesticate a creature that forms the family's food supply for a pet. When Jody runs to Pa Forrester for advice and support, Pa warns Jody that he must detach himself from his feelings for Flag in order to survive: "Why, love's got nothin' to do with corn. You cain't have a thing eatin' the crops" (406).

Rawlings's ending, though, is ambiguous. Yes, Jody must follow Pa Forrester's and Penny's advice, "Life knocks a man down and he gits up and it knocks him down agin" (426); but the tone of the novel's last few lines is wistful: "He found himself listening for something. It was the sound of the yearling for which he listened" (427). Even when he dreams, he thinks of the yearling and calls out to the deer: "It was not his own voice that called. It was a boy's voice. Somewhere beyond the sink-hole, past the magnolia, under the live oaks, a boy and a yearling ran side by side, and were gone forever" (428).

When *The Yearling* was published, Rawlings valued the responses she received from Barney Dillard, who called the book a "masterpiece" and said it made him "almost see old Slewfoot's tracks" (*Max and Marjorie* 346). But the comment that probably meant the most to her came from F. Scott Fitzgerald, who wrote: "The Marjorie Rawlings book fascinated me. I thought it was even better than 'South Moon Under' and I envy her the ease with which she does action scenes, such as the tremendously complicated hunt sequence, which I would have to stake off in advance and which would probably turn out to be a stilted business in the end. Hers just simply flows; the characters keep thinking, talking, feeling, and don't stop, and you think and talk and feel with them" (344).

## A Comparison of Hurston's and Rawlings's Fictional Works

Similarities in Hurston's and Rawlings's fiction exist, in spite of their radically different subject matters. Beginning with their first published stories and culminating in their masterpieces, *The Yearling* and *Their Eyes Were Watching God*, remarkable parallels can be drawn. Their early fiction is grounded in the reality of their fictional communities, whereas the later novels become more metaphoric in an attempt to address larger issues.

Both Hurston's "The Eatonville Anthology" (1926) and Rawlings's "Cracker Chidlings" (1931) concern the building blocks of community, that is, characters, their interactions, and the events that define them. For example, characters and situations that first appear in the "Anthology" are later mined for other works; notably, Mrs. Jody Clarke turns into Janie Starks in *Their Eyes*.

After the success of their early stories, Hurston's and Rawlings's first novels also run in parallel directions. In *South Moon Under* and *Jonah's Gourd Vine*, both authors present an anthropological picture of their communities. Hurston, of course, was a trained scientist, but Rawlings, too, became an avid student of the world around her. All of her work demonstrates her vast knowledge of plants and animal behavior, often acquired on hunting and fishing trips with seasoned hunters and fishermen. She also had success as a farm woman, taking care of an orange grove that was always at the mercy of the elements. In addition, she became an astute psychologist, observing and analyzing the actions of her neighbors around her. Both Rawlings and Hurston employ their observational skills to create fictional worlds in these two novels. But they also begin to explore a world beyond the everyday, by using metaphors that can suggest deeper meanings. Thus, the image of Jonah's gourd vine is used to explain John Pearson's insatiable, self-destructive desires, which prove to be a bottomless pit. The image of "south moon under" shows Rawlings's linking of human and natural phenomena. According to Samuel Bellman, Rawlings's novel presents "voluminous lore of the moon's phases and their importance in human affairs—hunting, planting, and certain other vital matters. There is a tide in the affairs of her characters, and the moon is one of its chief regulators" (32).

Finally, in *The Yearling* and *Their Eyes Were Watching God*, the pinnacle of their writing careers, Rawlings and Hurston become fully "conscious of the three layers of life, instead of the obvious thing before [their] nose[s]." They merely sketch out the overtly autobiographical material, while deepening its symbolism. Now in their forties, they have matured as writers and made their "peace with the universe and its laws"—if not in their lives, at least in their fictional worlds.

1. Main Street Eatonville today (photograph by author).

2. Site of Hurston residence in center of Eatonville (photograph by author).

3. Mathilda Moseley's home in Eatonville. Hurston stayed in this home when she returned to Eatonville (photograph by author).

4. Hurston at a national exhibit of the Federal Writers' Project in 1938 (photograph in the public domain).

5. Stetson Kennedy took this photograph of Hurston at a turpentine camp in Cross City, Florida, when she was doing Federal Writers' Project research in the spring of 1938 (photograph courtesy of Stetson Kennedy, Department of Special Collections, George A. Smathers Libraries, University of Florida).

5.

would be a mighty fine thing, the harried older women thought, if
more girls felt as Arvay did. Therefore, on that day of Arvay's re-
nunciation, when the girl had finished off by tearfully asking the
prayers of the congregation, for their earnest prayers that she might
hold out and never, never turn back, but to go on and on to greater
grace, "Amens" burst out all over the church. The pastor himself had
gotten to his feet and paid his young sister-in-law a great tribute.

 " This young girl's devotion to the cause of Christ makes me feel
ashamed", Reverend Middleton had stated with an apostolic look on his
face, " Here she is, much too young to be sent into the field as yet,
but ready and willing to go. Ready to go wherever the Spirit might
send her. Her stand ought to make me, and all of us grown folks feel
ashamed. And if you, my flock xxxx feel that you can spare me, I will
declare myself ready and willing to go."

 The flock had cried once more at the thought of the pastor's
offer to sacrifice himself, but it was felt that he could not be spared.
To compensate for this denial, the parsonage was re-painted, and five
dollars a month was added to his salary, bringing the total to seventy
dollars a month even.

 Five years had passed since Arvay had turned her back on the
world and all it's sins and snares. Arvay still played _____ _____ in
the Sunday School, and she took an active part in chu_____ _____ _____
she kept strictly to herself. It was not too _____ _____
the community soon put Arvay Henson down _____ _____ _____
" tetched." Nothing like her sister Raine _____ _____ _____
ever been robust, not to say a trifle _____ _____
was pretty in the ways that the _____ _____
full head of curly reddish ha_____ _____
_____ _____ full of ch_____ _____

6. A manuscript page of *Seraph on the Suwanee*, which was burned after Hurston's
death in 1960 (photograph courtesy of the Department of Special Collections,
George A. Smathers Libraries, University of Florida).

7. One of the last known photographs of Hurston in Fort Pierce, Florida, 1958–59 (photograph courtesy of Department of Special Collections, George A. Smathers Libraries, University of Florida).

8. Cross Creek, Florida (photograph by author).

9. Rawlings's farm home at Cross Creek (photograph by author).

10. A tenant house similar to the one in which Rawlings's black servants lived in Cross Creek (photograph by author).

11. Rawlings at work, mid-1930s (photograph courtesy of the Department of Special Collections, George A. Smathers Libraries, University of Florida).

12. Rawlings and her second husband, Norton Baskin, on a hunting trip, late 1930s (photograph courtesy of the Department of Special Collections, George A. Smathers Libraries, University of Florida).

13. J. T. Glisson, Rawlings's next-door neighbor at Cross Creek, at his home in Evinston, Florida, July 2007. His watercolor of Rawlings's home is on the wall (photograph by author).

14. Martha Mickens at Cross Creek, early 1930s (photograph courtesy of the Department of Special Collections, George A. Smathers Libraries, University of Florida).

15. Rawlings and Martha Mickens at Cross Creek, early 1930s (photograph courtesy of the Department of Special Collections, George A. Smathers Libraries, University of Florida).

16. Rawlings at home in Cross Creek, 1939 (photograph courtesy of the Department of Special Collections, George A. Smathers Libraries, University of Florida).

# 3

## Looking Back

Hurston's *Dust Tracks on a Road*
and Rawlings's *Cross Creek*

**A**FTER HURSTON AND RAWLINGS WROTE their great American
novels in the 1930s and succeeded in channeling their voices into
stories that captured the attention of both the public and critics, they
had difficulty switching genres from novels to their autobiographies,
*Dust Tracks on a Road* and *Cross Creek*, both published in 1942. Their
struggles in composing their life stories suggest the psychological conflict in constructing an accurate image of themselves and their communities. Rawlings complains in a 1938 letter to Maxwell Perkins that the
"material is treacherous" and that she does not know how to organize
*Cross Creek*. She debates with Perkins how open she should be about her
personal life. She wants to write a chronicle but does not want the narrative to be "confluent" or the content to be autobiographical (Rawlings,
*Max and Marjorie* 231). In an 11 February 1943 letter to Rollins College
president Hamilton Holt, Hurston complains that she "did not want to
write [*Dust Tracks on a Road*] at all, because it is too hard to reveal one's

inner self" (*Selected Letters* 478). In the construction of *Dust Tracks*, Hurston decides occasionally to veer away from the strictly autobiographical and mythologize her life story when it suits her purposes. For example, she gives herself a birthplace in Eatonville in the twentieth century, although census records and a family Bible show that she was born in Notasulga, Alabama, in 1891.

Hurston's propensity for stretching the truth and Rawlings's difficulty in structuring *Cross Creek* suggest that both authors were trying to redefine their self-identities. Their identification with Eatonville and Cross Creek had once been liberating, allowing them to escape from the restrictions and definitions of mainstream America. Both *Their Eyes Were Watching God* and *The Yearling* once reflected Hurston's and Rawlings's personae as chroniclers of vanishing American folk communities, but by the 1940s their memoirs also record the emergence of "alternative selves" that challenge this cultural identity. Furthermore, each woman assisted the other in giving birth to a new self.

## Hurston's *Dust Tracks on a Road*

Zora Neale Hurston's Eatonville is a place of the imagination in the sense that Gaston Bachelard in *The Poetics of Space* defines the way a person's inner projections can give meaning "to the visible world" (185). For Hurston, no place is more meaningful than Eatonville, which is the locus of her race consciousness and self-esteem. On the one hand, Eatonville is a symbol of the indomitability of the black spirit, her "racial health," in Alice Walker's terms. Hurston is "proud of her blood and proud of her people," Rawlings notes. On the other hand, nowhere does she don more masks than in her Eatonville stories and in her memoir of the town, *Dust Tracks on a Road*. Eatonville is a fictional construct that is rich enough to embody the essence of black culture, in Hurston's imagination, but the reality is that she left the town and thus can see it from many different perspectives. As a result, "Zora becomes an actor with many masks," notes Delia Konzett, "negotiating an essentially displaced and dynamic identity that is always in the process of transforming itself" (84).

Hurston's first transformation in *Dust Tracks* occurs in the opening lines: "I was born in a Negro town" (3). The fact that she was born in

Notasulga, Alabama, in 1891 is irrelevant in her creation of the myth of herself as a representative citizen of a town that has always been independent and able to govern itself. When she defines the town as "hitting a straight lick with a crooked stick," she is also defining herself as a person who tells the truth using poetic means. Throughout *Dust Tracks*, she tells the truth about her existence, but in the margins, off the printed page.

*Dust Tracks* begins with the founding of Eatonville as the dream of three white men who had been officers in the Union army. They decide to "try their fortunes in the unsettled country of South Florida" and found the town of Maitland in the "primeval forests," which had a legacy of violence: "This had been dark and bloody country since the mid-1700's. Spanish, French, English, Indian, and American blood had been bountifully shed" (4). "The Negro population of Maitland settled simultaneously with the white" (8), Hurston notes, and blacks were allowed voting privileges during the first election. According to Hurston, Tony Taylor, a black man, was elected mayor of Maitland, and another black man, Joe Clark, was elected town marshal. Hurston records what happens next: "But during that year, a yeast was working. Joe Clarke had asked himself, why not a Negro town? Few of the Negroes were interested. It was too vaulting for their comprehension. A pure Negro town! If nothing but their own kind was in it, who was going to run it? With no white folks to command them, how would they know what to do?" (9–10).

Clark discussed his ambitions with his white boss, Josiah Eaton, and Eaton, along with another white man, Lewis Lawrence, purchased land for the black town. On 18 August 1886, according to Hurston, Eatonville "made history by becoming the first of its kind in America, and perhaps the world. So, in a raw, bustling frontier, the experiment of self-government for Negroes was tried" (10). Hurston claims that "White Maitland and Negro Eatonville have lived side by side for fifty-six years without a single instance of enmity. The spirit of the founders has reached beyond the grave" (10–11). She then concludes in a more mythic tone and says that "The whole lake country of Florida sprouted with life" in the "late eighties" when "the stars fell" (11).

The opening chapter, "My Birthplace," presents Hurston's vision of the town. She shows the equality between whites and blacks, explains that they have always worked together in harmony, and claims that the life they brought to this area has replaced the bloody history of its past. In addition, Hurston rewrites her town's history. Missing from her mythic account are a number of salient facts. First, she is wrong about the date of the town's founding; it occurred a year later, on 18 August 1887. Second, the Maitland Historical Society, in its history *Maitland Milestones*, lists Josiah Eaton, not Tony Taylor, as the first mayor of Maitland. Although the *Maitland Milestones* does not mention black leadership in the founding of Maitland, Tony Taylor was chosen as an alderman. He was a member of the town's first council, but only because the new state constitution required a certain number of men (black or white) in order for a town to be incorporated and he was enlisted to fill the quota. Third, the Maitland city history points out that the town came into being because it was part of the Black Bear Trail, an Indian path that extended from Montreal to St. Petersburg; the Seminole Indians "camped by this trail." Thus, Maitland celebrates its Native American roots rather than its African American associations. Fourth, Hurston claims that the town was founded in harmony with its white benefactors, who wanted to actualize Joe Clark's ambitions of creating his own black town. In fact, a booklet published by the town of Eatonville on the occasion of its centennial tells a very different story:

> This all-Black community was an outgrowth of the white municipality of Maitland which had been incorporated three years earlier in 1884. It appears that the all-white community of Maitland found the Blacks and the area they inhabited to be somewhat "unsightly" and wanted them to move to another area. It was at this time that one Josiah Eaton, who had helped establish Maitland, offered to sell the Blacks a rather large parcel of land one mile to the west of Maitland.
>
> The land was bought by Joseph Clarke, who would be one of the first Mayors of Eatonville. Clarke in turn sold the land within the bounds of Eatonville (which was named after Josiah Eaton) to any Blacks who wished to settle there.
>
> It appears that Florida, and the Maitland area in particular, un-

like other southern states after the Civil War, took a more moderate attitude toward the Blacks who had finally been given equal rights under the 13th and 14th amendments. However, this was easier said than done and many Blacks suffered under the hands of local whites who did not want to lose their power. From all accounts it appears that this was not the prime factor in establishing the all-Black community of Eatonville. ("Town of Eatonville" 18)

Even the *Eatonville Speaker*, the city's weekly newspaper, printed a notice on 22 January 1889 announcing that land was for sale in the new town for people wishing to escape racism. Land had not been available previously, because "so great was the prejudice then existing against the Negroe [*sic*] that no one would sell the land for such a purpose." The title of the notice and its final exhortation emphasize racial difference rather than assimilation in the founding of the town: "Colored people of the United States: Solve the great race problem by securing a home in Eatonville, Florida, a Negro city governed by Negroes ... and not a white family in the whole city!" ("Town of Eatonville" 18).

Eatonville historian Frank Otey raises the "historical enigmas" of the period and wonders "why the freedmen seemed to suddenly want to break away from an economically thriving and racially harmonious town [Maitland] to risk possible failure in the chartering of another municipality." He also claims that Tony Taylor was the first mayor, but posits the notion that there may have been a "political rift" that caused the black men elected mayor and town marshal of Maitland to serve only one year. He also offers another explanation: "Joe Clarke had a long-standing desire to found a town and that lending support to the establishment of Maitland was merely his way of 'working the white folks'" (2).

Otey quotes Marjory Stoneman Douglas, who describes the terrible conditions under which blacks in Florida lived during this period. They struggled against immense prejudice and fought "to cling to a patch of land." Stoneman claims that many African Americans who tried to vote were thrown into chain gangs. But, the people of Eatonville escaped this fate because they ran their own town; they weren't forced to live in the "neglected "colored section" of a larger city:

To maintain the supply of convict labor, in addition to the usual murderers and criminals, local judges convicted as vagrants and sent to the chain gangs Negroes who had committed no crime but to vote, to demand justice, be ambitious, independent or rebellious in the face of the regained power of the white man. In some counties Negroes were sent to the chain gang for looking for work, for refusing to work under certain conditions, for trying to homestead or own land. Such courts kept no dockets or records. They took the place of the Klu Klux Klan [sic], silent since the federal investigation, in stamping out Negro participation in politics. (qtd. in Otey 5–6)

Douglas notes that "most Negroes had gone back silently to work for inadequate wages, living as they could in terribly restricted and neglected colored sections"—except for Eatonville, "the only town ever owned and run entirely by Negroes" (Otey 6).

In creating the story of her life and her community, Hurston shapes it into a vision of life as she sees it. Distorting the truth to fit the myth of black empowerment corresponds to Hurston's lifetime agenda of abolishing race as a consideration in judging human worth. Her self-identity and pride are founded on this rock of racial equality and on the notion that whites wish to help blacks because their lives are intertwined. On the other hand, the historical record paints a grim picture. In Hurston's defense, it is not surprising that she would wish to sweep all the unpleasant facts under the carpet and glorify the heroism of her town's founding fathers, which included her own father, Reverend John Hurston, the town's third mayor, who served from 1912 to 1916.

Parallel to the rewriting of her town's history in the first chapter of *Dust Tracks*, Hurston then shapes the story of her life in terms of self-empowerment and coexistence with white benefactors. This time, she dons the mask of the adorable "darkie" girl in telling the tale of her own childhood in her second published story, "Drenched in Light" (which appeared in *Opportunity*, the literary journal of the Urban League, in 1924), which she reworked as an autobiographical sketch for the chapter "The Inside Search" in *Dust Tracks on a Road*. In both the story and the autobiographical sketch, the young black girls are similar in character.

Both are swept out of their all-black world by fairy-godmother-type white women, who are entertained by their antics. In both pieces, the girl already has her eyes set on the far horizon; she spends her days taking "a seat on top of the gate-post" in order to "watch the world go by" (*Dust Tracks* 45). She "hails" the white travelers and begs to go "a piece of the way" down the road with them. She realizes that she causes "a great deal of amusement among them," yet she is so self-confident that her "self-assurance carr[ies] the point" (45). Her "brazen" behavior scandalizes her grandmother, who, remembering the days of slavery, yells at her: "You li'l sow, you! Git down! Setting up dere looking dem white folks right in de face!" (46). In *Dust Tracks*, the young Zora refuses to give in; she already feels like an outsider: "The village seemed dull to me most of the time. If the village was singing a chorus, I must have missed the tune" (46).

Contact with the white people complicates life for both Isis in "Drenched in Light" and young Zora in *Dust Tracks on a Road*. In the short story, Isis steals her grandmother's tablecloth and uses it as a shawl while dancing a jig at the nearby carnival. When her grandmother discovers her transgression, Isis runs away down the road, only to encounter the white people who had seen her dance. They call her their "little gypsy," and she volunteers to guide them to the white Maitland hotel. During the drive, she regales them with tales of her life as a princess and "her trips to the horizon, about the trailing gowns, the gold shoes with blue bottoms" (946). As they are taking her home, she asks, "Do you wanta keep me?" The white woman replies, "Oh, I wish I could, you shining little morsel" (946). Instead, she gives Isis five dollars to repay her grandmother for the ruined tablecloth and also to perform for her at the hotel, saying, "I want brightness and this Isis is joy itself, why she's drenched in light!" (947). The grandmother transforms herself into an obsequious "darkie," proudly sending Isis off with the white woman. The woman's husband seems more cynical about the whole episode, telling his wife, "you've been adopted," with "a short, harsh laugh." The woman replies: "Oh, I hope so. . . . I want a little of her sunshine to soak into my soul. I need it" (948).

In *Dust Tracks on a Road*, the white patrons reward young Zora with an invitation to their hotel after she has read the story of Persephone in class. Ironically, they ask her to read from *Scribner's Magazine*—Hurston will publish her last novel with Scribner's. The ladies give her as a reward a cylinder of "one hundred goldy-new pennies." Hurston recalls her ecstasy: "Perhaps, I shall never experience such joy again. The nearest thing to that moment was the telegram accepting my first book" (*Dust Tracks* 52). Later, after the ladies return to their homes up north, they send young Zora books, including Norse tales and Greek and Roman myths. She "resolves" to be like the powerful Hercules or Thor "as he sped across the sky in rumbling thunder, lightning flashing" (53).

Both of these pieces are full of racial overtones. The young black girl must perform entertaining acts in order to gain the notice of white people who happen to wander into her black world. Hurston, writing these sketches as an adult, never mentions the white people who may have been rude or cruel; instead, her childish persona sees them as powerful, giving, and kind. They notice and reward her specialness; yet, once rewarded, she stands out from the other black girls, who are understandably jealous. Viewing her younger self—drenched in light, trailing princess gowns, and shining like "a morsel"—the adult Zora can perceive herself above the fray of white women who use her to forget their cares or to assuage their guilt about race or who are "curious" about her existence, or white men who have "harsh laughs."

Black male authors found irksome the mask Hurston wore while addressing whites. Wallace Thurman's *Infants of the Spring* (1934) casts Hurston as Sweetie May Carr, a writer better known "for her ribald wit and personal effervescence than for any actual literary work. She was a great favorite among those whites who went in for Negro prodigies" (229). If Sweetie May had a white audience, "she would launch forth into a saga of the little all-colored Mississippi [Florida] town where she claimed to have been born. Her repertoire of tales was earthy, vulgar, and funny. Her darkies always smiled through their tears, sang spirituals on the slightest provocation, and performed buck dances when they should have been working" (229).

Thurman allows Sweetie May to describe her mode of operation:

"Being a Negro writer these days is a racket and I'm going to make the most of it while it lasts. Sure I cut the fool. But I enjoy it, too. . . . the only way I can live easily until I have the requisite training is to pose as a writer of potential ability. *Voila!* I get my tuition paid at Columbia. I rent an apartment and have all the furniture contributed by kind hearted o'fays. I received bundles of groceries from various sources several times a week . . . all accomplished by dropping a discreet hint during an evening's festivities. . . . About twice a year I manage to sell a story. It is acclaimed. I am a genius in the making. Thank God for this Negro literary renaissance. Long may it flourish!" (229–30)

Another enduring portrait of Hurston was penned by Langston Hughes in his autobiography, *The Big Sea* (1940). Hughes and Hurston had been close friends, traveling all over the South together, commiserating on their treatment by their patron, Charlotte Osgood Mason, and encouraging each other's literary efforts—until they had a falling out over their collaboration on the play *Mule Bone*. Hughes describes Hurston once again as someone who panders to whites:

Of this "niggerati," Zora Neale Hurston was certainly the most amusing. Only to reach a wider audience, need she ever write books—because she is a perfect book of entertainment in herself. In her youth she was always getting scholarships and things from wealthy white people, some of whom simply paid her just to sit around and represent the Negro race for them, she did it in such a racy fashion. She was full of side-splitting anecdotes, humorous tales, and tragicomic stories, remembered out of her life in the South as a daughter of a travelling minister of God. She could make you laugh one minute and cry the next. To many of her white friends, no doubt, she was a perfect "darkie," in the nice meaning they give the term—that is a naive, childlike, sweet, humorous, and highly colored Negro. (238–29)

Hughes, of course, also received "things" from wealthy white people, notably financial support from Mason. But in this passage he overlooks the benefits he has received from white patronage in order to keep the focus on Hurston as someone who he thinks has sold out her race. In addition, he contributes to the legend that she is more of a performance artist than a true writer, that she has compromised her art by her associations with white people. Susan Edwards Meisenhelder judges Hurston similarly: "Hurston thus reveals the complexities of white patronage and initiation into a white world. Instead of fleeing from the potential psychic damage such relationships could inflict, she depicts herself enjoying the gifts and avoiding the price" (151).

This view is unfair; nevertheless, throughout her life Hurston gravitated toward women of influence whom she admired. Some of these women were benevolent, such as Fannie Hurst, Ethel Waters, and Jane Belo; others, such as Mary McLeod Bethune and Mason, treated her badly, often under the guise of helping her out. Meisenhelder claims that Hurston's friendship with Rawlings was motivated by Hurston's desire to "play the darkie" in order to gain favors from Rawlings. Rawlings's account of Hurston's visit to Cross Creek "provides the quintessential portrait of Hurston successfully presenting herself to a potential white patron as a colorful, amusing, even brash—but unthreatening—black woman who 'has no use for the Left Wingers who consider her a traitor' and who 'puts full responsibility for negro advancement on the negroes themselves'" (93). Meisenhelder continues: "Whereas Hurston's relationship with Rawlings—her own obsequiousness and Rawlings's condescension—is a discomfiting one, it is important to remember that (like Isis in "Drenched in Light"), Hurston had much to gain from it" (93).

As mentioned previously, Carla Kaplan suggests that Hurston may have pursued her friendship with Rawlings in order to initiate and advance a film career (*Hurston: A Life in Letters* 435). While visiting California, Hurston worked as a "story consultant" for Paramount Pictures in October 1941. When producer Arthur Hornblow took her to lunch, Hurston reported that she was "elated" and eagerly reminded herself of her credentials, maybe in order to boost her confidence in getting her own work produced (436). But nothing came of these nibbles. When her star refused to rise in Hollywood, Hurston must have left California deeply disappointed that another creative outlet for her work was closed. She moved back to Florida in early 1942 and threw herself into revising *Dust Tracks on a Road*.

In *Dust Tracks*, Hurston describes how much writing means to her: "I have come to know by experience that work is the nearest thing to happiness that I can find" (285). At the time she met Rawlings, Hurston was experiencing one of the happiest periods of her life, because she had found "a quiet place to write" in St. Augustine. She felt she was "working harder, and more consistently now than ever in [her] life" (*Hurston: A Life in Letters* 472). Rawlings, too, often commented in letters that she was nothing without her work.

Both writers felt that they were at a crossroads in their work after the publication of their masterpieces. Autobiographies tend to dredge up old memories and force a reevaluation of one's self and direction later in life. Hurston, especially, had a frustrating experience with *Dust Tracks*. Even though she received a special award for her memoir—the thousand-dollar Anisfield-Wolf Book Award for the best book on race relations—she knew her true feelings had been censored by her publisher and that what was left was not genuine.

Thus, *Dust Tracks on a Road*, originally meant to be Hurston's portrait of the artist as a young woman, turned out not to be, significantly, a portrait of the woman she had become. The three chapters that the editors at Lippincott's excised were seemingly written with her mask down (or, at least, slipped aside a bit), thus expressing her true feelings. When she writes to Hamilton Holt how "hard" it is "to reveal one's inner self" (*Hurston: A Life in Letters* 478), she may have been referring to these sections.

On the other hand, many critics take Hurston at her word and believe that she never reveals her "inner self" in *Dust Tracks*. Carla Kaplan calls *Dust Tracks* "one of the most un-self-revealing autobiographies ever written" (*Hurston: A Life in Letters* 436). Alice Walker disparages the false voice she hears behind the words: "For me, the most unfortunate thing Zora ever wrote is her autobiography. After the first several chapters, it rings false." Walker goes on to excuse Hurston for her "dependency" on others, which is "a sign of her powerlessness, her inability to pay back her debts with anything but words" (qtd. in Hemenway xvii). Hurston is, indeed, poetic and hyperbolic in her descriptions of Mason, with whom she says she has "a psychic bond," but she can also turn around and be scathing in her criticism, as when she records Mason's angry words at one of Hurston's transgressive acts: "'You have broken the law!' Her tongue was a knout, cutting off your outer pretenses, and bleeding your vanity like a rusty nail. She was merciless to a lie, spoken, acted or insinuated" (*Dust Tracks* 177).

Nevertheless, Hurston was revealing herself in *Dust Tracks*—but her audience was not listening to her or could not listen to her. They expected her usual colorful anecdotes from Eatonville, but she no longer knew "what her editors and white audience expected," according to Hemenway (287). Furthermore, even though Hurston had changed as a person and had moved on to more international concerns, an editor at Lippincott's scrawled across the bottom of a page of her manuscript: "Suggest eliminating international opinions as irrelevant to autobiography" (Hemenway 288). Hurston acquiesced in the censorship, because of her fatalistic view of the way publishing worked in those days. "Rather than get across all of the things which you want to say," she once told an interviewer, "you must compromise and work within the limitations [of those people] who have the final authority in deciding whether or not a book shall be printed" (qtd. in Hemenway 286–87).

The three cut chapters appear as an appendix to Robert Hemenway's edition of *Dust Tracks on a Road*, published in 1984. These passages, according to Hemenway, "reveal a writer at work, one who benefited from her editor's advice, but one who also had her true feelings considerably distorted by the editorial process" (*Dust Tracks* 288). Hemenway believes that these sections "display a more self-assured, irreverent, and politically astute figure than the Zora Neale Hurston of the published book" (287).

The first excised chapter, which Hurston wrote while she was in Haiti in 1937, contains material that was meant to go into the published chapter "My People, My People!" The published version is considerably watered down, and Hurston generalizes her examples: "the well-mannered Negro" is embarrassed by his "brother in black," who boards a train or bus and "find[s] other Negroes on there with their shoes off, stuffing themselves with fried fish, bananas and peanuts and throwing the garbage on the floor" (*Dust Tracks* 215). In contrast, in the excised portion she personalizes the people by referring to "a brown young woman, fresh from the classic halls of Barnard College" (like herself), who is "escorted by a black boy from Yale" (291). They have just attended a Marian Anderson concert, along with an audience of white people, and assure themselves that "The Race is going to amount to something after all. Definitely!" (292). They then board a subway train, and their senses are assaulted by two "scabby-looking Negroes" who "come scrambling into the coach" and sit beside them. The men, who are "dirty and smelly," "woof, bookoo, broadcast, and otherwise distriminate [*sic*] from one end of the coach to the other" (292). According to the narrator, the two men "consider it a golden opportunity to put on a show" while "Barnard and Yale sit there and dwindle and dwindle" (293).

This anecdote satirizes both the Barnard-Yale couple and the two street performers. It also makes the point that the phrase "My People, My People!" can be read either as praise or as opprobrium, thus proving how in flux a definition of African Americans is. Hurston is also using this anecdote to deconstruct the attitudes of the white people who observe this scene in the "Jim Crow coach" (294). According to Hurston, no one in this scenario has the correct view toward race. Each person is misjudging the other and making assumptions based on racial stereotypes.

Hurston further complicates the issue by using this anecdote and other examples to define African American qualities, much as she lists black modes of expression in "The Characteristics of Negro Expression" (1934). In this excised chapter, Hurston claims that blacks share the following stereotypes: first, "they can't agree on a single, solitary thing" (296); second, they use "six big words where one little one would do" (298); third, they have "no memory of yesterday, nor no concept of tomorrow" (298–99); fourth, they "never steal more than a dollar and a quarter," even if a thousand dollars is sitting in a pile next to them (299); fifth, they call the monkey their brother, based on all the stories they tell "to poke a little fun at" themselves (299); sixth, they love to imitate; and seventh, they love a show: "We love to act more than we love to see acting done" (304).

By enumerating these stereotypes, Hurston pokes fun at the prejudiced reader. After she goes through the list, she pulls the rug out from under the racially biased person by driving home her main point, which has to do with the relativity of any racial classifications: "What we think is a race is detached moods and phases of other people walking around. What we have been talking about might not exist at all. Could be the shade patterns of something else thrown on the ground—other folks, seen in shadow" (304). Her meaning, too, is a pattern thrown on the ground, to be deciphered by those able to separate the substance from the shadow. Her meaning seems indirect only to those readers who cannot read her message. Hemenway's judgment that *Dust Tracks* "can be a discomfiting book" that has "harmed Hurston's reputation" was the general view of early readers. They critiqued her, because *Dust Tracks*, "like much of her career . . . often appears contradictory" (276). But Hurston was trying to show that the notion of a monolithic view of race is simply "a mirage," as she explains in "My People! My People!": "'Race Solidarity' looked like something solid in my childhood, but like all other mirages, it faded as I came close enough to look. As soon as I could think, I saw that there is no such thing as Race Solidarity in America with any group" (218).

Delia Konzett further explains this view: "These lies or contradictions point not so much to 'untruths' in general (exaggerations, story-telling) but 'untruths' upholding single viewpoints as 'truths.' These lies are seen especially in matters of 'race,' with its various and shifting constructions" (85). In fact, Hurston's only consistency regarding race is the celebratory exuberance and self-esteem expressed in "How It Feels to Be Colored Me," as David Headon notes: "No 'double consciousness' for her, no measuring of oneself with the tape of the white world. . . . [Her characters] celebrate instead of plotting revenge, characters who want to love, discover and transcend, rather than commit murder" (28–29).

The second excised chapter, "The Inside Light—Being a Salute to Friendship," speaks exuberantly on another subject about which Hurston feels passionate—friendship. The published chapter "Two Women in Particular" reduces Hurston's circle of friends to Fannie Hurst and Ethel Waters, a representative white woman and a black woman. Hurst is presented as a frivolous woman who invites herself to tea, "mak[es] up characters to play with," and "behave[s] like a little girl." In contrast, Waters is portrayed as a great female black artist whom Hurston senses has "great humanness and depth about her" (243). Even though Hurston had a longer history with Hurst, she seems to have bonded more deeply with Waters, perhaps as a fellow female black artist: "We exchanged confidences that really mean something to both of us. I am her friend, and her tongue is in my mouth. I can speak her sentiments for her, though Ethel Waters can do very well indeed in speaking for herself" (245).

Although the portraits of Waters and Hurst are revealing, the excised chapter gives a broader sense of the breadth of Hurston's circle of friends and what they mean to her. These relationships were reciprocated and not dependent or transitory, as Walker claims. In the chapter, Hurston proves the opening sentiment: "[Friendship] is a wonderful trade, a noble thing for anyone to work at" (307). She then describes her friends and what they mean to her. Carl Van Vechten, for example, "has bawled me out more times than anyone else I know. He has not been one of those white 'friends of the Negro' who seeks to earn it cheaply by being eternally complimentary" (309). Jane Belo, a fellow anthropologist, is another example of a genuine friend. She had worked on research projects with Hurston in South Carolina and also spent "years in Bali studying native custom." Hurston says: "I also wonder at times why she liked me so much" (312). Katharane Edson Mershon, with whom Hurston was staying when she wrote this chapter in 1941, was "a person of immense understanding" (314) who "called in the doctors and cleared the malaria out of my marrow" (316). Mershon had also spent nine years in Bali, "conducting a clinic at her own expense" (315). Hurston ends the chapter by saying "I have had friends" and explains: "Perhaps no human being has ever explored [friendship's] limits. Anyway, God must have thought well of it when He made it. Make the attempt if you want to, but you will find that trying to go through life without friendship is like milking a bear to get cream for your morning coffee. It is a whole lot of trouble, and then not worth much after you get it" (321).

In a letter dated 2 November 1942, Hurston expresses to Van Vechten her regret that her publisher did not allow her to express her true feelings for him: "My best to you, darling Carl. I owe you *so* much. I wrote a chapter in my new book dedicated to friendship, but the publishers deleted it. In it, I tried to show my inside feelings for certain people, because I am not sure that I have ever made it clear how I feel" (*Hurston: A Life in Letters* 467–68).

The third excised chapter, "Seeing the World as It Is," is the most radical of the censored material, but it is the work that most reveals the opinionated, globally conscious woman that Hurston had become in the early 1940s. The title of the watered-down version of this chapter, the last in *Dust Tracks*, is "Looking Things Over," which sounds vague, unfocused, and trivial. In contrast, the title "Seeing the World as It Is" implies that Hurston is explaining her worldview, that is, that her subject is more global and universal than her local concerns about the village of Eatonville. As she explains, "Lord, give my poor stammering tongue at least one taste of the whole round world" (330–31).

Hurston begins "Seeing the World as It Is" with a description of the scars she has received from life. She sounds like she is laying out her credentials in order to prove that she has the right to speak with authority. She describes her tough times in mythic metaphors straight out of Eatonville: "My knees have dragged the basement of Hell and I have been in Sorrow's Kitchen, and it has seemed to me that I have licked out all the pots" (322).

She then reiterates her usual message that race should not matter—"Negroes are just like anybody else" (329); it is the individual who counts: "I found that I had no need of either class or race prejudice, those scourges of humanity. The solace of easy generalization was taken from me, but I received the richer gift of individualism" (323). She points out that she "cannot accept responsibility for thirteen million [black] people," because "Every tub must sit on its own bottom regardless" (324–25). Further, she rejects any concern for the past: "I turn my back upon the past. I see no reason to keep my eyes fixed on the dark years of slavery and the Reconstruction. I am three generations removed from it, and therefore have no experience of the thing" (331–32).

Rather than worrying about the past, she zeroes in on the present and accuses the world of perpetuating slavery: "But I know that the principle of human bondage has not yet vanished from the earth. I know that great nations are standing on it" (338). She wants to sound the alarm and communicate that the survival of humanity depends on eliminating race consciousness: "What the world is crying and dying for at this moment is less race consciousness" (326).

She then comments on current politics. Writing before the Japanese attack on Pearl Harbor in 1941, she compares Japanese imperialistic ambitions to the United States' treatment of China (341). She also criticizes U.S. politics at home and suggests that "President Roosevelt could extend his four freedoms to some people right here in America before he takes it all abroad" (342). American society, in fact, is corrupt, according to Hurston: "One hand in somebody else's pocket and one on your gun, and you are highly civilized. Your heart is where it belongs—in your pocketbook" (343).

Hurston goes further toward establishing a tone of empowerment in this chapter than in the published version. First, she says she does not want to "join in a protest for the boss to provide me with a better hoe to chop his cotton with. Why must I chop cotton at all? . . . I will join in no protests for the boss to put a little more stuffing in my bunk. I don't even want the bunk. I want the boss's bed" (345). She goes on to say: "I can get no lift out of nominating myself to be a peasant and celebrating any feasts back stairs. I want the front of the house and I am going to keep on trying even if I never satisfy my plan" (345–46). Second, she even advocates the use of violence in order to change the world: "Why not take a stronger position? . . . I am not bloodthirsty and have no yearning for strife, but, if what they say is true, that there must be this upset, why not make it cosmic?" (346). Hurston seemingly ends on an upbeat note. She appeals to Dame Nature, who has the power both to destroy and to create: "May I never do good consciously nor evil unconsciously. Let my evil be known to me in advance of my acts, and my good when Nature wills" (348).

In contrast, the ending to "Thinking Things Over" is frivolous and superficial. She offers the "right hand of fellowship and love" to her readers, whom she hopes will become "kissing-friends" (286). Maybe, she suggests, they then can "breed a noble world in a few hundred generations or so" (286). The final sentence of *Dust Tracks* is curious: "Maybe all of us who do not have the good fortune to meet, or meet again, in this world, will meet at a barbecue" (286). The vague, flippant tone suggests that this event will probably never occur.

Obviously, Hurston hated having her voice silenced, even though she was resigned to the racism that existed in American publishing at the time. This type of censorship had to affect the way she regarded her work. Hemenway claims that the result was that Hurston lost touch with her fellow Eatonville citizens: "*Dust Tracks* eventually exposes Hurston's uneasiness over how to move beyond the Eatonville voice and, by implication, how to explain her fame and her townspeople's obscurity" (279).

I sensed this unease in 1989 when I interviewed the people who had known Hurston and who were still living in Eatonville. Like Harriet Moseley, nearly all of them emphasized that they had loved Hurston as a daughter of the town (and daughter of the popular Lucy Potts Hurston) but hated the way she had portrayed them in fiction. Hurston notes that after her mother's death in 1904, her life as a wanderer began: "That hour began my wanderings. Not so much in geography, but in time. Then not so much in time as in spirit" (*Dust Tracks* 89). When she leaves her home, she realizes: "I was on my way from the village, never to return to it as a real part of the town" (94). She would return to the town again and even lived in her own home at Tuxedo Junction in the 1930s. She usually stayed at the homes of her mother's friends, particularly Armetta Jones and Mathilda Moseley. She interacted with the community, and people recalled how friendly she was. She even cast Eatonville people in her play *From Sun to Sun*, which she produced at Rollins College in 1933. Clara Williams remembers that Hurston had "an outgoing personality, and, as far as children were concerned, she was a very nice person because whenever she came up the hill she always had something to give us" (Lillios 18). Williams says that Hurston would gather the children around her: "She'd sit down and she'd tell us stories and things about places she had been. . . . She just had everyone's attention when she came" (18). Williams remembered a day when Hurston rounded up the children and directed them to eat watermelon so that a photographer could take photos of them. When her father heard that she was being used in that way, he told Hurston off. When asked how the townspeople felt about Hurston, Williams laughingly remarked: "She'd written some things about Eatonville and when she came back, [the townspeople] said they were going to fix her" (19).

Annie Davis, whose father was Will Davis, the husband of Armetta Jones, describes Hurston:

> She was just Zora. She never looked over none of her people because she had more education. She never looked over the lower class that was under her. She never did. She was always Zora. She was always happy. She was always rejoiced. She didn't care what you had to sit down to eat. She always made herself welcome. She wasn't one of those high-class people. To look at her, the type of woman she was, you could never tell by the way she treated you.

She always was nice. She was always kind. When she spoke to any of her people she always spoke nice. She just wanted to put in her book her childhood on up. (Lillios 23)

Davis confirms the idea that some people in town did not like Hurston, but she feels that Hurston "wasn't doing nothing but telling the truth": "You know how these slums and places are . . . outdoor toilets, pumps in the backyard, chickens, hogs, and cows and everything. She come out of a slum. I read some of that in her books" (Lillios 23–24). Davis also mentions that Hurston would sit on the side porch of her parents' home and write her books: "She'd always go off and be by herself and she'd be writing, humming little songs. She was just a nice, quiet person" (24).

In the Daytona Beach area, Lynn Dawkins has documented much harsher black perceptions of Hurston when she taught at Bethune-Cookman College in 1934. Dawkins conducted extensive interviews with Dr. Annie Mae McClary Walker, a civil rights leader, pioneer of Head Start, and founder of university African American studies programs who was also a close friend of Hurston's from 1929 to 1948. Walker insinuates that Hurston was a lesbian, because Hurston associated closely with Walker's sister, Lulu, an acknowledged lesbian, and slept in close quarters on a houseboat with a white woman. Walker reports that her sister and Hurston would hang out in jook joints and "meet the paydays," that is, stand on street corners and solicit sex from men who had just received their pay (144). Because of Hurston's allegedly bad reputation, Walker's father did not allow her to befriend Hurston:

Certainly the blacks on campus looked down on her, not only because of her appearance, but because Zora hung out at the jooks, where respectable people just didn't go. Down at those noisy corner saloons, lower-class blacks congregated around juke boxes to sneak in moonshine . . . and dance. When couples got juked up enough, the establishment rented bedrooms for 25 cents. . . . As blacks denounced her as an outcast mostly because of her association with the jooks and street people, but I loved and respected her. . . . Only white people would accept Zora's unusual moral standards, but even they rejected her after she came back from the West Indies. She was really into hoodoo and the study of Zombies, and into the Yoruba religion. (144)

All of these personal anecdotes may or may not be true; they certainly depend on the teller's perspective. But they do suggest how Hurston was simultaneously an insider and an outsider in her own culture. Hurston was in a difficult position in her writing career in the early 1940s. Her own people did not want to read what she had written about her community, and white publishers did not want her to venture too far out of her folk milieu.

Thus it is possible that when Rawlings and Hurston met, they may have discussed possible directions that Hurston could go in her work. After all the criticism and censorship that *Dust Tracks* had engendered, a way out was to bypass racial issues altogether. In a 2 November 1942 letter to Carl Van Vechten, Hurston writes about her career plans, which include moving away from her usual subject matter: "Having been on the writing staff at PARAMOUNT for several months, I have a tiny wedge in Hollywood, and I have hopes of breaking that old silly rule about Negroes not writing about white people. In fact, I have a sort of commitment from a producer at RKO that he will help me to do it. I am working on the story now" (*Hurston: A Life in Letters* 467).

It was not until 1947, two months before Perkins died, that Hurston signed on with Scribner's; she published *Seraph on the Suwanee*, her next novel—with a cast of white characters—in 1948. *Seraph on the Suwanee* tells the story of a poor white couple, Arvay and Jim Meserve, who struggle to make a living and finally succeed. The novel was praised by critics for its "positive picture of Southern white culture" and its earthy qualities: "as earthy as a vegetable garden planted in rich soil, and as wholesome" (Meisenhelder 94). Meisenhelder compares the book to *Cross Creek* and finds many parallels between the two works: "On the surface Hurston seems to have paid careful attention to Rawlings's work. In fact, the basic situation and characters of *Seraph on the Suwanee* strikingly parallel one of Rawlings's sketches in *Cross Creek*, that of Tom Glisson, a poor Southern white who rises above his poverty. Like Jim Meserve, Tom Glisson has no education, but 'he talks with a flair for the picturesque and the dramatic'" (93).

Meisenhelder even compares *Seraph on the Suwanee* to Rawlings's *The Yearling* and its focus on southern white males, "the male-bonding ritual of the hunt," and the way it "bitterly criticize[s] a female figure, who lurks on the boundaries of this world as an impediment to male desires" (94). The problem with this argument is that one can just as easily say that *The Yearling* copies certain aspects of *Their Eyes Were Watching God*, such as the struggle the protagonists have establishing their individuality in the face of domineering people close to them; their confrontation with nature's power; and climactic scenes that involve animals—Slewfoot versus the rabid dog in *Their Eyes*. One could go farther back in time and show similarities between "The Eatonville Anthology," which Hurston published in 1926, and "Cracker Chidlings," which Rawlings published in 1931. The point is that Hurston and Rawlings were dealing with the same subject matter and with the same viewpoint, one that highlights nature's power, the courage of ordinary people in the face of adversity, and the empathetic treatment of their characters. Stetson Kennedy in his essay "The Magic Circle" points out that both women were writing at a time when black and Cracker cultures intermingled in Florida: "Notwithstanding certain airs put on by folks in the Big House, the fact remains that Cracker culture, influenced in good measure by Black culture (it is a well-kept secret that Florida was 48% Black at the time of the Civil War) has constituted the Mainstream in our State as it has in the rest of the South. (How else do you suppose Atlanta's pre-integration baseball team, the 'Black Crackers,' got their name?)" (4).

It is always difficult to prove influence. We can only speculate that Hurston's contact with Rawlings led to her association with Scribner's and, probably, to her defiance of custom in her last novel with its cast of white characters. Just as Rawlings became more racially conscious after she met Hurston, Hurston became more racially active. For example, Hurston supported the black signal corpsmen at her school, Florida Normal, in 1942, when a controversy arose over their living conditions. She did not hesitate to write to Walter White, the executive secretary of the NAACP. She begins her letter: "Well, the Negroes have been bitched again!" She goes on to explain that "The dissatisfaction is *tremendous*," because four men who were outspoken about being "swindled out of their $30 for board and getting baloney sandwiches and tea" were dismissed from the campus by the president of the school. Hurston concludes her letter by urging White to help: "I feel that the whole body of Negroes are being insulted and mocked. Please send someone to look into things" (*Hurston: A Life in Letters* 469–70). Hurston left the school before the issue was resolved in the men's favor.

She continued her advocacy of service people by joining the Florida Negro Defense Committee in 1943 and 1944, and she assisted Mary Holland, the wife of the governor, in working on the Recreation in War project, in which she spoke about her travels and life experiences to black GIs stationed in Florida. In her essay "Crazy for This Democracy," published in *Negro Digest* in 1945, she ends with a commitment to action: "I give my hand, my heart and my head to the total struggle. I am for complete repeal of All Jim Crow Laws in the United States once and for all, and right now. For the benefit of this nation and as a precedent to the world. . . . Not in some future generation, but repeal *now* and forever!!" (948–49).

Thanks to friends such as Rawlings, who encouraged her to keep writing about what was close to her heart, Hurston continued to advocate for change. She did not seem to care if she angered people in the process and even made outrageous statements such as "the Jim Crow system works," which won her no friends. But she never gave up her dream of one day living in a world in which race was not a factor. As she proudly tells a reporter: "I don't see life through the eyes of a Negro, but those of a person" (Hemenway 289).

## Rawlings's *Cross Creek*

Rawlings's life in Cross Creek began in 1928 when she left mainstream America for frontier Florida. Besides her avowed desire to change her career from journalist to creative writer, Rawlings, in a 24 October 1936 letter to F. Scott Fitzgerald, confesses another motive: "I don't understand people like us—and what little I do understand, terrifies me. That's why I write, gratefully, of the very simple people whose problems are only the most fundamental and primitive ones. I have probably been more cowardly than I'd admit, in sinking my interests in the Florida backwoods, for the peace and beauty I've found there have been definitely an escape from the confusion of our generation" (*Selected Letters* 122).

Rawlings was referring to the confusing times in which they were living. She was old enough to remember the Great War, she was living through the Great Depression, and, with the rise of Hitler's Germany, the warning signs of another world war were already on the horizon. No wonder she would want to escape imaginatively to Cross Creek and describe it in terms of its idyllic beauty: "[Cross Creek] was a primitive section off the beaten path, where men hunted and fished and worked small groves and farms for a meager living, where the lean, sun-browned women did their washing outdoors in iron kettles over smoky pine fires. . . . And the country was beautiful, with its mysterious swamps, its palms, its great live oaks, dripping gray Spanish moss, its deer and bear and raccoons and panthers and reptiles" (*Uncollected Writings* 344).

*Cross Creek* opens with a vision of harmony among all the residents of the Creek who live in this paradise: "We are five white families; 'Old Boss' Brice, the Glissons, the Mackays and the Bernie Basses; and two colored families, Henry Woodward and the Mickenses" (9). They all share a common characteristic, as the narrator notes when she recalls a conversation with Black Kate:

> People in Island Grove consider us just a little biggety and more than a little queer. Black Kate and I between us once misplaced some household object, quite unreasonably.
> I said, "Kate, am I crazy, or are you?"
> She gave me her quick sideways glance that was never entirely impudent.
> "Likely all two of us. Don't you reckon it take somebody a little bit crazy to live out here at the Creek?" (9)

In the midst of this idyllic description, the words "mad" and "queer" jump off the page. "Queer," particularly, is not necessarily used in its contemporary association with homosexuality, but as an indicator of the "strange, peculiar, eccentric." "To queer," as an intransitive verb, also means "to spoil." Annette Trefzer suggests that Rawlings's use of "queer" is "crucial" in presenting "an unruly and possibly countercultural community identity." She concludes: "As a writer, Rawlings explored the strategy of queering communal and personal identities as one way to cross sexual and racial boundaries" (72). Trefzer gives as an example Rawlings's suggestion to her black servant, Adrenna, that they should "trap a good [black] man," one who can work on the farm by day and have sex with Adrenna by night. When this man is shot by Adrenna's lover, he says, "Cross Creek is the most queerest place and the queerest people I've ever knowed" (208). Rawlings's purpose, according to Trefzer, is to present "the Creek as a community of suspect 'others' who, precisely because of their alterity, are able to provide a 'home' to the woman writer" (73).

These "suspect others" share other qualities: they are all "individualists"; they have "chosen a deliberate isolation"; they "need and have found only very simple things," namely, "flowering and fruiting trees," "a certain blandness of season," the song of birds," the sound of rain coming across the *hamaca*, and the sound of wind in trees"; and they need "a certain remoteness from urban confusion" (10–11). Rawlings's narrator concludes with a statement that suggests that the landscape itself has shaped their being and determined who they are: "There is of course an affinity between people and places" (10). J. T. Glisson also describes the effect the setting of the Creek has on its residents: "The Creek folks were like the lakes. They could lay quiet and calm for weeks, basking in the subtropical sun, and then suddenly break loose and kick up all hell before settling back as if nothing had happened" (2). The fact that they are living in an isolated place gives them the psychic space to "break loose," if the spirit moves them, according to Glisson:

> Everyone is a character if they have the room and opportunity to be one. And most certainly the Creek was the perfect spot for characters. Everyone had one or more titles: "meanest," "nicest," "best catfisherman," "laziest," "most pregnant," "most profane," "stingiest." None of the titles were meant to hurt. They represented the distinction we associated with idiosyncrasies, local humor, and respect for individuality. To some degree there was family love involved, as in, "He may be a son-of-a-bitch, but he is my brother." We were family. (3)

The land itself seems to have magical properties that transform humans as they move through it. The narrator says that if one enters the wood or grove, one moves "out of one world and in the mysterious heart of another" (15). Fittingly, "For This Is an Enchanted Land" is the title of chapter 2. In addition to magic, the grove can evoke a sense of "terror," as when the narrator realizes that her fate, through love, is tied inextricably to the land—"for the joining of person to place, as of person to person, is a commitment to shared sorrow, even as to shared joy" (17).

Rawlings originally wanted to portray the Creek to show its more sinister side, as she explains to Perkins in a 31 March 1931 letter. When she proposes to use the hammock country at the north end of Orange Lake (Cross Creek is at the south end) as the setting of *Golden Apples,* she tells him about "a strange, unearthly stream that has overflowed into the hammock itself." The river is called, "inexplicably, the River Styx." To the British-exile protagonist of her second novel, *Golden Apples*, "the strange small river would indeed seem another Styx, transporting him from life into death" (*Max and Marjorie* 37). As mentioned in the discussion about *Golden Apples*, Rawlings compares the river to a beautiful woman "capable of a deep evil and a great treachery." Neither can be trusted: "Back of the lushness is something stark and sinister" (*Max and Marjorie* 37).

The sinister element, of course, is starvation. "All of life [in Cross Creek] is geared to the threat of hunger. This is literal," Rawlings reports to a medical officer in 1951 (*Selected Letters* 362). In the essay "Florida: 1928–1953," Rawlings admits that after her divorce, she too knew what it felt like to be hungry: "I was alone at the Creek. There were bad years for the grove, years of freezes and low prices. . . . I was down one day to a box of crackers and a can of tomato soup" (*Uncollected Writings* 345).

Many of the sketches in *Cross Creek* deal with poverty and hunger. "The Pound Party," for example, tells of the narrator's innocent joy in being invited to a welcome party by the Townsend family when she moves to the Creek, only to realize that she is the sole guest and is expected to bring the food. Observing the many Townsend children, she notices how emaciated they look: "[They] were thin, grave boys and very capable. They moved slowly, like old men, and had the look of age that hunger puts on children" (52). The narrator also notes that "Their green color came from a lifetime of hookworm," which she tries to treat with free medicine from the state. When asked what they would do with a dollar, one boy answers, "I'd have all I want of rich folks' rations—light bread and jelly" (52).

Hunger, though ever-present, is kept at bay. Rawlings tells how the people of Cross Creek help each other or are clever enough to find enough food to eat. The Creek is similar to Baxter's Island in *The Yearling*, which is "a fortress ringed around with hunger" (43). Martha Mickens, one of the black residents of the Creek and the narrator's servant, explains that even though hunger is present outside the perimeter of Cross Creek, the good land surrounding the Creek provides enough food for the inhabitants to stave off starvation: "Ain't nobody never gone cold-out hongry here. I'se seed the grove freeze to the ground. I'se seed it swivvel in a long drought. But Sugar, they was grove here. . . . as long back as tongue can tell. . . . And they'll be grove here right on, after you and me is forgotten. They'll be good land to plow, and mast in the woods for hogs, and ain't no need to go hongry. All the folks here ahead o' you has fit cold and wind and dry weather, but ain't nary one of 'em has goed hongry" (29).

In the chronicle, Martha functions as a woman whose words of wisdom reassure the narrator and help her understand the Creek's cosmic cycles: "I remembered the things the old black woman said, and I was comforted, sensing that one had only to hold tight to the earth itself and its abundance. And if others could fight adversity, so might I" (29). Through Mickens's guidance, the development of Rawlings's connection with and empathy for her fictional characters and her real-life Cracker neighbors become the hallmark of her work. In 1936, when she was writing *The Yearling*, Rawlings realized that this "element of sincerity given by [her] own interest and sympathy" in her characters was her strength as a writer (*Max and Marjorie* 251).

According to noted human-rights activist and author Stetson Kennedy, however, Rawlings's sympathetic treatment of Cross Creek's inhabitants does not accurately reflect the reality of the time. As the only person alive who was friends with both Hurston and Rawlings, Kennedy admits that his own writing was influenced by both women, but he soon felt that "the realist within me was rearing its head" and needed "to tell it like it was." He critiques both women for ignoring the realities of life:

> Admittedly, the pictures painted by both women were a bit on the rosy side, Acadian [*sic*] even. But even in Acadia [*sic*], the necessities of life are none the less necessary. Those were the "root hog or die" days of the Great Depression, and life for many whites and

blacks was one of "grits without gravy." Then, too, both women studiously ignored the Jim Crow system of apartheid which permeated every aspect of life. Somehow Rawlings' whites never lynched, and Hurston's blacks never got lynched. Having said all of this, however, I hasten to add that even so Florida was about as close to Acadia as you could get, and in places it still is. ("The Magic Circle," unpublished manuscript, University of Florida Libraries)

As someone who was brave enough to infiltrate the Ku Klux Klan in the 1930s and 1940s and expose their nefarious activities, Kennedy has painstakingly documented (in his book *Southern Exposure*) the Klan's role in inciting racial violence and mayhem in central Florida in the early 1940s, the period in which Hurston and Rawlings were trying to establish a friendship. The Klan was reveling in the race-based evil that the Nazis were spewing forth, but they finally remained patriotic to the American cause in World War II. During 1942–43, when Hurston and Rawlings were communicating with each other on a regular basis, Kennedy records a great deal of Klan activity in central Florida, mainly directed against labor unions. On 30 January 1943 the Klan broadcast over the local Orlando radio a "call for all Klansmen" to mobilize; the next day, they paid for a help-wanted ad in the *Orlando Sentinel-Star* that exhorted their followers: "4,000 of the 8,000 Klansmen from Orange, Seminole, and Osceola counties—there is work to do" (181). On 15 September 1943 in Apopka, just outside Orlando, a parade of Klansmen drove through the black part of town, threatening union members at a citrus packing house who were to vote in an election the next day (181).

Throughout the South, Klan activity at that time was running rampant to such an extent that, Kennedy claims, "In matter of peonage, feudalism, exploitation, and denial of suffrage to her own citizens, the South is 100 per cent as fascistic as was Nazi Germany" (191). In the mid-1940s, Kennedy feared that "native-born fascism" would "sally forth to infect the entire nation if the forces of democracy do not combine to cauterize it" (191). Even today, four Klan groups exist in Florida—two near Cross Creek in Ocala and Silver Springs—according to Mark Potok, director of the Southern Poverty Law Center's Intelligence Project (Eckinger).

Although Rawlings does not compare the South to Nazi Germany, as Kennedy does, her letters to her husband reflect the racism of the times.

Today's reader winces every time she calls one of her servants a "nigger."
When her maid, Idella Parker, displeases her, Rawlings says that Parker
has become "pure nigger" (*The Private Marjorie* 405); when Parker has
a toothache, it "makes her cross and *very* niggery" (266); when Parker
angers her, Rawlings says, "Idella has been having a high old nigger time"
(471); and Rawlings complains to Baskin that Parker *"snapped* at me,
*simply all nigger"* (483).

Rawlings's racism carries over to the pages of *Cross Creek*. Throughout the memoir, Rawlings continues with the theme of the strength of
the Crackers' human spirit, but, perversely, the narrator begins to obsess
over her difficulty in finding black servants to work for her. In the most
shocking chapter, entitled "Catching One Young," Rawlings describes
the ordeals:

> I bought Georgia of her father for five dollars. The surest way to
> keep a maid at the Creek, my new friends told me, was to take over
> a very young Negro girl and train her in my ways. She should be
> preferably without home ties so that she should become attached
> to me. My friends traced a newly widowered father of a large fam-
> ily that he was unable to feed as a unit. He was happy to "give"
> me Georgia, with no strings attached. A five-dollar-bill sealed the
> bargain. Two months of life with her made me wonder why he had
> not given her to the first passing gypsy caravan, or drowned her
> decently.
>
> It is possible that in catching one young, I had picked from too
> early a litter. (85)

Today's reader may detect Rawlings's wry sense of humor, but the racism
explicit in "buying" another human being is shocking. In this passage,
the narrator of *Cross Creek* functions like the plantation owner of a by-
gone era, wheeling and dealing in human flesh. Yet, the narrator is also
mocking herself for appearing to be so desperate. In his introduction to
*The Private Marjorie*, Rodger Tarr concludes that Rawlings's views on
race are "disturbingly contradictory" (4):

> Rawlings's racism is particularly frustrating, because, although it
> was not unusual in her time, we expect more from her. . . . Rawlings
> acted as a champion of the blacks at Cross Creek and by extension

as a spokesperson for the cause of equality nationwide. She lectured the editor of a Jacksonville newspaper on his racial bias; she stayed in the president's house at Fisk University to call attention to her position; and she repeatedly debated with Norton [Baskin] (and others) the best way to advance the cause of equality. . . . And yet, while Rawlings chastised her closest friends for their racism, in the next breath she would call her "Perfect Maid," Idella Parker, a "nigger," or refer to her ancient servants, Will and Martha Mickens, as "Nigger Will" and "Nigger Martha," or, more incredibly, dispatch her good friend Zora Neale Hurston to the "nigger" quarters to sleep when she visited Rawlings at Cross Creek. Such actions make no sense, particularly within the context of her Herculean efforts to stem the tide of racism. On the subject of race, Rawlings is an enigma. (4–5)

Rawlings's actions and views on race must, of course, be placed in the context of her times. Many critics condemn her for her frequent use of the word "nigger" and the prejudiced way she portrays her servants, but they fail to realize that Rawlings evolved from being a blatant racist to becoming a champion of black civil, economic, and human rights. It took her a long time to conquer her innate racism. In the chapter titled "Black Shadows," the narrator takes a broad view as she attempts to understand the situation of the African Americans. She begins with a disclaimer: "I am not of the race of southerners who claim to understand the Negro." She admits that she goes along with the crowd and agrees with its "platitudes": "The Negro is just a child. The Negro is carefree and gay. The Negro is religious in an amusing way. The Negro is a congenital liar. There is no dependence to be put in the best of them" (189).

The narrator then breaks away from the multitude's way of thinking by trying to look at social reality from the viewpoint of the blacks:

Back of these superficial truths lies the mystery of the primitive African nature, subjected precipitously first to slavery and then to so-called civilization, the one as difficult and unjust as the other. The Negro today is paid instead of being rationed. He is left to shift for himself for the most part instead of being cared for. In the South his wages are a scandal and there is no hope of racial development until racial economics are adjusted. Meantime, he continues to be, ostensibly, childish, carefree, religious, untruthful and unreliable. Back of it all is a defense mechanism as ingrained as the color of his skin. (189)

Unfortunately, this sentiment is not developed further; the narrator goes on to relate incidents in which her servants are childish, carefree, and unreliable. She complains: "The long line of Negroes has come and gone like a string of exploding firecrackers, each one arriving on the smoking heels of another and departing as violently. Most have gone in insanity, mad love affairs, delirious drunkenness and shootings. Their shadows lie long and black against the pattern of the Creek" (191).

When she goes to North Carolina "to cool the malaria in [her] blood and begin a book," on her return she sacks her black servants, Raymond and Kate, "for going wild" in her absence and for not taking care of the farm. The narrator is particularly angry because her brother, Arthur, is coming to visit and she wants to spend the day hunting with him and "com[e] home at night to an orderly house and a waiting and edible dinner" (193–94). When Arthur sees the narrator's domestic state of affairs, he suggests they confront the unruly servants: "I've seen what you have to put up with. We're going over to the tenant house and run that black ape off" (195). When they burst into the bedroom of the tenant house, they find three people in bed—a clothed Kate and a naked "sweetheart" and a naked Raymond, on either side of her. In the comic scene that follows, the naked men begin "a strange community dance" in search of their clothes and then run off down the road, never to be seen again. The narrator feels "sad" that she has lost the chance to remold these people into good servants—until she discovers that Kate has "turned into a thief" by stealing money from her brother's wallet (198). She partly blames herself for making "a grave mistake": "I have expected that, given justice and kindness, a reasonable attitude toward their problems, and wages higher than the customary ones, they could carry considerable responsibility and learn to discipline themselves" (190). She had thought Kate and Raymond would have the self-discipline to be responsible, "what most of us manage so painfully and so inadequately for ourselves" (190). In other words, her attitude is demeaning and condescending toward Kate and Raymond, whom she feels are incapable of managing their own lives.

To reinforce her philosophy regarding black servants' ineptitude, she gives another example in the chapter "Black Shadows." This anecdote concerns Kate's successor, Adrenna, who happens to be Martha Mickens's daughter. Adrenna's flaw is that she is man-crazy. The narrator describes her effect on the local men: "when she swung that shingle butted rear down the road, the Negro men followed and were entranced" (199). Adrenna suggests that she and the narrator share a man. The narrator explains: "Her efforts to trap a man, who should please me by day and her by night, fell between two stools. One by one she lured them in, and one by one they were incompetent in one capacity or the other" (199). She finally finds a man, Samson, and the narrator pays for the wedding, although she knows that "three more or less legal husbands were still in the offing" (201). Even though Samson turns out to be useless in the fields, life seems to settle down—until the narrator leaves once again only to return to find trouble. The sheriff informs her that Samson has been shot and that Martha Mickens's son-in-law, Henry Fountain, is the culprit. The narrator feels that Adrenna, "the butt-switcher, was back of it all" by "egg[ing] Henry on" (205). She then sees "the whole Creek lined up against [her]," because she seeks to make Henry pay for his crime at a trial. The case is dismissed for "lack of evidence," even though the narrator calls the proceedings a "mockery." As she and her neighbors exit the courthouse, she tells them: "if there's ever any trouble at the Creek again, it won't ever reach a court. I'll take care of it. And if there's any shooting, I'm going to do it" (211).

Another version of the story exists, radically different in content and tone from Rawlings's account, written by another eyewitness to the shooting that occurred on 1 January 1940. In *The Creek*, J. T. Glisson writes about Henry Fountain's shooting of B. J. Samson and tells his version of the shocking event. In doing so, he proves how different Rawlings was from her neighbors. Implying that she manipulated reality, Glisson says that she "turned a simple catastrophe into a downright disaster, or at least that is the way it appeared to me" (130). As a boy, Glisson regarded Henry Fountain as his dear friend. They worked together in the fields and talked for hours. Fountain was a mentor to the young Glisson and spoke to him like an adult. Glisson even attributes his inspiration for becoming an artist to Fountain's "spellbound" appreciation of his drawings. When Fountain got into trouble with the law for shooting Samson, Glisson says, "I was saddened then and still am that his love for his family and his desire for self-respect was [were] the cause of all the trouble that descended on him" (131).

Interestingly, Glisson's and Rawlings's stories differ radically regarding the shooting. Glisson shows no racial bias in his account as he relates how his father, Tom Glisson, protected Fountain when he got into trouble and allowed him to stay in the family's garage while they made plans. Tom Glisson even helped Fountain escape to his sister's farm in Georgia while racial tensions were high in the neighborhood, and he facilitated Fountain's return when his trial began. J. T. Glisson points out that Rawlings was partly to blame for the troubles, because she hired Samson in the first place and, as an outsider, did not know the inner workings of the community. Tom Glisson explains to him about Samson: "He's trouble, that's what he is. Miz Rawlings should know better than to bring anybody from the city to Cross Creek, especially a Negro, into Martha's clan" (139). When Samson has been shot and is lying on the ground, J. T. Glisson feels "nothing but anger toward the outsider" (139). In this statement, Glisson considers the blacks to be part of the Creek's community, whereas in Rawlings's chronicle they are definitely a race apart. Glisson tells how Samson, as an outsider, had been "thrust on us, and now he held all of us hostage. His fate would determine whether our lives at the Creek would ever return to normal" (140). Samson held the community hostage because the Creek people knew that Samson started all of the trouble by making "advances toward Sissie [Henry's wife] deliberately to provoke Henry" (141). Samson then "pulled a switchblade and cursed Henry, called him a ignorant nigger. He forced Henry away from the truck with the switchblade and drove off with Sissie and Drenna" (141).

In Rawlings's account, however, she was not privy to the cause of the shooting and guesses that Adrenna is behind all the trouble. She was also not told that Tom Glisson had talked to the sheriff behind her back and arranged for Fountain to get out of jail and escape to Georgia. Furthermore, Fountain is treated like an adult in Glisson's account of the story; Tom Glisson explains his actions in these terms: "Henry is a grown man, and he made the decision to do what he did knowing when a feller makes his bed, he has to lie in it" (142). J. T. Glisson notes how the whole community, in defense of Fountain, had risen up against Rawlings. When she threatened to swear out a warrant, "Everyone at the Creek, including the blacks, tried to talk her out of doing it. For someone from the Creek to swear out a warrant, especially against anyone else from the Creek, was to be in league with the government against us" (144). Under Tom Glisson's leadership, the blacks and the whites at the Creek met together to decide what was best for all of them. Tom Glisson respected the blacks' opinions by asking them, "How do you want it to come out?" (145). Interestingly, Rawlings was excluded from this meeting. When the group decided they wanted Fountain back—but not Samson—Tom Glisson was able to speak to the judge, who "threw the whole mess out of his court" (149). Fountain was relieved, summing up the experience: "I found out I sure has got some good friends here at the Creek" (149).

The fact that there are two versions of the same story shows the slippery nature of memory. Rawlings's husband, Norton Baskin, admits that "there was a lot of fiction" in *Cross Creek*: "Every story and every human in there was true to life, but Marjorie had a little O. Henry ending to each story. And everything in there happened to somebody, but not to this person. Because for instance, there was a succession of nine maids and Negroes around there, including old Martha, but these were all condensed into each. And everything that happened to each, it happened to one of them. It was certainly true to Marjorie's book" ("Gentleman Story-Teller" 35).

From the inception of *Cross Creek*, as a successor to "Cracker Chidlings," her first published story with *Scribner's Magazine*, Rawlings struggled with her Creek material, wondering how truthful she should be with it, what her role should be in the narrative, and how to organize it. Ultimately, she adopts a view similar to Quincey Dover's in "Cocks Must Crow," a short story she published while working on *Cross Creek*: "Now I got to put this together the best way I can. I ain't like them story writers can make a tale come out as even as a first-prize patchwork quilt. Life ain't slick like a story, no-ways. I got to remember this, and remember that, and when I'm done it'll make sense" (256).

Another problem Rawlings faced with telling the story of the Creek was how to handle her own dark vision of nature. She realized early on that to get published by Scribner's she had to follow Maxwell Perkins's view that authors should bring out the valiant, inspiring qualities in human nature so that "natural human perseverance and courage" will prevail in the "struggle against nature" (*Max and Marjorie* 34). Rawlings agrees with this expectation, writing to Perkins that "from the human if not the cosmic point of view, the courage of these people is . . . important" (34). In another letter to Perkins, Rawlings says that she "likes to see people bucking something solid, instead of their own neuroses" (346).

When Perkins asks Rawlings, "Is there any chance that you will write a novel?" (*Max and Marjorie* 36), she replies in a 31 March 1931 letter that she is "vibrating with material like a hive of bees in swarm" and says, "I see four books very definitely" (37). She easily visualizes the books: first, there will be "a novel of the scrub country" (which becomes *South Moon Under*); next, another novel, called "Hammock" (*Golden Apples*); then, she mentions the genesis of *Cross Creek* and says that she has composed "a dozen or so completed sketches," which are "really 'Cracker Chidlings,'" and can be "grouped under some such heading as 'Cracker Town' indicating the village psychology" (41); and, finally, in her detailed description of Leonard Fiddia (Lant in *South Moon Under*) as a "boy as indigenous to the scrub as the deer" (40), she presents the germ of an idea that would lead to *The Yearling*.

Rawlings let the idea of *Cross Creek* lie dormant for several more years until after she published *Golden Apples* in 1935. When Perkins asks her about doing "the boy's book" next, she replies:

> There is one Florida book that will surely be done, I don't know how soon. One I had thought would not be possible because I hadn't done it when the material struck me freshly. Yet mellowness, not freshness, is the requisite. It will be non-fiction, called "Cross Creek: a Chronicle." It will not be a confluent narrative, (for the reason that I do not wish to write my personal story) but made up into chapters. . . . It will be as quiet in tone as anyone could wish for! Some of the material is violent, but it will be interesting to tell it in a matter of fact and quiet way. It will not be a book to sit down

and "do," but one accumulated. Some of the material has been done several years, needing re-writing, of course. Sketches, stories, narratives, essays, laid here at the Creek, done with no special use in mind. But all with a certain, what shall I say, out of the world flavor, catching, I hope, the quality that has made me cling so desperately and against great odds to this place. . . . It is possible it will be ready in a year or two and will fill in until I have a novel ready for you. (*Max and Marjorie* 231)

Hurston, too, recognizes that it may sometimes be useful to present reality indirectly. In *Their Eyes Were Watching God* she uses a striking image to describe the mingling that occurs when producing "out of the world flavor." She compares it to "the piece of string out of a ham. It's not ham at all, but it's been around ham and got the flavor" (64). Rawlings struggled for years to define the elusive quality that made the Creek, Cross Creek. She obsessed over the form of the book, deciding to write a non-confluent—that is, non-chronological—narrative mirroring the hidden currents of the Creek itself, and regarding the tone, hoping to keep the tone "quiet" and, perhaps, more poetic. While she is writing the book, Perkins assures her in his letters that she can "move things around" as long as she gives "the poetic truth" (*Max and Marjorie* 476). Poetic truth in Rawlings's work means the awareness of nature and its universal workings. According to Rodger Tarr: "Rawlings's creations owe a great deal to the narrative strength and moral legacy of Romanticism. She believed in what she called 'cosmic consciousness,' what we call Transcendentalism" (introduction to *Max and Marjorie* 23). Rawlings also shares in the romantic poets' interest in exotic states of being, reminding the reader that Coleridge's depiction of Salt Springs in "Kubla Khan" was inspired by William Bartram's journals of his travels through Florida. Calling *Cross Creek* a "*queer*" book in a 23 September 1941 letter to Perkins, Rawlings expresses her hope that "its effect on readers would be to take them into a totally strange world, and that they should feel a certain delight and enchantment in the strangeness" (*Max and Marjorie* 499). Perkins responds: "'Cross Creek' may be queer, but it is lovely, and it is human," and he concludes that it is a "very rare book" that "makes one feel better" (499). On the other hand, Rawlings's dark conception of the landscape and her frank treatment of her Cracker neighbors and black servants eliminated the possibility that her book would be received in a "quiet" or "matter of fact" way.

After *Cross Creek* was published in 1942, Rawlings met Hurston. Their friendship marked a turning point in Rawlings's views on race. Rawlings had employed black servants; however, Hurston was the first black person whom Rawlings came to know intimately as a friend and as a professional writer. Hurston's distinctive personality worked on Rawlings's innate sense of empathy and began to change Rawlings's decades-old racism.

It is unclear how much clarification on the race issue Rawlings received from her husband, Norton Baskin, who had to resolve his own feelings about blacks. Baskin, in an interview with actor Peter Coyote, recounts his horror as a child when he stumbled on a man being lynched: "When I was about eleven years old, I sauntered along down the railroad track and down there witnessed a lynching. I would never get over it. They strung this Negro up by his heels and then somebody cut his testicles off. I really got back at some distance. I just couldn't watch that thing. You talking about sick, I really was" (Baskin, "Peter Coyote Interviews" 30). The man had been accused of raping a white woman, although no one had any proof against him. Baskin said the event made him "sick and a sickness that [he] never did get over" (31). His racial ambivalence is evident when he tells Coyote, on the one hand—"I don't want [blacks] socially. I never had 'em in my home, but to me it's wrong anyway, to mistreat one" (31)—yet, on the other, he tells Coyote about the numerous times he aided and supported his black "cooks and bellboys and people like that—the doormen"—who worked in his hotels. "I'd do anything in the world for 'em," he claims (31).

Rawlings had some of the same ambivalent feelings about race that her husband did. It is difficult to understand why Baskin would say, regarding blacks, "I never had 'em in my home," since Rawlings always employed black servants, who were in her home and around Baskin all day long when he was staying at the farmhouse. A reader cannot help but note the irony. Rawlings, too, displays her ambivalence in *Cross Creek* as she enumerates, on the one hand, her many struggles with her black servants, often insulting them by using racial epithets, and, on the other, her desire to make their lives better by paying them decent wages, giving them money when they are in trouble, taking them to the doctor when they are ill or injured, coming to their defense when they have broken the law, and giving advice when needed. Donald Wilson claims that Hurston made the offer in order to be close to her, because in those racially charged times it was impossible for Hurston to make an extended personal visit to the farmhouse.

Even after she became acquainted with Hurston, Rawlings struggled to achieve a more humane stance on race. Everyday incidents around the farm seemed to be her stumbling blocks. In letters to Baskin she describes the frustration she has had babysitting her servant Sissie's three children while the adults go into town to shop: "I am whipped down by three little nigger babies" (*The Private Marjorie* 211). She goes on to call the children "three little blackbirds," "the tar babies," and "the three little pickaninnies" (211–13). But the children turn the tables by pretending to be Rawlings and acting out incidents in which Rawlings orders her servants to serve her: "Every now and then through the nightmare that was the afternoon, Martha would suddenly 'be' Mis' Baskin, and high saccharine notes would announce the dearth of wood or what-not" (212). The children, then, ask, "We is to mind you just like you was our Mama, isn't we?" If they are to behave as if she were their mother, they then leap to a new game and pretend that she *is* their mother, and much to Rawlings's horror, they call her "Mama" (212). Rawlings can hardly wait for Sissie to return to retrieve her children, having had her fill of being the mother of three black children. She recalls: "And if anybody wants the help or the love of three nigger babies, they may have my share" (213). This anecdote shows how Rawlings is forced to look at the black children's reality as they subversively turn the tables on her, but she also allows herself to be regarded humorously. Of course, she is being facetious as she tells this story to Baskin; nevertheless, the reader questions her transformation regarding race.

Actions also contribute to the definition of character, and Rawlings does take steps to prove that she has evolved. In an article titled "The Evolution of a 'Southern "liberal"': Marjorie Kinnan Rawlings and Race," C. Anita Tarr describes various actions that Rawlings took in her public and private lives to stand up for her beliefs. First, in a letter dated 27 November 1943, Rawlings describes her new way of thinking about race:

"I have forced myself to take the final mental leap about the Negroes. There is no question but that . . . we must go all out for 'full equality'. . . . Anything else is the height of hypocracy [*sic*]" (unpublished letter, Scribner's Archives, qtd. in C. A. Tarr 158). Second, in an undated letter written in 1943 to an editorial writer of the *Florida Times Union*, Rawlings is explicit in her beliefs:

> Don't you see, can't you see, that segregation denies a man or woman something more important than "justice" or "opportunity," and that is self-respect, freedom from being made to feel subtly inferior, from being, after all, and finally, an outcast. Most of us now know enough of psychoanalysis to understand the devastation [when a person] . . . is made early to feel inferior. . . .
>
> I can only tell you that when long soul-searching and a combination of circumstances delivered me of my last prejudices, there was an exalted sense of liberation. It was not the Negro who became free, but I. I wish and pray for your own liberation. It is almost a religious experience. No man is free as long as another is enslaved, and the slavery of the spirit is more stringent than that of the body. (*Selected Letters* 237–38)

In the letter, she quotes Eleanor Roosevelt's words regarding social equality: "Why, that's something that can't be legislated. It is something you have with your own friends" (*Selected Letters* 238).

Shortly thereafter, Rawlings follows Mrs. Roosevelt's advice and tests out her new views on her friends at a dinner party. In a 16 February 1944 letter to her husband describing the party, Rawlings says that when someone made a "typical southern and ugly anti-Negro remark," she found herself "expounding moral principles for dear life. . . . and I might as well have turned a rattlesnake loose, for the effect it had—especially on my popularity" (*The Private Marjorie* 269). One man at the party, a formerly good friend, tells her, "You have never been hated in your life as you are hated here tonight." When Rawlings returns home in tears, she recounts the evening's events to Idella Parker, who scolds her: "Please, don't ever do a thing like that again. You can't do any good, and it just isn't worth it" (269). But Rawlings does not follow Parker's advice; in a 14 April 1944 letter to her husband she says that, once her lawsuit is settled, she plans "to go all out on the question of Negro rights" (327–28).

Rawlings next defended blacks' social equality in a sketch she wrote for the Writers' War Board in 1944; the sketch was rejected because the board felt it was "too controversial" (*Selected Letters* 254). In a 7 March 1945 letter to Edith Pope, Rawlings writes that she has just returned from Florida A&M, the "colored" college at Tallahassee, where she "spoke on a program honoring Mary Bethune. It was a fascinating experience and I am more than ever ashamed of the people who try to hold the Negroes back" (*Selected Letters* 263). In 1946, when the National Equal Rights League demanded that *The Yearling* be taken off a reading list at a school in the Bronx, Rawlings defended the use of "nigger" as a sign of the times, but she approved the word's removal in the School Book Edition of 1947 (C. A. Tarr 150). In 1948 she agreed to speak at Fisk University in Nashville, Tennessee, and even stayed in the university president's home. Anita Tarr quotes from an unpublished letter dated 24 May 1948 in which Rawlings describes her Fisk visit: "I was no longer conscious of race or color—only of individuals—and I met some of the most brilliant minds and charming personalities I have ever known" (159).

Ernest Bass, who knew Rawlings while he was growing up, provided the following story from the late 1940s, which shows that Rawlings was expressing her views to the Cross Creek community as well as the public at large:

When the Berry Family owned the Cross Creek Fish Camp in the late 1940s, they made their fishing camp and cabins a "white only" establishment. When Rawlings heard about this turn of events, she took herself in a hurry and huff down to the camp and cornered Mr. Berry on the end stool at the counter in the café. She dressed him down in her strongest possible language, laced lavishly with profanity, for discriminating against "colored people" who, according to her, had as much right to fish in Orange Lake or Lochloosa Lake as white people did. Berry was polite to her, but finally she hit a raw nerve, and he began cussing back at Rawlings. "If you want a god-dammed fish camp for the niggers," he said, "then you put one in for them. You own property on the Creek too, you know. Now get the hell off my property and don't be in too big of a hurry to come back." She had not made a convert. (4)

The development of Rawlings's consciousness about race was one outcome of the publication of *Cross Creek*. Another outcome was totally unexpected and devastated Rawlings for at least five years afterward. Rawlings agonized over her problematic stance as narrator and her ability to find the "right approach" in blending her real-life experiences into the narrative. When she finally finished the book, she called the ending "nauseating." In a 12 December 1941 letter to Perkins, she also mentions another concern: "I too have done a great deal of worrying about the libel possibilities. I am making a great many minor changes and deletions that will take care of much of the problem. It is simply impossible to tell how people will accept being written about. The Negroes, Snow, Old Boss, the Glissons, the Bernie Basses, Zelma the census taker, are perfectly all right" (*Max and Marjorie* 506).

Rawlings asked Perkins to let her know if there was anything "dangerous" in the book. He replied that he thought the chapter "Black Shadows" might be problematic but that overall he feels that the people portrayed in the book "would be pleased by it" (*Max and Marjorie* 511). Rawlings assures him that she would not have any trouble with the blacks in her book, because "no case of libel by a negro against a white would even reach a southern court" (514). Little did she think it would be her friend Zelma Cason, a census taker, who would take offense and, ultimately, bring her grievance to the Florida Supreme Court. Cason objected to Rawlings's description of her in chapter 5: "Zelma is an ageless spinster resembling an angry and efficient canary. She manages her orange grove and as much of the village and county as needs management or will submit to it. I cannot decide whether she should have been a man or a mother. She combines the more violent characteristics of both and those who ask for or accept her manifold ministrations think nothing of being cursed loudly at the very instant of being tenderly fed, clothed, nursed or guided through their troubles" (56). Acton notes that Cason also objected to Rawlings's "references to her as 'my profane friend Zelma,' and giving appropriately edited examples of Zelma's famous cussing" (31).

Rawlings's "invasion of privacy" trial lasted five years and became famous in Florida legal history. On 8 January 1943, Cason filed her libel suit against Rawlings and asked for $100,000 in damages for defamation of character and the pain and suffering caused by Rawlings's having written, among other things, that she "cursed loudly." Cason's lawyers were Judge and Kate Walton of Palatka, and Rawlings's were Philip May of Jacksonville and Sigsbee Scruggs of Gainesville. The case was so complicated that the charge was changed from libel to invasion of privacy. In August 1943 a local judged ruled that "the lawsuit was groundless, and entered judgment in favor of Marjorie without a trial" (Acton 33). Cason appealed, and the case went to the Florida Supreme Court. The state supreme court, after a highly dramatic trial, reversed the lower court's verdict. On 23 May 1947, Cason won her suit for "invasion of privacy"—and Rawlings was fined one dollar plus costs ($1,050.10). According to Patricia Acton, "Zelma had, indeed, proved that her privacy was invaded. She was not a public figure, and she had not consented to have her story told in a book. . . . But the Court also had some bad news for Zelma. Although she was entitled to judgment in her favor, she had not proved that she suffered any damages as a result of the invasion of privacy" (38). Acton reports that the final legal document related to the case was filed on 9 August 1948.

Even though Rawlings had to pay Cason only a dollar, the psychological toll was enormous. Not only did she have to pay more than eighteen thousand dollars in legal fees, but she also paid a heavy price in lost time and wasted energy. After *Cross Creek* was published in 1942, it took Rawlings eleven years to publish another book, *The Sojourner*, which appeared in 1953, shortly before her death. The trial marked Rawlings's turning away from her original source material, perhaps because she was fearful of being sued again (she backed out of doing a sequel). In addition, her imaginative life was changing. Although she published a few Cross Creek stories in the 1940s, Rawlings began to look outside her rural world to a more international arena.

During World War II, Rawlings's husband enlisted in the American Field Service and was sent to the India/Burma theater in 1943. During his absence, she poured her energy into writing nearly daily letters to him and also to U.S. soldiers stationed abroad. Rawlings had come to the notice of service people after her books were distributed in the Armed Services Editions; people stationed abroad who read *The Yearling, Cross Creek,* and *South Moon Under* felt these books were highly evocative of home and the pleasures of living close to nature. In his introduction to

*The Private Marjorie*, Rodger Tarr points out the value of this work: "If history should credit Rawlings with anything beyond her literary contributions, it should credit her with enriching the lives of hundreds of service people by writing detailed responses to their letters of appeal" (17). Even today, as executive director of the Marjorie Rawlings Society, I receive e-mails from people throughout the country who have discovered letters Rawlings wrote to their parents during the war. Tarr notes that Rawlings would often receive more than one hundred letters a week and felt it was her duty to answer every one of them.

## A New Definition of Self

In the 1940s, both Hurston and Rawlings had exhausted the possibilities their communities could offer them as writers and were seeking a way to construct their selves in different terms, based on entirely new "images of their own creation." The mood of the country had shifted away from an interest in primitive rural life and toward the world war. Work on their memoirs dredged up personal issues that were exacerbated by the times in which the two women lived. Hurston and Rawlings were seeking to redefine themselves because the 1940s were full not only of global challenges but also of difficult personal ones. Rawlings had severe medical problems, particularly diverticulosis, which sent her to the hospital on numerous occasions. She also had to deal with recurrent malaria, a broken neck due to a fall from a horse, and problems with her weight. The war also took much of her attention; she often was a spotter for German aircraft off the Florida coast and was devastated when her husband enlisted in the American Field Service. Baskin served in Burma for eighteen months until he contacted amoebic dysentery and, finally, returned home to Florida. Rawlings's psychic energy was further tapped when she diverted her creative energies to writing to her husband and countless other service people. She also had to contend with her lawsuit and the upheaval that this emotional ordeal created in her own life and in the lives of her Creek neighbors. Rawlings believed that she was representing all authors in their right to portray the "truth" any way they wished in their fiction and felt that this was a cause worth fighting for.

It is likely that Hurston and Rawlings were drawn to each other because they were facing similar hardships during the 1940s. Hurston also had medical emergencies and was hospitalized on several occasions. She returned from her Latin American anthropological forays with tropical illnesses. She constantly struggled to pay her bills and often did not eat well. She also became embroiled in politics during the war years and continued to fight against special treatment for blacks—a highly unpopular stance. Her life, too, took a tragic turn when she had to spend time in the courts defending herself against the false child molestation accusations in 1947.

It is no wonder, therefore, that in their memoirs both Hurston and Rawlings were trying to reflect the changes through which they and the world were passing in the 1940s. Peggy Whitman Prenshaw sees Rawlings's voice in *Cross Creek* as that of a woman who is "ready in her own voice to say the world into being, ready to construct, to incarnate knowledge in her story. Not as man, but as independent woman. . . . like being the boss of Walden Pond or Yoknapatawpha County" (19). Rawlings would have hated having her work compared to Faulkner's, but in the 1940s, at the time they met, both Hurston and Rawlings were seeking a new self-definition that would give them a sense of empowerment as authors.

# 4

# The Road Ahead

Hurston's and Rawlings's Last Works

**T**he 1940s were a time of terrible troubles for both Zora Neale Hurston and Marjorie Kinnan Rawlings. After the success of their Eatonville and Cross Creek works in the 1930s, both women turned away from their original source material in search of new ways to define themselves as writers and as human beings. In the process they faced devastating personal struggles, including the drying up of their wellspring of folklore at a time when the country was fighting a world war; innumerable medical emergencies; trials that took a high toll in time, energy, and resources; rejection from their publishers; and deepening depression that made everyday life a challenge. Just as Rawlings reached out to service people, Hurston sought to adapt to the changing times by turning outward to politics and journalism. A sign of Hurston's troubled state of mind appears in the apology she wrote on 30 July 1947 to her old friend Carl Van Vechten for not looking him up when she was in New York: "The place was too much of a basement to Hell to suit me. Everybody busy hating. . . . Not hating anyone, I felt entirely out of place. I am afraid that

I got a little unbalanced. I got so it was tortu[r]e for me to for to meet people, fearing the impact of all the national, class, and race hate that I would have to listen to" (*Hurston: A Life in Letters* 551). Hurston, stuck in a "basement to Hell," and Rawlings, trapped in what her husband called an "ivory dungeon," nevertheless continued to struggle to do work that was meaningful and truthful to whom they had become.

## Hurston after *Dust Tracks on a Road*

After the publication of *Dust Tracks on a Road*, Hurston met with failure after failure at her publisher's office. She had moved beyond the Eatonville material and was searching out various aspects of black experience that fit her better at this stage of her life. She ranged from trying to envision what it was like being a white person in *Seraph on the Suwanee* to ruling an ancient kingdom as King Herod did in the first century B.C.

Hurston also sent to Lippincott many less successful projects on which she was working. She reports to Van Vechten on the first one, titled "Mrs. Doctor," which was rejected and does not survive in manuscript: "I wanted to do a serious one on the upper strata of Negro life, and had it two-thirds done, when I think Lippincott, (timid soul) decided that the American public was not ready for it yet" (*Hurston: A Life in Letters* 529). She then started another novel, for which she gives Van Vechten the plot summary: "So I have done a book on my native village, starting with the material of Mule Bone and weaving a story about a village youth expelled from town by village politics going places, including Heaven and Hell and having adventures, and returning after seven years to achieve his childhood ambition of being a fireman on the railroad, and the town hero" (529). This manuscript, also lost, may have been an early version of *The Lives of Barney Turk*. Lippincott found it sloppy and strained, according to Robert Hemenway (*Hurston: A Life in Letters* 529 n. 4). After this failure, her novelette "The Golden Bench of God," which was about the life and work of Madame C. J. Walker and her daughter, A'Lelia Walker, was also stillborn.

About a decade ago I met with Jean Parker Waterbury, Hurston's former literary agent, who died in 2008, in St. Augustine and asked her if she had any idea what happened to these lost manuscripts. She did not possess any copies of the manuscripts, nor did she know their fate; unfortunately, the manuscripts have also disappeared from Scribner's and Lippincott's files. Hurston's lost book manuscripts may have even been consumed in the conflagration on her front lawn after her death.

### Seraph on the Suwanee

Given the fact that her new novels based on Eatonville and the black experience were rejected, Hurston decided to turn to a completely new area for her, the world of white Crackers in west Florida. Hoping to interest Hollywood and tap into subject matter with which Rawlings had been so successful, Hurston creates the story of a married couple, Jim and Arvay Meserve, who struggle for years with traditional gender roles in their relationship. Jim starts their married life working in the turpentine camps in Sawley, a town on the Suwannee River. After their first child is born, he moves to Citrabelle, south of Polk County, to work in the citrus groves. Finally, he ends up working his shrimp boats off of New Smyrna Beach.

Hurston learned about the turpentine industry when she spent time doing research in camps near Cross City, Florida, while working for the Federal Writers' Project in late spring 1939. Pamela Bordelon claims that Hurston drew on her "impressions and information" from this field experience in order to shape "powerful scenes and characters for *Seraph on the Suwanee*" (Hurston, *Go Gator* 42). She accompanied John McFarlin, a turpentine foreman who rode through the woods checking on his crew's progress. In her short essay "Turpentine," Hurston describes what it was like to "ride the wood" with McFarlin. Her depiction of him is straightforward: "He was a sort of pencil-shaped brown-stained man in his forties" who describes his work in the woods as "kind of lonesome" (129). McFarlin, though, is no model for Jim Meserve. He lacks the depth and power of personality that Hurston invests in Meserve: "Jim had a flavor about him. He was like a hamstring. He was not meat any longer, but he smelled of what he had once been associated with" (7). Jim dominates every social setting in which he finds himself. He calls himself "Peter Rip-Saw, the Devil's high sheriff and son-in-law" (19).

The portrait of Jim Meserve bears striking similarities to Rawlings's hero Bill Boyle in "Lord Bill of the Suwannee River." It is not known whether Hurston had read Rawlings's story or discussed its contents with her before she wrote *Seraph on the Suwanee*, but the parallels are evident. Rawlings wrote "Lord Bill" in 1931 and submitted it to *Scribner's Magazine*, only to have it rejected. She also sent it to the *Atlantic* and received this note from the editor: "[it is] rather a pity that you haven't told a genuine story instead of piecing together these scraps of legend" (Silverthorne 69). The story was eventually discovered by Gordon Bigelow and published posthumously in the June 1963 issue of *Southern Folklore Quarterly*.

Rawlings based her story on the real-life character of William E. Bell, a railroad building foreman, who had died fifteen years before she began her research in Trenton, Florida. Just like Jim Meserve, everything about "Lord Bill," as Bell was called, was larger than life. In Rawlings's sketch, one citizen claims that Lord Bill is "king around here, absolutely king" (113), and is the size of "two Teddy Roosevelts." The narrator compares him to "Henry the eighth" by declaring: "He loved money and power and men and railroads and food and drink and jesting. Life spread all these things before him on the broad table of the Florida frontier and he bolted them raw. He had some connection with the sources of things" (115).

Like Jim Meserve, Lord Bill owns a boat, which is a "floatin' palace," and travels up and down the river "straddlin' the stern and shuckin' hisself oysters" (108), in the words of residents who are awed by his presence in their midst. An old-timer tells the narrator that Lord Bill "look[s] like Stone Mountain moving" (108). The narrator is impressed: "He wanted a town, so he built a town in a cornfield. He wanted to see the wilderness under cultivation" (110). Jim Meserve is also considered a king among men, an empire builder like Jody Starks in *Their Eyes Were Watching God*. Jim assists in the destruction of a swampland behind his house by developing it into a community and then builds a shrimping business. Wherever he applies his energies, he changes the landscape.

Lord Bill's reputation is particularly enhanced by his black employees. Although he is "feared" by them, he is also revered, as Bill's "own man" Tobe recounts: "They worshiped his person and his power. They loved him because he took care of them" (119). Rawlings touches on the blurring of racial lines brought about by the strength of Lord Bill's personality whenever he mixes with his men: "Everybody, blacks and white company and Lord Bill, had such a good time the camp was in a delirium all night. Big nights" (121). This erasure of racial elements also occurs in *Seraph on the Suwanee*. Jim Meserve develops a close, lifelong relationship to his employee, Joe Kelsey, who figures prominently in the turning points in *Seraph*'s plot.

Even though *Seraph on the Suwanee* focuses on the lives of white Crackers, Hurston found a way to comment on the complexity of black-white relations in the United States. She found plenty of material on this subject while working for the Federal Writers' Project in 1938 and 1939. According to Bordelon, Hurston based the story partly on her research. Bordelon claims in *Go Gator and Muddy the Water* that "Hurston's FWP writings show her to be a serious anthropologist whose career had just hit its stride. The massive FWP research engine supplied background material for Hurston's last novel, *Seraph on the Suwanee* (1948), a seminal connection that has never been established. Indeed, the connection between Hurston's FWP experience and *Seraph* is so complete that one can find passages where Hurston lifted sentences from her FWP field notes and placed them in the mouths of her novel's characters" (x).

In other words, Hurston lifts sentences from the black people she met in the field and places their words in the mouths of her white characters. Besides blurring the lines between races, Hurston does the same with class. First, she makes a distinction between rich and poor classes in the characters of Jim and Arvay Meserve. Jim is described as privileged because of his class: "The man was Jim Meserve, whose ancestors had held plantations upon the Alabama River before the War. In that respect, Jim Meserve differed from the rest of the inhabitants of Sawley, who had always been of the poor whites who had scratched out some kind of an existence in the scrub oaks and pines, far removed from the ease of the big estates" (7).

Arvay, on the other hand, is a poor white, and she feels like an outsider when compared to Jim. She thinks she is not good enough for him, since she comes from a background in which "there was ignorance and poverty, and the ever-present hookworm. The farms and the scanty flowers in front yards and in tin cans and buckets looked like the people" (1). In a slippage of categories that further complicates the boundaries between blacks and whites, Arvay explains her family's status to Jim: "You [Jim], come from some big high muck-de-mucks, and we ain't nothing but piney-woods Crackers and poor white trash. Even niggers is better than we is, according to your kind" (126). Chuck Jackson points out that in this society Arvay is considered "white trash," which he identifies with qualities that are symbolic of deterioration, specifically, "deformity, feeble-mindedness, albinism, alcoholism, miscegenation, and criminality" (642).

According to Jackson, in Hurston's work, "racial categories always intersect with other categories, and the fluidity of the body always messes up any clean and proper understanding of the self" (641). The fluidity of the body as it relates to racial categories is seen in the pivotal rape scene, in which the black Joe Kelsey urges Jim to break Arvay sexually the way one would break a horse. Jim is unsure what Arvay's motives are for marrying him, and therefore he is receptive to Joe's suggestion: "Most women folks will love you plenty if you take and see to it that they do. Make 'em knuckle under. From the very first jump, get the bridle in they mouth and ride 'em hard and stop 'em short. They's all alike, Boss. Take 'em and break 'em" (46).

Delia Konzett interprets this scene as "a complex cross-racial patriarchal bond" that illustrates "the overlapping dynamics of gender, class, and race" in the novel (121). Joe, though Jim's employee, places himself on an equal footing when giving advice about sexual matters, whereas Arvay as a white female is a victim of both men's way of thinking. The result is that no one's position in the scheme of things is fixed, undercutting the rigidity of racial, gender, and class lines.

Another example occurs years later after Arvay marries Jim and has children with him. Once again, Joe Kelsey is complicit in the blurring of boundaries. Jackson points out that Joe is Hurston's vehicle for introducing "a black voice into the white trash narrative in order to critique its obsession with racially inherited traits" (651). When Arvay and Joe are discussing the musical abilities of Arvay's son, Kenny, Joe puts on a mask to compliment Arvay for her's son's talent, saying that it comes from her genetics, not from his own instruction. Joe assures her: "Kenny took to it [music] because he brought that talent in the world with him. He got that part from you. . . . What's bred in the bones'll be bound to come out in the flesh. Yeah, that boy come here full of music from you" (250). By juxtaposing this scene with a previous one in which Joe tells a lie, Jackson is convinced that Joe is just "messing with" Arvay. Hurston's purpose in this exchange between Arvay and Joe is to "hyperbolize Arvay's whiteness and to amplify the *acquisition* (rather than natural inheritance) of cultural traits as integral to racial identity" (650).

Later, when Arvay burns down her ancestral home, that "evil, ill-deformed monstropolous accumulation of time and scum" (306) that had caught a "distemper" from the people who had lived in it, she seems truly to have erased all the remnants of her old identity, with its false assumptions about race, class, and gender: "She was no longer divided in her mind. The tearing and ripping and useless rending was finished and done. She had made a peace and was in harmony with her life" (307–8). The new Arvay, at peace with herself at the end, is merely a "benevolent angel in the house," according to Jackson, who argues that Hurston is inserting a "level of facetiousness" in the conclusion. Arvay's contentment with remaining a dutiful wife to Jim and her feeling maternal at the end of the novel still baffles critics, who want her to be transformed just as Janie Crawford is at the conclusion of *Their Eyes Were Watching God*. The fact that Arvay is able to meet "the look of the sun with confidence," even though she is "meant to serve" and is content to "snuggle down again beside her husband," may mean that she has become more self-confident and is now ready for a fresh start in life, because she is in tune with nature's rhythms. Or, another interpretation is that she has knuckled down to her identity as Jim's mate, no more than a "slave" to him, as Hazel Carby notes in the foreword to *Seraph* (xv). Calling the novel "a very modern text," Carby says that it "speaks as eloquently to the contradictions and conflict of trying to live our lives as gendered beings" (xvi). Konzett concurs: "In *Seraph* Hurston articulates what she sees as the unspoken golden rule of the South and thus lays bare a messy system in which traditional oppositions of perpetrator and victim, master and slave, white and black, overlap and are at times indistinguishable from one another" (115).

Thus the novel can be seen as advocating a new way of looking at race, class, and gender in the South. Konzett explains: "Hurston did not believe she was leaving her black folk culture behind. . . . Instead, she saw herself as depicting and imagining a transcultural New South, in which the sociocultural bonds between blacks and whites are acknowledged, leading to a better understanding of the complex relationships between the two races" (116).

## "Herod the Great"

Besides her prophetic *Seraph on the Suwanee*, Hurston was also turning further afield—all the way to Israel, thousands of years back in time, to tell the history of the Jews from the Exodus to the "final destruction of Jerusalem by the Roman emperor Titus." She conceived of the idea as early as 12 September 1945, as she reports to Van Vechten: "the story I am burning to write is one that will be highly controversial. I want to write the story of the 3000 years struggle of the Jewish *people* for democracy and the rights of man" (*Hurston: A Life in Letters* 529).

Shortly after *Seraph on the Suwanee* was published, Hurston submitted an outline to Scribner's for a book about "the history and philosophy of the Hebrews." Its title was to be "Just Like Us," and it would "bring about a revision of our Sunday School literature, and alter the slovenly and inimical attitude towards the modern Jew" (qtd. in Hemenway 343). One of the chapters concerned Herod the Great, the ruler of Judea from 37 to 4 B.C. According to Hurston, Herod "made friends and matched wits with Pompey, Crassus, Marc Anthony, Julius Caesar and Augustus Caesar and never came off as second best" (343).

Hurston soon became fixated on Herod the Great, who seems like a highly unusual subject for the author from Eatonville. Hemenway explains Herod's appeal to Hurston: Herod allied himself with the Jewish people against their priests and was to Hurston a symbol of democracy (343). Furthermore, Hurston has grandiose plans for her biblical work and brags to Van Vechten, "It is the biggest story in the world" (*Hurston: A Life in Letters* 532). In mid-1954 she asked Winston Churchill to write the introduction to the book, but he declined because of ill health. She even dreamed that her story was the stuff of epic movies, which were popular at the time, in the style of Cecil B. DeMille. She writes to Jean Parker Waterbury: "It needs Hollywood. It is a great story, really, and needs to be done. The man [Herod] had *everything*, good, bad and indifferent. Handsome, dashing, a great soldier, a great statesman, a great lover, he dared everything" (qtd. in Hemenway 343–44).

Hurston's obsession with this one image led her to isolate herself. On 19 August 1951 she writes to Jean Parker Waterbury: "All I can say is that now and then I am attacked by a spell of withdrawal. Something keeps me from communicating with the outside world. . . . I have decided that it a sort of creative pregnancy period that makes me like that" (*Hurston: A Life in Letters* 673).

The key to understanding her obsession with Herod comes in a letter to her editor at Scribner's, Burroughs Mitchell, dated 2 October 1953. Hurston first apologizes for not writing: "No. I have not been asleep all this time. I have been passing through the most formative period of my whole life. Under the spell of a great obsession. The life story of HEROD THE GREAT" (*Hurston: A Life in Letters* 702). She then communicates her immense enthusiasm for Herod and tries to sell Mitchell on the novel: "Herod is a magnificent character" (702). She points out that Herod does not deserve his reputation as the murderer of "all the babies in the hope of catching the infant Jesus in the dragnet," because Herod died four years before Christ was even born. To back up this claim, she tells Mitchell that she has done an immense amount of research and read the works of "Flavius Josephus, Titus Livius, Eusebius, Strabo, and Nicolaus of Damascus"—probably none of whom her editor has read. She explains her view of Herod's magnificence: "The story, [Herod's] actual life, has EVERYTHING. He is set forth by all writers of his time as a man of the greatest courage, of high intelligence, one of the handsomest men of his time, capable of the greatest and most faithful friendship . . . and his strength of character. Perils which would have de[s]troyed lesser men elevated Herod" (702–3).

Hurston livens up the story of Herod's life by mentioning his friendship with Marc Anthony and his rejection of Cleopatra's sexual advances. She also adds interest to his story by claiming that Herod paved the way for Christ: "He trampled upon the Pharisees and the corrupt Sanhedrin" and "highly honored the sect of the Essenes," which created "a matrix for the growth of christianity" (703). She ends her letter by promising,

"Not only a swell book is inherent in the theme, but a most magnificent movie" (703).

On 3 June 1955, Hurston writes to Mary Holland at length about her Herod manuscript and explains why she is attracted to such a figure. At first she had considered Herod "nothing but a mean little butcher," but when she researched him more she discovered that he was "a highly cultivated, Hellenized non-Jew, the handsomest man of his time, the greatest soldier" (*Hurston: A Life in Letters* 730). In her letter to Holland, she keeps repeating what an "extraordinarily handsome figure of a man" Herod was and claims that he was a "celebrated lover (though very faithful in marriage)" (731). She admits that her project is a "hard, tough, assignment" but thinks "it should be done," because "Nobody has thrown sufficient light on that First century B.C. with it's [*sic*] all-important implications for present-day Western civilization" (733).

The fall came quickly when Scribner's rejected the manuscript in August 1955; Mitchell called the book "disappointing." But, Hurston responded in a 12 August letter: "please, please do not think that I feel badly about the rejection. I was astonished myself how easily I felt. Perhaps it is because I have such faith in the material and now my conviction that I can handle it. All is well" (*Hurston: A Life in Letters* 742). She is baffled by his statement that "the work does not represent that first century B.C."; she tells him that she "spent so much time in research."

Hemenway has another explanation for the rejection; he feels that Hurston knew the first century B.C. only too well, for she was escaping into it: "The first century B.C. had become a haven for an author who found herself without any way to publish her work. As events dealt harder and harder blows each year, she burrowed deeper into antiquity, as if the manuscript provided a way to avoid the unpleasant reality of her diminished circumstances. She not only maintained her enthusiasm, but also developed a recurring vision of growth in the writing" (344–45).

On 28 June 1957, Hurston writes to her ex-husband, Herbert Sheen, that although others may feel she has failed, "As for myself, I have gone through a period that might appear outwardly unprofitable, but in reality extremely important. A taking-in-period like the gestation of a prospective mother. Now, I am ready to give forth again. I feel that I have made phenomenal growth as a creative artist" (*Hurston: A Life in Letters* 755). She tells him that she now has "a greater competence with the tools of my trade than formerly." Hemenway comments: "The pathos in such remarks is that the Herod the Great manuscript left at her death evinces no such growth. . . . her failing powers were not equal to the task. Zora's manuscript suffers from poor characterization, pedantic scholarship, and inconsistent style; the whole performance touches the heart by revealing a talent in ruins" (345).

After the rejection, Hurston—alone and in failing health—continued to work on the Herod manuscript. She was forced to leave her beloved rental home at Eau Gallie, Florida, when her landlord decided to sell the house. She eventually moved to Fort Pierce, Florida, when C. E. Bolen, the publisher of the *Fort Pierce Chronicle*, invited her to write for the local black newspaper. Dr. C. C. Benton, her Fort Pierce landlord and friend, in an interview with Alice Walker, gives an upbeat description of Hurston in her last year of her life: "She was always studying. Her mind—before the stroke—just worked all the time. She was always going somewhere, too. She once went to Honduras to study something. And when she died, she was working on that book about Herod the Great. She was so intelligent! And really had perfect expressions" (qtd. in Walker 310).

Hurston suffered a stroke in early 1959, and Benton told Walker how badly she had deteriorated: "She couldn't really write much near the end. She had the stroke and it left her weak; her mind was affected. She couldn't think about anything for long" (Walker 311). Sadly, in the last recorded letter Hurston wrote, on 16 January 1959, she asks Harper Brothers if they have "any interest in the book I am laboring upon at present—a life of Herod the Great. One reason I approach you is because you will realize that any publisher who offers a life of Herod as it really was, and naturally different from the groundless legends which have been built up around his name[,] has to have courage" (*Hurston: A Life in Letters* 771). Hurston was forced to enter the St. Lucie County Welfare Home near Fort Pierce, Florida, where she died on 28 January 1960 of "hypertensive heart disease."

In her memoir, *Dust Tracks on a Road*, Hurston's attitude toward death reflects her innate courage and belief in the oneness of all being: "When the consciousness we know as life ceases, I know that I shall still be part and parcel of the world. I was a part before the sun rolled into shape and burst forth in the glory of change. . . . Why fear? The stuff of my being is matter, ever changing, ever moving, but never lost" (279). Hurston had faith in the natural workings of the universe, a faith that surmounted divisions of color, religion, and culture; and she bravely expressed her beliefs even when they were criticized. Many have called her a woman ahead of her time who has finally come into her own.

When Hurston died, Marjorie Adler wrote an article that describes Hurston's background and notes that she had died without enough money to pay for a funeral. The article was picked up by the UPI and, according to Adler, "the major publishing houses and her bigtime friends sent donations." And so, on 7 February, ten days after her death, Hurston, dressed for burial "in a pale pink, fluffy something," had the kind of funeral she despised. Three ministers—two Baptist, one Methodist—spoke; afterward, flower girls followed the coffin out of the Peck Funeral Chapel. Hurston was buried in an unmarked grave at a small segregated cemetery, the Garden of Heavenly Rest. Weeds and sandspurs still cover the ground, but it is a place of peace and rest.

*Time* magazine and the *New York Times* printed obituaries, and Hurston would have been pleased that both publications got the date and place of her birth incorrect. Old friends such as Fannie Hurst and Carl Van Vechten were deeply affected by the loss of their former companion. Van Vechten wrote to Hurst: "I discover as sometimes happens too late, that I loved the girl. Zora was put together entirely different from the rest of mankind. Her reactions were always original because they were her OWN. When she breezed into a room (she never merely entered) tossed a huge straw hat (as big as a cartwheel) on the floor and yelled, 'I am the queen of the Niggerati,' you knew you were in the presence of an individual of the greatest magnitude" (qtd. in Kroeger 340).

When looking at the end of Hurston's life, the key word is "courage"—the last recorded word that she wrote. After her Eatonville era, she bravely walked a path that was uniquely her own. She tirelessly tried to publish novels in the 1940s, but when her ideas fell flat with publishers she had the inner fortitude to try a new direction. Writing about Herod would never be popular with commercial publishers or their audiences. The subject is simply too esoteric, remote in time, and obscure to westerners. Hurston dedicated herself to learning about this era, the first century B.C., and became an expert in the history, philosophy, religion, and politics of this period. What she was trying to do did not fit a genre—it certainly did not fit the genre of the folklore novel by which people knew her. She was trying to write a work of nonfiction that describes not only the cradle of civilization but also the birthplace of spiritual ideas. "Herod the Great" is vast in scope, ambitious in its goals, and occasionally brilliant. The reason why scholars do not discuss it in depth is because, first of all, the references in it are obscure and arcane. One would have to be a scholar of Middle Eastern history and religion to place Hurston's ideas in context. Second, because Hurston kept rewriting, there are many different versions of the manuscript. For example, the manuscript has five parts and is 269 pages in length. Part 1 has two introductions, and part 2 has four introductions and six prefaces. Third, the manuscript was badly damaged by the fire and water from the burning of her papers after her death; luckily, a fireman passed by and rescued the remnants of her work. The manuscript is difficult to read, not only because of its tattered condition but also because Hurston moves from idea to idea, thus breaking the continuity of the narrative.

Another fascinating aspect of the Herod manuscript is the portrait of Herod himself. As Hurston explains, "A biography of HEROD THE GREAT would be extravagantly justified by the intense personal drama of his life. As a story for story's sake, perhaps unsurpassed in human history. It climbs to the very summit of triumph, and plumbs the depths of tragedy. In fact, the man known to history as HEROD THE GREAT appears to have been singled out and especially endowed by some diety [*sic*] to attract the lightning of fate" (unpublished manuscript, University of Florida Libraries). This portrait is similar to those of other great men or father figures who possess great power and are scattered throughout Hurston's work, beginning with the white man who cut her umbilical cord. Even though Hurston gravitated toward white women of influence, she was still her father's child, as noted in the section on *Jonah's Gourd Vine*.

In *Dust Tracks*, young Zora, seeking a substitute father, turns to a nameless white man "of many acres and things" who passed by her house on the day she was born and "cut the navel cord." He becomes like a spiritual father, who does not abandon her and shows up at pivotal moments of her life. She describes him as the "one person who pleased me always," mainly because he gave her advice about life, including the unfortunate wording "Snidlets, don't be a nigger" (41). In a note, Hurston explains that "The word Nigger used in this sense does not mean race. It means a weak, contemptible person of any race" (41). The white man explains to the young Zora: "Niggers lie and lie! Any time you catch folks lying, they are skeered of something. Lying is dodging. People with guts don't lie. They tell the truth" (41). He also advises her not to let anyone spit on her or kick her and tells her that "If anybody ever do one of those things to you, kill dead and go to jail" (42).

Carla Kaplan speculates on the role of the white man in Hurston's life: "Why did Hurston choose to repeat—or invent—that story in her autobiography? Was she positioning herself as a daughter of two worlds, black and white? Was she suggesting that white patronage—for good or ill—had always been a feature of her life? Did she want her life to read like a racial fairy tale? Or to make a parody of American fairy tales of race?" (*Hurston: A Life in Letters* 36–37).

A possible answer is that the white man was actually Hurston's grandfather, John Hurston the first, according to Barbara Speisman. Born in Alabama, he owned a small plantation with slaves, including Hurston's father, who was born into slavery in 1861. John Sr. disappears from census records in the late 1800s; thus, it is possible that he left Notasulga for Florida with his son. The slim evidence for this comes in a 17 May 1932 letter that Hurston wrote to Charlotte Osgood Mason: "My father was a mulatto but he was born in Alabama and moved here while young, following his employer and father who settled in the white community" (*Hurston: A Life in Letters* 256). If Hurston grew up with her white grandfather in her life as her mentor and soul mate, then her views on race become completely understandable. Also, her dedication to Herod is a way to make her life come full circle: to end it the way she began it, connected to a man "endowed by some diety [*sic*] to attract the lightning of fate."

## Rawlings after *Cross Creek*

Rawlings's later years involved just as much mental and physical struggle as Hurston's. After the complications that the publication of *Cross Creek* brought into her life, Rawlings then tormented herself for ten years over the writing of her last novel, *The Sojourner*, which takes place in the southern Michigan landscape of her maternal grandfather's home. It is the bleak story of the Linden family's life in the "terrible bog" of their farm as they struggle with the elements and their betrayal of each other.

Rawlings began writing *The Sojourner* in 1943, when she was left alone by her husband's enlistment in the American Field Service during the war. His departure made her feel utterly "flattened out about it," she reports to Perkins. She complained that she could not focus on her work, because she was continually worried about him and diverted a great deal of her creative energy into lengthy letters that she wrote to him. Perkins remained patient, always sending her encouragement and suggestions, but "the inspiration was simply not there," according to Rodger Tarr (introduction to *Max and Marjorie* 16).

Over the decade she worked on the novel, Rawlings made many false starts and lamented that she had writer's block to Perkins. "None was right," she writes in an essay. "I had not yet discovered that I must renew my northern contacts" (*Uncollected Writings* 348). By this time, Rawlings made the decision to leave Cross Creek and move north, at least for part of the year. She discovered the charms of Van Hornesville, New York, first as a guest of Mr. and Mrs. Owen Young, and then in her own home, which she purchased and restored. Even though this change of scenery refreshed her, the lingering effects of the "invasion of privacy" trial in the mid-1940s impeded her progress on the book.

These impediments were nothing, though, compared to what awaited Rawlings on 17 June 1947, when she received a telegram from Scribner notifying her that her beloved editor had died of pneumonia. Rawlings never recovered from the loss of Perkins's kind and wise guidance. As she explained to Bernice Gilkyson on 9 July, "It was startling to realize . . . how much we wrote *for* him, and certainly with his judgment constantly in mind. I dream about him often and wake up in tears" (*Selected Letters* 300). Tarr claims that her "career declined rapidly" after Perkins's death, mainly because Rawlings "lacked the ego" of Hemingway, who was able to continue on without Perkins (introduction to *Max and Marjorie* 20).

Rawlings faced a final challenge two weeks before she finally planned to complete the novel in February 1953—"a heart attack caught [her] alone at Cross Creek" (*Uncollected Writings* 348). She was able to recover, but her brush with death may have given her the dark vision that allowed her to finish the book.

## *The Sojourner*

Rawlings cast herself in the role of the main protagonist, Ase Linden, and chronicled his family life in upstate New York over a period of nearly eighty years, from the end of the Civil War to the late 1930s. Ase works the family farm for all of these years, without owning it. His older brother, Benjamin, had as a young man run off to seek his fortune in the West, with the deed to the family farm in hand. Ben also left behind his girlfriend, Nellie Wilson, who ends up marrying Ase. Together they produce five children and steadily make their lives prosper. Unfortunately, Ase's mother lives with them and poisons their existence. A bitter, deranged, angry old woman, she eventually causes the death of Ase's favorite child, Doll, by leaving her outside in a blizzard. Ase never recovers from the loss of Doll, whose death adds to his sorrow over the disappearance of his brother. At the end of the novel, Ase travels west to meet up with his brother, after receiving a note from his brother's landlady informing him that Ben is on his deathbed. Ase arrives in time to reconcile with his brother (and receive the long-lost deed) before Ben succumbs to a heart attack. As he is flying back east on a plane, Ase also dies of a heart attack.

Rawlings claims that she "so identified with him [Ase] that I felt the same soaring release that came to him at the end of the novel." After saying his final farewell to his brother, Ase, now in the plane, feels a connection with the cosmos as he looks down at the earth. He observes the "battered planet" on which we live and realizes that it "could not last forever," but he is also certain that "Something in man was surely eternal, if only his awareness of eternity" (312). He experiences a kind of self-awareness and sorrow as his heart attack begins: "It had been so brief a sojourn, not even a full century. He had been a guest in a mansion and he was not ungrateful. He was at once exhausted and refreshed. His stay was ended. Now he must gather up the shabby impedimenta of his mind and body and be on his way again" (313).

This passage alludes to 1 Chronicles 29:15: "For we are strangers before thee, and sojourners, as were all our fathers: our days on the earth are as a shadow, and there is none abiding." The entire novel is permeated by this dark vision of life, which is tragic and deterministic. Samuel Bellman notes the epistemological gloom that surrounds Ase and argues that he is an existentialist: "Asahel's predicament—which can never be resolved while he lives—is that something like a deep feeling of personal loss, perhaps a painful lack of affection from his closest kin . . . impoverishes his life. Nothing seems to belong to him—neither wife, children, land, nor house: 'He was a stranger'" (125).

In one of her drafts of the novel, Rawlings planned a sad ending for her protagonist: "I knew the man; I thought I saw the outcome of his life, which I had planned to end in a noble and unselfish suicide. Yet suicide, however unwarranted, is always an admission of defeat, and Ase Linden, after a life of frustration, would not accept it, and he soared to an ending that was more triumphant than I had believed possible for him" (*Uncollected Writings* 356). The ending soars, because Ase, after a lifetime of alienation, finally feels the oneness of all things: "All life seemed to him contained in the beginning and the end, if there had ever been a beginning and if there would ever be an end. Time was, must be, timeless. As from a great enough height a landscape would show no detail, so from a far enough distance all time would be seen to exist simultaneously. He felt this in his inner mind and spirit" (152–53).

Ase's awareness is similar to Einstein's notion of the continuum, in which past, present, and future blend together in the wholeness of being. In this novel, more than in any of her others, Rawlings seeks to describe this cosmic connection. She admits to Reverend Arthur MacGillivray, S.J., on 20 September 1952 that the book has "a religious feeling that will probably be missed entirely by the average reader" (qtd. in Bellman 128).

In the midst of her struggles with the composition of *The Sojourner*, Rawlings was nearly suicidal; therefore it is not surprising that she would consider having her protagonist, Ase, commit the act. While living in New York, she wrote on 27 July 1949 to her friend Norman Berg about her despair: "Oh Norman, I have been in such anguish. I came closer to killing myself than ever before, except once, last Sunday night. I have always felt that without my writing, I was nothing. And the writing was going so badly. But I made myself wait, and now it is going better" (*Selected Letters* 336). A couple of weeks later, Rawlings learned that her close friend Margaret Mitchell had died after being hit by a car in Atlanta. She writes to her husband of her desperation: "I begin to disintegrate, either from taking drinks too early, or from frustration over the writing. My inability to write for several days came from the shock of finding myself once again off-key. I see now that all I have to do is tear up two pages, and start over. . . . I have always considered myself on the side of the angels, and if I manage to avoid suicide, it will be because I cannot bear to depress others, but my secret feeling is that we are past saving" (*The Private Marjorie* 540–41).

A year later she was still in despair, as she relates in a 12 April 1950 letter to her husband: "I became so distressed yesterday when I wasn't able to pick up work on my book. I go crazy when I work too long at a time, and I go crazy when I interrupt myself and lose my train of thought. I go crazy, period" (*The Private Marjorie* 569). Two months later, on 10 June 1950, she admits to Baskin, "I am not so brave any more after fighting hard for so many years, I must be taken care of, or down a whole bottle of Phenobarbitol" (574). Two years later, on 4 June 1952, she is still in the grips of her depression and tells her husband that she has "never had so long a period of depression" (640).

Rawlings discussed her depressed condition with Robert Frost, who was a close friend in New York, on one of his visits to her home. Rawlings reports on their discussion regarding suicide to Baskin: "Robert Frost and I had discussed our spells of depression and that I had said to Robert that what kept me going was the feeling that one was obligated to fight in one's small way on the side of the creative, not the destructive, forces, and Robert said, 'I've never quite committed suicide. I figure as long as you can *make* [underlined three times] something, if it's only a basket, the whole business is worth while'" (*The Private Marjorie* 648).

Rawlings's experience with deep sadness gave her a feeling of empathy for the emotional difficulties of other writers. In a 31 July 1953 letter to Baskin, she describes how writers can help one another: "This horrible thing that gets me in its grips is of course a form of mental illness. No one knows a thing about it who isn't subject to it, and such another person could scarcely help, except that everybody could cry together. I have just finished the Sherwood Anderson letters, and he went through the same thing. A great part of it is the writer-not-at-work" (*The Private Marjorie* 686).

Surely, Rawlings's experience with her own despair helped her understand Hurston's struggles. The money she sent to Hurston, along with warm letters of support and encouragement, must have helped to alleviate the black woman's lonely struggle with work that had no audience.

The "Queer Stories"

While struggling to write *The Sojourner*—a book in which she no longer believed or which failed to represent her inner thoughts—Rawlings turned to what she called her "queer" stories. "Queer" does not mean "homosexual" to Rawlings; instead, she is referring to the experimental, more psychologically dark stories she was writing in the mid-1940s. Her "queer" stories include four published in the *New Yorker*—"Jessamine Springs" (1941), "The Shell" (9 December 1944), "Black Secret" (8 September 1945), and "Miriam's Houses" (24 November 1945). On 4 October 1945 she writes to Perkins that she is working on two more "queer" stories, but her agent, Carl Brandt, is unable to sell them even though she says that "One of them I think is all right." She reports: "'Town and

Country' took one of the queer stories. Counting the four stories that have been in 'The New Yorker,' there are seven that I should not be ashamed of, and when I have about ten, I should hope that you would like them well enough to make a book of them" (*Max and Marjorie* 585). It is not known which two stories Rawlings was working on at the time of this letter. *Town and Country* did not publish "Miss Moffatt Steps Out"; it appeared in the February 1946 issue of *Liberty* magazine.

A good example of Rawlings's "queer plane" is "The Shell." A nameless girl, intellectually challenged and as symbolically empty as the seashells she loves to touch, waits on the shore for her husband, who is missing in action in the war. She has been left in a beach house by her husband, under the protection of a black servant who runs off to join a boyfriend. The girl's only relative, a sister, hates her so much for her beauty that she, in the husband's words, "beats her as I wouldn't beat a dog." He sadly comments on the sister's cruelty to his wife: "It seems to me you can hurt a child's mind that way" (*Short Stories* 341). Years later, the memory is only a "fog" to the girl, and now she wanders along the shore, longing for her husband. She picks up a little shell that is "broken and imperfect. It was too small and fragile, now that it was empty, to have survived the buffeting of great forces" (342). Holding onto the shell, the girl realizes that her beloved husband is across the sea, so she walks into the water, hoping to reach him. The narrator coolly recounts the girl's death in such an ironic, indirect way that the reader's imagination has to take over: "A smooth body brushed past her, nudging her with a hard nose, and then another. She opened her hand and the little empty shell dropped from it and spiralled down through the water, to reach the sand and be thrown by the tide on the beach again, still further to be broken. The shell was worthless, and had been even when there was life within it. But it was a pretty little thing and it was a pity that it should be quite destroyed" (343). The girl's death is the iceberg, the unexpressed event that haunts the reader after the story is over.

In "Black Secret," Dickie, a boy of seven, is dreaming of lions in his parlor when he overhears his mother and her friend Mrs. Tipton talking about a secret. His mother's friend keeps saying, "Men are beasts," and the rest of the conversation is enigmatic to the young boy:

His mother said, "The rest of us must just thank God for ours."

"If anyone could be sure, Mrs. Merrill."

His mother's voice fluttered like a butterfly.

"You mustn't say such things, Mrs. Tipton. My Richard . . . I thank God every night. I don't know what I've done to deserve such—such devotion." (*Short Stories* 346–47)

Dickie assumes that the secret is somehow related to the black female servants in the house, but he does not learn the truth about the secret until he goes to the black barbershop down the street and overhears that his uncle has fathered a child with a black servant. Dickie feels at once that "a cyclone [is] on him" and starts sobbing. The black barber thinks he is sick and gives him a coin to make him feel better. As he clutches the penny, the boy feels that "It [is] wet and sticky with sweat from the black hand and from his own" (351).

In this story, racism is the iceberg just below the surface, and Dickie senses that his whole world is based on a substance that can melt. The narrator is ambiguous about the reasons behind Dickie's emotional turmoil. Does he question his father's faithfulness? Is he upset because his tidy, genteel world has collided with the poverty-stricken, racially oppressed world of the servants who live in his home? What are the implications of miscegenation in his life and the connection to a cousin who is half black? The narrator implies at the end, though, that black and white lives are linked for better or worse, even in the passing of a penny from one hand to the other. In the case of Dickie and the barber, it seems as if it is for the better, as the black man envelops him in kindness and concern.

"Miriam's Houses" also involves a secret about what occurs in Miriam's houses. Here, Helen, the protagonist, does not discover the truth until forty years have passed. As a child, she had been fascinated with her friend Miriam and Miriam's houses, which seem to change every month or so. Only later, when she walks into one of the houses, does memory kick in, like Proust's madeleine, and she deduces that Miriam's mother had changed houses in order to skip out on her rent every month or so. Furthermore, the various gentleman callers, whose personal effects were visible in the houses, were there to pay visits to Miriam's mother, a prostitute. After thinking back on Miriam and her houses, the narrator wonders in amazement: "My knowledge had come to me after forty years." But then she asks herself, "Ah, but when had it come to Miriam?" (*Short Stories* 358). The poignancy of Miriam's lost innocence can only be imagined, but the fact that it took the narrator forty years to realize the facts of life implies that she, too, has been living in a state of naïveté and ignorance for her whole lifetime.

"Miss Moffatt Steps Out" also deals with a woman who shelters herself from reality. Miss Moffatt hides from herself the fact that she is living like a hermit. Her only outlet is her teaching, and to "bring a greater enthusiasm to her classes" she ventures out one day to observe soldiers "home from the wars" marching in a parade. As she is watching the parade, a sergeant notices her on the sidelines, steps out of line, "bow[s] in front of her, chuckle[s], 'Hiya, babe,'" and steps back into formation. This random incident is enough to change Miss Moffatt's life. She is in a state of shock and realizes: "It's my own fault that I'm so lonely. I don't go out to people. When I did, today, it happened. Someone *responded* to me. I must *participate*" (*Short Stories* 362). She resolves that very evening to go out to dinner alone to the local hotel, which is "magnificent." The evening is a disaster: she spends too much money, no one notices her, the waiters are snooty and ignore her, and she leaves before the musicians even begin playing. In spite of the dismal reality, she decides to "go home in glory, as the state division had returned." And, she will teach her students "that one human being must be kind to one another, one race, one nation to another, or the world was lost" (367). Once again, Rawlings's narrator gives the reader no indication how to respond to this woman. Miss Moffatt's message is sound, but it comes from a woman who is so out of touch with reality that she has no idea how to rejoin the world. The narrator makes us wonder, Is the world doomed because of the ignorance of people like Miss Moffatt? Is there any way for her to change?

Perkins did not want Rawlings to spend her time working on these stories, since he was concerned that she was working on them at the expense of progressing on *The Sojourner*. She admits that this is so in her 4 October 1945 letter: "I have laid by the book again, but without undue anxiety. It is truly bad as it stands and I cannot let you see it" (*Max and*

*Marjorie* 585). A month later, Rawlings complains to Ellen Glasgow: "I am in a dreadful state of mind, from being unable to do anything with a novel that has been long on my mind, and on which I have made eight or nine beginnings. In one version, I did about a quarter's book-length, and was so depressed that one night I tore it all into irretrievable shreds" (*Selected Letters* 275). Calling her own work "pure tripe," Rawlings praises Glasgow for doing work that "is so much more important than mine" (275).

Perkins was certainly invested in keeping Rawlings on track as one of Scribner's most successful novelists. Not wanting to come down too hard on her for straying into more experimental fiction, he mildly praises it, while urging her to return to her Quincey Dover stories: "I certainly did read 'The Shell' and I think it is a beautiful story. 'The Pelican's Shadow' I admired too, for it was extraordinarily effective. I'll look out for 'Dark Secret' but I do think a book could be made of such stories in the end,— Of course, as you know, I have always hoped you would get Quincey Dover into a book. Won't you some time?" (*Max and Marjorie* 581).

Perkins's lack of enthusiasm for Rawlings's experimental fiction must have worried, or at least discouraged, her. His inability to regard her in any way other than as the commercially viable storyteller from Cross Creek must have constricted her spirit. Her other audiences did not appreciate her straying off into unfamiliar territory either. When *Cosmopolitan* rejected "Miriam's Houses," Rawlings says she could have "killed" her agent, Carl Brandt, for "even submitting it to such people." Rawlings claims that "the editor said that they loved the story, but it was too far out of line for them and 'would shock the already sagging girdles off our matrons.' The irony is that the story is completely moral and literally God-fearing" (*Max and Marjorie* 574). The *New Yorker*, which was publishing the stories, labeled them "terribly experimental," which is, at the least, ambiguous. Rawlings, though, interpreted this label to be "just possibly, it may be good!" She admits that "It is all stuff certainly very different from my Florida stories and books" (*Max and Marjorie* 580). Even though she may "hope for a small succes d'estime," she realizes that her new stories "might alienate some of the readers of the more sweetness-and-light books" (584).

By this time, Rawlings had outgrown her persona as the narrator of

*Cross Creek.* In a 9 December 1946 letter to Norman Berg, she writes of her disgust when fans come up to her and act as if they know who she is: "Readers think of me so much as The One Friend, and my flesh crawls when they approach me, which would never happen to The Friend" (*Selected Letters* 289–90). She even parodies herself in the hilarious "Yesterday's Woman: An Exclusive Interview by Lollie Popp Twitters." Twitters describes her first view of "the bitch" of Cross Creek, the author of "Rotten Apples" and "The Blasted Buck": "Mrs. Rawlings is a big-butted woman with a shuffling step and uncombed hair straggly about her neck." When Twitters asks how she works best, Rawlings responds, "Tight as a tick" (48–49).

Most likely, Rawlings would prefer to think of herself as someone in the same league as one of the "Big Boys," the classic authors in the Modern Library series. She complains to her husband: "It seems asinine to turn out my trivial tripe when the Big Boys have already said about all that needs saying. It makes me feel like a rag-picker, pawing through the cosmic dump" (*The Private Marjorie* 149). No doubt she wanted to be the equal of Perkins's other great American authors. She greedily read their works as soon as Perkins sent them to her and enjoyed analyzing the narratives with Max. Rawlings particularly admired Hemingway's work and loved spending time with him, not only deep-sea fishing off of Bimini but also socializing with him and Martha Gellhorn at Norton Baskin's restaurant at Marineland in St. Augustine and at her home on Crescent Beach.

Given Rawlings's admiration for Hemingway's gritty approach to the surface of things, on the one hand, and his genius at capturing the underlying "unexpressed" emotion, on the other, it is not surprising that she may have tried to follow his example as she explored new literary horizons after the publication of *Cross Creek.* She calls her "queer" works ("The Shell," "Black Secret," "Miriam's Houses," and "Miss Moffatt Steps Out") "sad, ugly stories." And if they were to be collected in a volume, she says, "the title should probably be "Gall and Wormwood." In a letter to Norman Berg she confesses: "I don't know out of what sadistic, frustrated depths they come, and they are not pretty, though I hope they are telling" (*Selected Letters* 267). The stories not only deal with the harsh reality of life but also give a sense that there is something huge beneath the surface of things. While writing *Golden Apples*, Rawlings tells Perkins, in a 9 August 1934 letter, how she is able almost unconsciously to slip into this other world beyond the world of appearances, which is "definitely *off-key*, into a queer plane that is without reality. . . . Perhaps I just let a haze of words, of imperfect conceptions, carry me along, without focusing sharply and accurately enough" (*Max and Marjorie* 155).

It is hard to tell whether Rawlings was headed in a new creative direction with her "queer stories." For some reason, she never fully developed her work in "the queer plane." After her publication of *The Sojourner*, she turned her efforts to writing a biography of Ellen Glasgow.

# Afterword

Time ran out for both Hurston and Rawlings. Hurston was seeking to expand her vision of the world outward by studying King Herod and the dawn of civilization. Rawlings, too, had outgrown her Cross Creek mentality, perhaps as a result of the devastating "invasion of privacy" trial. Her vision turned more inward, as she explored the demons inside Ase Linden and revisited the distant past of her childhood. Nevertheless, finding new horizons was difficult for both women, mainly because other people—agents, editors, audiences—were unwilling to accept the changes they were going through. These people regarded the changes—and the literary works that were being produced as a result—as failure or decline. Robert Hemenway, for example, criticized Hurston's obsession with Herod, believing that she was moving away from her essential self and primary material: "The subject was running away from its author; she no longer could control 'the spell.' When her Scribner's editors said that the manuscript had to be cut and focused, she resisted, unable to give up so much of her research. She had become possessed. . . . Zora was riding for a fall" (344). Carla Kaplan discusses other critics, such as Hemenway, who "write off this period of her life as a time of collapse and confusion, 'a talent in ruins'" (*Hurston: A Life in Letters* 591). Bellman criticizes Rawlings's last work, *The Sojourner*, in the same vein: "Mrs. Rawlings clearly was no longer in her element when she depicted [her characters'] lives. Her message comes through somehow, but the story is weak in many places, and the characterization is often flat—in fact, painfully unimaginative" (119).

Instead of looking at this period in their lives in a negative light, we must see Hurston and Rawlings as evolving, spinning in a gyre upward to a new sense of self. Fortunately, revisionist readings of their works are now being published. For example, Deborah Plant in *Zora Neale Hurston: A Biography of the Spirit* (2007) celebrates Hurston's lifetime achievement: "We have a more profound sense of Hurston's courage and resilience, and a more profound respect for her intellect, ingenuity, creative genius, political activism, and literary production. Aware of the challenges she faced . . . one wonders at her consistently positive outlook, enthusiasm, and extraordinary productivity" (2).

In their introduction to Rawlings's *Uncollected Writings*, Rodger Tarr and Brent Kinser denounce those critics who would deny Rawlings a place in the canon of American literature: "Their neglect" of her is a "disgrace," compromising "the integrity of their work." They conclude: "Rawlings is no less an American treasure than Kate Chopin, Zora Neale Hurston, Ellen Glasgow, and Eudora Welty—to name but a few. . . . How can we say it more bluntly? Rawlings's work demands inclusion, significant inclusion, in any discussion of twentieth-century American literature. She was a bright star among the shining stars—in the words of Wallace Stevens, 'a very remarkable woman'" (14).

In time, the literature that Hurston and Rawlings produced in the latter part of their lives will also be vindicated. In the end, they both returned to their roots and were preoccupied with subjects close to their hearts. They no longer felt a need to write what other people wanted them to write. Hurston's study of King Herod satisfied her longing to analyze the nature of power, the birth of a religion, and the creation of an empire. Her fixation on Herod becomes understandable in light of new archaeological discoveries about his life and death. He was featured on the cover of the December 2008 *National Geographic* after Israeli archaeologist Ehud Netzer discovered his tomb on the Herodium in April

2007. The author of the article, Tom Mueller, explains the contemporary fascination with this ancient ruler: "Throughout his life [Herod] blended creativity and cruelty, harmony and chaos, in ways that challenged the modern imagination" (40). Who would not be fascinated by a man who was the image of the Antichrist in the Middle Ages, who killed three sons and a beloved wife (but not the Jewish male infants)? Hurston must have also been attracted to his eclectic life story: he worked for the Romans as king of the Jews; his mother was an ethnic Arab, and his father was an Edomite; he was raised as a Jew; he was chosen by the Greeks to be the president of the Olympic Games; and he was an empire builder, who created the Northern Palace at Masada and the Second Temple in Jerusalem. He was, above all, the image of the multicultural person, someone who crossed boundaries, brought people and ideas together, and sparked a new religion.

While Hurston's cosmic vision expanded outward, Rawlings's contracted. Without the leavening influence of Maxwell Perkins, who urged her to create uplifting endings to her novels, Rawlings allowed her vision to turn darker and darker. Her struggle to write the story of Ase Linden in *The Sojourner* also reflected her own private demons and despair. Yet, she is to be commended for turning away from the abyss and choosing to "make something," as her beloved friend Robert Frost advised her to do. She was well under way with her next project, the biography of Ellen Glasgow, when she suffered a ruptured aneurysm and died on 14 December 1953.

Unfortunately, Hurston's and Rawlings's lives were cut short, so we will never know what they may have created in the years to follow. And they, too, were aware that their goals may have been unattainable. In the final extant letter that Hurston wrote to Rawlings in the fall or winter of 1948, Hurston claims that her goal in life "still eludes" her and laments, "I am in despair because it keeps ever ahead of me." She thanks Rawlings for lending her money during the period of her legal difficulties and concludes, for once with her mask seemingly down: "Oh, my dear, so much has happened to me since that time. I have had to go through a long, long, dark tunnel to come out to the light again. But I had the feeling all the time that you believed in me and that I had better git up and git or you would feel let down" (*Hurston: A Life in Letters* 575, 577).

All the dark events in Hurston's and Rawlings's lives, with time, transformed and have "come out to the light again." Rawlings's "invasion of privacy" trial was a battle fought for all authors' freedom of expression. Her letters to service people won her and Cross Creek fans worldwide. These letters are currently being passed on to a new generation that is moved by her generous spirit. Hurston's insistence that she is not "tragically colored" and her belief that she belongs to "no race and no time" is an ideal to which we Americans have moved closer. And, their courage in confronting their adversities and their struggle to redefine themselves is a beacon of light in the history of American literature.

Fiercely independent, strong willed yet tenderhearted, passionate about literature's ability to understand human nature and to stand as a buffer against the evils of the world, Hurston and Rawlings were women ahead of their time. They, unfortunately, did not always have the audiences that appreciated their forward-looking ideas. Instead, they found solace and solidarity in each other. As Hurston's last letter suggests, they were each other's best inspirations.

# Works Cited

Acton, Patricia N. "The Author in the Classroom: The *Cross Creek* Trial of Marjorie Kinnan Rawlings." *Marjorie Kinnan Rawlings Journal of Florida Literature* 1 (1988): 29–40.

Bachelard, Gaston. *The Poetics of Space*. Boston: Beacon, 1969.

Baker, Houston A., Jr. *Blues, Ideology, and Afro-American Literature: A Vernacular Theory*. Chicago: University of Chicago Press, 1984.

Baker, Lee D. "Franz Boas Out of the Ivory Tower." *Anthropological Theory* 4 (2004): 29–51.

Barthes, Roland. "The Death of the Author." *The Discontinuous Universe*. Ed. Sallie Sears and Georgianna W. Lord. New York: Basic Books, 1972. 7–12.

Baskin, Norton. "Gentleman Story-Teller: A Conversation with Norton S. Baskin." Interviewed by Carolyn and Jack Fleming. *Marjorie Kinnan Rawlings Journal of Florida Literature* 15 (2007): 31–123.

———. "Peter Coyote Interviews Norton Baskin for the Movie *Cross Creek*." *Marjorie Kinnan Rawlings Journal of Florida Literature* 5 (1993): 19–38.

Bass, Ernest "Buddy." "Marjorie Rawlings: The Second Generation." *Marjorie Kinnan Rawlings Journal of Florida Literature* 15 (2007): 1–14.

Bellman, Samuel I. *Marjorie Kinnan Rawlings*. New York: Twayne, 1974.

Bettelheim, Bruno. *The Uses of Enchantment*. New York: Vintage, 1977.

Bigelow, Gordon E. *Frontier Eden: The Literary Career of Marjorie Kinnan Rawlings*. Gainesville: University Press of Florida, 1966.

Boyd, Valerie. *Wrapped in Rainbows: The Life of Zora Neale Hurston*. New York: Scribner, 2003.

Bruccoli, Matthew J. *Fitzgerald and Hemingway: A Dangerous Friendship*. New York: Carroll & Graf, 1994.

Carby, Hazel V. Foreword to *Seraph on the Suwanee*, by Zora Neale Hurston. New York: Harper & Row, 1991. vii–xviii.

———. "The Politics of Fiction, Anthropology, and the Folk: Zora Neale Hurston." *New Essays on "Their Eyes Were Watching God."* Ed. Michael Awkward. New York: Cambridge University Press, 1992. 71–94.

Cirlot, Juan Eduardo. *A Dictionary of Symbols*. New York: Philosophical Society, 1962.

Dawkins, Lynn. "Zora in Hot Water—On and Off the Houseboat." *Florida Studies* 1 (2005): 143–48.

Douglas, Ann. *Terrible Honesty: Mongrel Manhattan in the 1920s*. New York: Farrar, Straus and Giroux, 1995.

duCille, Ann. *The Coupling Convention: Sex, Text, and Tradition in Black Women's Fiction*. New York: Oxford University Press, 1993.

———. "The Intricate Fabric of Feeling, Romance and Resistance in *Their Eyes Were Watching God.*" *All about Zora: Proceedings of the Academic Conference of the First Annual Zora Neale Hurston Festival of the Arts, January 26–27, 1990*. Ed. Alice Morgan Grant. Eatonville, Fla.: Four-G, 1999. 132–52.

Eckinger, Helen. "Fruitland Park Cop Linked to Klan Quits." *Orlando Sentinel* 7 February 2009: B1+.

Evans, Harry. "Marjorie Kinnan Rawlings: Part One." *Family Circle* 7 May 1943: 18.

Fitzgerald, F. Scott. *Tender Is the Night*. New York: Scribner, 1962.

Gannon, Michael. *Florida: A Short History*. Gainesville: University Press of Florida, 1993.

Gates, Henry Louis, Jr. *The Signifying Monkey*. New York: Oxford University Press, 1988.

George, Rosemary. *The Politics of Home: Postcolonial Relocations and Twentieth-Century Fiction*. Cambridge: Cambridge University Press, 1996.

Gilmer, Mary Dudley. *Marjorie Kinnan Rawlings in the Mountains: The Story behind "A Mother in Mannville."* Banner Elk, N.C.: n.p., 2004.

Gilroy, Paul. *The Black Atlantic: Modernity and Double Consciousness*. Boston: Harvard University Press, 1993.

Glisson, J. T. *The Creek*. Gainesville: University Press of Florida, 1993.

———. Personal interview. 10 May 2007.

Headon, David. "'Beginning to See Things Really': The Politics of Zora Neale Hurston." *Zora in Florida*. Ed. Glassman and Seidel. Orlando: University of Central Florida Press, 1991. 28–37.

Hegeman, Susan. "Franz Boas and Professional Anthropology: On Mapping the Borders of the `Modern.'" *Victorian Studies* 41 (1998): 455–84.

Hemenway, Robert. *Zora Neale Hurston: A Literary Biography*. Urbana: University of Illinois Press, 1977.

Huggins, Nathan Irvin. *Harlem Renaissance*. New York: Oxford University Press, 1971.

Hughes, Langston. *The Big Sea: An Autobiography*. New York: Hill and Wang, 1940.

Hurston, Zora Neale. "Characteristics of Negro Expression." *Zora Neale Hurston: Folklore, Memoirs, and Other Writings*. Ed. Cheryl Wall. New York: Library of America, 1995. 830–46.

————. "Crazy for This Democracy." *Zora Neale Hurston: Folklore, Memoirs, and Other Writings*. Ed. Cheryl Wall. New York: Library of America, 1995. 945–49.

————. "Drenched in Light." *Zora Neale Hurston: Novels and Stories*. Ed. Cheryl Wall. New York: Library of America, 1995. 940–48.

————. *Dust Tracks on a Road*. Ed. Robert Hemenway. Urbana: University of Illinois Press, 1984.

————. "The Eatonville Anthology." *Zora Neale Hurston: Folklore, Memoirs, and Other Writings*. Ed. Cheryl Wall. New York: Library of America, 1995. 813–25.

————. *Go Gator and Muddy the Water: Writings by Zora Neale Hurston from the Federal Writers' Project*. Ed. Pamela Bordelon. New York: Norton, 1999.

————. *Jonah's Gourd Vine*. New York: Harper & Row, 1990.

————. *Seraph on the Suwanee*. New York: Harper & Row, 1991.

————. *Their Eyes Were Watching God*. New York: Harper & Row, 1990.

————. *Zora Neale Hurston: A Life in Letters*. Ed. Carla Kaplan. New York: Doubleday, 2002.

————. *Zora Neale Hurston: Folklore, Memoirs, and Other Writings*. Ed. Cheryl Wall. New York: Library of America, 1995.

————. *Zora Neale Hurston: Novels and Stories*. Ed. Cheryl Wall. New York: Library of America, 1995.

Jackson, Chuck. "Waste and Whiteness: Zora Neale Hurston and the Politics of Eugenics." *African American Review* 34 (2000): 639–60.

Kennedy, Stetson. "The Magic Circle." Unpublished manuscript, University of Florida Libraries.

————. *Southern Exposure*. Boca Raton: Florida Atlantic University Press, 1991.

Konzett, Delia Caparoso. *Ethnic Modernisms: Anzia Yezierska, Zora Neale Hurston, Jean Rhys, and the Aesthetics of Dislocation*. New York: Palgrave Macmillan, 2002.

Kroeger, Brooke. *Fannie: The Talent for Success of Writer Fannie Hurst*. New York: Times Books, 1999.

Lewis, David Levering. *When Harlem Was in Vogue*. New York: Oxford University Press, 1989.

Lillios, Anna. "Some Excursions into Zora Neale Hurston's Eatonville." *Florida in Florida*. Ed. Steve Glassman and Kathryn Lee Seidel. Orlando: University of Central Florida Press, 1991. 13–27.

Lowe, John. *Jump at the Sun*. Urbana: University of Illinois Press, 1994.

*Maitland Milestones*. Maitland, Fla.: Maitland Historical Society, 1976.

Malone, Ann Patton. *Sweet Chariot*. Chapel Hill: University of North Carolina Press, 1992.

McKay, Nellie. "Race, Gender, and Cultural Context in Zora Neale Hurston's *Dust Tracks on a Road*." *Life/Lines*. Ed. Bella Brodzki and Celeste Schenck. Ithaca: Cornell University Press, 1988. 175–88.

Meisenhelder, Susan Edwards. *Hitting a Straight Lick with a Crooked Stick: Race and Gender in the Work of Zora Neale Hurston*. Tuscaloosa: University of Alabama Press, 1999.

Mitchell, Olga Fenton, and Gloria Fenton Magbie. *The Life and Times of Joseph E. Clark: From Slavery to Town Father (Eatonville, Florida)*. Eatonville, Fla.: Four-G, 2003.

Mueller, Tom. "The Holy Land's Visionary Builder: Herod." *National Geographic* 214 (2008): 34–59.

Nolan, David. Personal interview. 20 March 2008.

Orser, Frank. "Tracy L'Engle Angas and Zora Neale Hurston: Correspondence and Friendship." *Southern Quarterly* 36 (1998): 61–67.

Otey, Frank M. *Eatonville, Florida: A Brief History of One of America's First Freedmen's Towns.* Winter Park, Fla.: Four-G Publishers, 1989.

Parker, Idella. *Idella: Marjorie Rawlings' "Perfect Maid."* Gainesville: University of Florida Press, 1992.

Patterson, Orlando. *Rituals of Blood: Consequences of Slavery in Two American Centuries.* Washington, D.C.: Civitas/Counterpoint, 1998.

Plant, Deborah G. *Every Tub Must Sit on Its Own Bottom.* Urbana: University of Illinois Press, 1995.

———. *Zora Neale Hurston: A Biography of the Spirit.* Westport, Conn.: Praeger, 2007.

Pope, Edith. Uncollected papers. University of Florida Libraries, Special Collections.

Prenshaw, Peggy Whitman. "The Otherness of Cross Creek." *Marjorie Kinnan Rawlings Journal of Florida Literature* 4 (1992): 17–24.

Rawlings, Charles. Transcript of unpublished interview with Jean Wardlow. University of Florida Libraries.

Rawlings, Marjorie Kinnan. "Cocks Must Crow." *Short Stories by Marjorie Kinnan Rawlings.* Ed. Rodger L. Tarr. Gainesville: University Press of Florida, 1994. 252–72.

———. "Cracker Chidlings." *Short Stories by Marjorie Kinnan Rawlings.* Ed. Rodger L. Tarr. Gainesville: University Press of Florida, 1994. 28–40.

———. *Cross Creek.* New York: Simon & Schuster, 1996.

———. "Jacob's Ladder." *Short Stories by Marjorie Kinnan Rawlings.* Ed. Rodger L. Tarr. Gainesville: University Press of Florida, 1994. 41–107.

———. "Lord Bill of the Suwannee River." *Short Stories by Marjorie Kinnan Rawlings.* Ed. Rodger L. Tarr. Gainesville: University Press of Florida, 1994. 108–23.

———. "Marjorie Rawlings Tells Story of Her Long Struggle to Write." *The Uncollected Writings of Marjorie Kinnan Rawlings.* Ed. Rodger L. Tarr and Brent E. Kinser. Gainesville: University Press of Florida, 2007. 343–47.

———. *Max and Marjorie: The Correspondence between Maxwell E. Perkins and Marjorie Kinnan Rawlings.* Ed. Rodger L. Tarr. Gainesville: University Press of Florida, 1999.

———. *The Private Marjorie: The Love Letters of Marjorie Kinnan Rawlings to Norton S. Baskin.* Ed. Rodger L. Tarr. Gainesville: University Press of Florida, 2004.

———. "Regional Literature of the South." *The Uncollected Writings of Marjorie Kinnan Rawlings.* Ed. Rodger L. Tarr and Brent E. Kinser. Gainesville: University Press of Florida, 2007. 272–79.

———. *Selected Letters.* Ed. Gordon E. Bigelow and Laura V. Monti. Gainesville: University Press of Florida, 1983.

———. *Short Stories of Marjorie Kinnan Rawlings.* Ed. Rodger L. Tarr. Gainesville: University Press of Florida, 1994.

———. *The Sojourner.* New York: Scribner, 1953.

———. *South Moon Under.* New York: Scribner, 1933.

———. *The Uncollected Writings of Marjorie Kinnan Rawlings*. Ed. Rodger L. Tarr and Brent E. Kinser. Gainesville: University Press of Florida, 2007.

———. *The Yearling*. New York: Collier Macmillan, 1967.

———. "Yesterday's Woman: An Exclusive Interview by Lollie Popp Twitters." Ed. Rodger Tarr. *Marjorie Kinnan Rawlings Journal of Florida Literature* 14 (2005–6): 45–51.

Reich, Kathleen. "Rollins College's Animated Magazine and the Hamilton Holt—Marjorie Kinnan Rawlings Correspondence." *Marjorie Kinnan Rawlings Journal of Florida Literature* 8 (1999): 51–62.

Silverthorne, Elizabeth. *Marjorie Kinnan Rawlings: Sojourner at Cross Creek*. Woodstock, N.Y.: Overlook Press, 1988.

———. Personal interview with the author. 5 December 2008.

Speisman, Barbara. "A Tea with Zora and Marjorie." *Marjorie Kinnan Rawlings Journal of Florida Literature* 1 (1988): 67–100.

Tarr, C. Anita. "The Evolution of a `Southern "liberal"': Marjorie Kinnan Rawlings and Race." *Marjorie Kinnan Rawlings Journal of Florida Literature* 15 (2007): 141–62.

Tarr, Carol A., and Rodger L. Tarr. Introduction to *Cross Creek*, by Marjorie Kinnan Rawlings. Jacksonville: South Moon Books, 1992. vii–xvii.

Tarr, Rodger L. Introduction to *Max and Marjorie: The Correspondence between Maxwell E. Perkins and Marjorie Kinnan Rawlings*. Ed. Rodger L. Tarr. Gainesville: University Press of Florida, 1999. 1–24.

———. Introduction to *The Private Marjorie: The Love Letters of Marjorie Kinnan Rawlings to Norton S. Baskin*. Ed. Rodger L. Tarr. Gainesville: University Press of Florida, 2004. 1–17.

Thurman, Wallace. *Infants of the Spring*. New York: Macaulay, 1932.

"Town of Eatonville Centennial 1887–1987." Eatonville, Fla.: Town of Eatonville, 1987.

Trefzer, Annette. "Floating Homes and Signifiers in Hurston's and Rawlings's Autobiographies." *Southern Quarterly* 36 (1998): 68–76.

Verdon, Michel. "Franz Boas: Cultural History for the Present, or Obsolete Natural History?" *Journal of the Anthropological Institute* ns 13 (2007): 433–51.

Wainwright, Mary Katherine. "The Aesthetics of Community: The Insular Black Community as Theme and Focus in Hurston's *Their Eyes Were Watching God*." *The Harlem Renaissance: Revaluations*. Ed. Amritjit Singh et al. New York: Garland, 1989. 233–43.

Walker, Alice, ed. *I Love Myself When I Am Laughing. And Then Again When I Am Looking Mean and Impressive: A Zora Neale Hurston Reader*. New York: Feminist Press, 1979.

Washington, Mary Helen. Foreword to *Their Eyes Were Watching God*, by Zora Neale Hurston. New York: Harper and Row, 1990.

Will, Lawrence E. *Okeechobee Hurricane: Killer Storms in the Everglades*. Belle Glade, Fla.: Glades Historical Society, 1990.

Wilson, Donald. Personal interview with the author. 30 November 2006.

Woodson, Jon. "Zora Neale Hurston's *Their Eyes Were Watching God* and the Influence of Jens Peter Jacobsen's *Marie Grubbe*." *African American Review* 26 (1992): 619–35.

Wordsworth, William. "Ode: Intimations of Immortality." *Norton Anthology of English Literature*. 8th ed. Vol. 2. New York: Norton, 2006. 306–12.

# Index

Anna Lillios is associate professor of English at the University of Central Florida. She edited the collection *Lawrence Durrell and the Greek World*. She is the editor of *Deus Loci: The Lawrence Durrell Journal*, the coeditor of the *Marjorie Kinnan Rawlings Journal of Florida Literature*, and the director of the Zora Neale Hurston Electronic Archive. She is the executive director and trustee of the Marjorie Kinnan Rawlings Society. She received the 2008 Distinguished Colleague award from the Florida College English Association.